Contents

Preface to the Ninth Dutch Edition, 2012

This ninth edition was completely revised and expanded with a few new chapters. Since the publication of the first edition of this book in 1996, I have spoken hundreds of times about this subject to parents, teachers and other educators in many countries. Countless people have told me that this book has been a great support for them in bringing up their teenagers, but also in processing and developing insight into their own teenagehood. Many questions, stories and encounters shared with all these people have helped me realise that we are all searching for an understanding of what happens to us in the turbulent period of the teen years.

Because understanding means keeping pace with changing conditions in time, I have now updated the book to reflect the perspective of 2012. A new chapter on the digital era was necessary, and have included more about divorce and composite families. I have also used this opportunity to add thoughts regarding dyslexic teenagers that have often come up when I have been speaking on the topic of teenagehood. I have also included several stories I often tell in my lectures, and which have had an appreciative response.

A woman told me that after attending one of my lectures on the teen years she had visited her old father. She had had a troubled relationship with him for a very long time due to what she had experienced because of him when she was a teenager. After the lecture she understood her father a little better, and she had mended her connection with him. Fortunately he was still alive. Stories and reactions like this have inspired me to continue writing and speaking.

I thank all my readers and listeners for their questions and often intimate stories. They show that *the narrow path to inner freedom* continues to be quite a challenge, for young people and for those who care for them and educate them!

Jeanne Meijs

Preface to the First Dutch Edition, 1996

The insights related in this book are the result of my experience and work with young people over many years. I have been allowed to share in their struggles and doubts, their despair and joy, and their path of development. These form the basis of this book.

Teenagers are fascinating to me. They are directly engaged and live in the totality of life. The incredible adventure of the soul that is enacted in these years, and which forms the foundation of adulthood, is always new and different.

The insights in this book are not intended as dogmas, but as hypotheses with which parents can go to work. When they have engaged with them and lived with them, the words can grow into truths they have lived through and made their own. Young people experience such truths as authentic and helpful.

I hope that these insights may be enriching not only for parents, teachers and others who work with young people, but also for all those who attempt to solve the riddle of their own youth. They who understand their roots understand their fruits!

For people who are searching for the red thread of meaning in the lives of their children, and in their own lives, the intellect does not suffice. The heart also requires nourishment. This is the reason I have included a number of stories to illustrate the text.

Jeanne Meijs

PART 1

TEENAGEHOOD: UNDERSTANDING THE JOURNEY

The seeker of truth
Finds much delusion.

Yet, to experience the true,
The soul will keep on searching.

Introduction

The Soul and the 'I'
(From the Publishers of the English-language Edition)

In anthroposophical understandings of the human being, a distinction is made between the physical body, the soul and the 'I'. (Life forces, or the etheric body, are another element, but these are not dealt with in detail in this book.)

The soul holds all the impressions we have of the world and the people around us, all our cultural influences and habits – our thinking and feeling and will.

Our 'I' is our spiritual and moral centre, the part that makes judgments and decisions, that loves others. The 'I' takes responsibilities and directs all the other parts.

These parts of the human being are important in this book because vital changes occur in the soul and the 'I' during the teenage period of development. Meijs tells us that the tasks of teenagehood are to free the soul, and for the teenager's own 'I' to gradually take over from the parent's 'I' the task of directing their life and choosing their future path.

We enter teenagehood with a soul full of influences from the outside – from our world and from other people. These are the impressions we have gathered through childhood. Once we are teenagers, we need to free ourselves of the sense of influence from the outside. Much of the behaviour and many of the characteristics we think of as typically teenage are helpfully understood as part of the massive project of throwing out all the soul content we have gathered through childhood, and taking back only what we can make or claim as our own. This project frees the soul, enabling the teenager to become an adult who feels self-determined on the inside.

Our 'I' does not fully develop until the teen years. With its development comes increasing autonomy and the capacity to take responsibility for ourselves, and indeed for others. It is our 'I', our spiritual core, that knows where and how we will find meaning in life, and so can guide us towards our life's questions and purpose. This finding of future direction and of a place in wider society is crucial to the later years of teenagehood.

Teenagehood: A narrow path

Bringing up a child is a much-discussed undertaking. You begin, but you never know what will be asked of you along the way. It is an undertaking that constantly changes, both in form and content. This is obvious when you look at the concrete situations in which you live together with your child. Every phase of their growth asks something different from you. Moreover, every child has different talents and an individual character, and their unique way of developing and pace of development vary all the time.

How long does it take to bring up a child? Generally speaking, children become independent around their twentieth year. They have left home, they have their own world, and they do not expect – nor tolerate – their parents acting as their educators.

In some cultures it is still the tradition that sexual maturity signals the time when children are declared to be adults. They are given in marriage or undergo initiation ceremonies that represent the bridge between childhood and adulthood. Puberty and teenagehood with all their trials, risks and challenges, are, in such cultures, reduced to a period of a few days or weeks. The child is taken into the soul of the people or family, and experiences the common soul content as their own. People then live inwardly out of a feeling of 'we', in which the developments and interests of the group are experienced as their own personal development and interest.

In our culture, children form a more individual soul life in the course of a teenagehood that lasts seven years. This lays the foundation for a subsequent strong, living experience of their own individuality.

Our connection with family and folk is not as close as in those cultures with a brief teenage period. We feel inwardly capable of choices and growth that deviate from the group to which we belong. In our time and culture, we seek a longer, more individuated path of development. And as parents we accompany our children to their 'life maturity' rather than to their sexual maturity.

During their child's teenage years, parents are no longer carried by their maternal and paternal instinct. Your young child can still feel in a sense a part of you, but this is less and less the case during the teenage years. Those who educate and care for teenagers depend on sources of true human love, free of egoism. Depending on pure human love is something akin to walking on a narrow edge – you often fall off. When that happens you are lacking in that beautiful, pure strength; your human love leaves you in the lurch, often at times when you desperately need it! This emotional cliff-edge is part of why the teenage period is often experienced as the toughest one by parents and educators.

Teenagehood is a narrow path for growing children, but also for yourself as a parent. Before you know it you have lost the straight path, and lost yourself in a way of dealing with your child in which love is hard to find. Every insight into the path of your child may help you avoid this, for wisdom and love go hand in hand.

The Three Great Periods of Growth, and Beyond

Every child is unique, and therefore the handling of every child's upbringing must be 'tailor-made' to fit, yet fortunately it is still possible to describe general periods of development that children must go through, each in their own individual way. The entire period of upbringing and education is divided into three great periods of about six to seven years. In the first period the emphasis is on physical care; in the second the right opportunities need to be created for children; and in the third period a balance needs to grow between keeping your distance from your child and remaining involved.

THE FIRST PERIOD: FROM BIRTH TO THE SEVENTH YEAR

This is a time of building, and the strongest, clearest demands on a parent are for physical care. The need for good nourishment, healthy sleep, care during illness, and protection from danger are largely self-evident. You may reflect on *how* you provide these things, but *that* you *will* respond to your child's needs and that this feels like your role as a parent doesn't need much examination. Attention and warmth are also self-evident needs. The obvious dependence of young children makes a strong appeal to adults. Small children evoke the best in us; they connect with the light in us.

After the first seven years, children have learned to eat, stand, walk and speak. They have learned what is okay and what is not. The baby body, gift of heredity, has been remodelled into a more individual body. With the change of teeth, the child concludes this phase of the conquest of its own body: the building period is finished.

In these early years, the parents experience their child strongly as 'their own'. Everything that lives in the souls of the people in its household lives also in the child. Young children vibrate in sympathy with the inner life around them. For parents, a young child is physically still *their* child: a strong physical bond forms part of the feeling life of both parent and child. This causes natural parenthood, which strongly colours this period.

THE SECOND PERIOD: FROM THE SEVENTH TO THE FOURTEENTH YEAR

This is not so much a period of building, but of extending. Children continue to grow in everything, both in outer and inner aspects. They collect forces from everywhere, and an unbelievable liveliness accompanies the school child. On the sports field and at home, in school and in the neighbourhood, climbing trees or running with each other, they grow out of their clothes and finally out of being a child.

This period demands much less physical care than the first, but just as much warmth and attention, which gives children opportunities to grow, and ensures that the necessary life forces can indeed be taken in. Parents and teachers create circumstances for children to learn to use all these forces in constructive ways. In sports and games, in hobbies and friendships, in all their activities, children grow as a result of the opportunities parents, educators and carers provide for them.

In this period it is less obvious that you have to accompany your child, give your attention or listen. You feel that this becomes more difficult, and that it is more and more a question of making conscious choices about what you are willing to do. They'll live anyway, won't they?

In this phase the parents continue to experience their child as 'their own', but now and then there are moments of estrangement: you don't know your child in this way; you don't understand her or him, or you are irritated without really good reason. You still carry the care and responsibility, and yet you no longer feel responsible for everything in the same way as before. There are more and more instances when you think: 'You did it to yourself; those are the consequences of your own behaviour.'

And so the child grows out of your direct influence and control. The first two periods are now past and, with them, your self-evident, natural parenthood.

THE THIRD PERIOD: FROM THE FOURTEENTH TO THE TWENTY-FIRST YEAR

This is a period of remodelling. In principle it runs from the fourteenth to the twenty-first year, but these days many children are in a hurry (or we hurry them up) so that teenagehood comes earlier and earlier – the children wrestle themselves away from their parents earlier.

At puberty, children become sexually mature; the girl becomes a woman, the boy a man. In principle, they are then physically the equals of their parents. Adulthood calls them, but they are not yet free; their soul is in all aspects – in thinking, feeling and the will – still completely permeated with those who accompanied them. Physically they may be adults, inwardly they are only at the beginning of the struggle for an independent existence. This struggle makes children vulnerable. It is tough to be on your own inwardly without stumbling, or to have to seek support from something you want to get rid of. It is a time of running the gauntlet, and therefore I call teenagehood *a narrow path to inner freedom*.

In this phase children require little physical care and direct attention. Indeed, they increasingly reject attention and object to being accompanied by you or indeed by any adults. As a parent you experience almost bodily that your child loosens her or himself from you. Often this comes with soul pain and struggle. No longer is this young person 'your' child in a literal sense; the child is in search of her or himself. Teenagers are learning to think abstractly, to make their own choices, and to look for an orientation in life. They learn to work and come in touch with the nice and not-so-nice aspects of money and sexuality. They learn to keep their own soul content safe, and strip it of all that does not fit their own growing individuality.

Until puberty, physical and life forces received from the parents were living in the child. Now, however, this is no longer the case, and that makes things more difficult for the parents. Many parents notice that they are able to give much more to their own children, when they are young, than to the children of someone else. That is because your own child is, in a sense, still part of yourself. In the first two periods of development, what we lack in deep human love is still supplemented by our love for ourselves.

In the third period it becomes more difficult to give children what they need. In addition, the children will often reject you and make things even more difficult for you through their behaviour. While your child thus struggles in teenagehood, all too often you yourself struggle to preserve your love for your child. Most parents are acutely conscious that this is exactly the phase when children need this love so greatly. For just as the small child enters into a relationship with the light in us, the teen will look for our shadow side. This causes estrangement and creates distance, often in extremely painful ways.

THE PERIOD OF SELF-EDUCATION: FROM THE TWENTY-FIRST TO THE TWENTY-EIGHTH YEAR

You could say that in the first three phases children fight for their existence: first to make their physical bodies their own, then to make their life forces their own, and finally to liberate and individualise their souls. After the twenty-first year follows a period of self-education that lasts approximately seven years.

In the first two periods children struggle together with their parents, even though it does not always look like that. In the third period children are forced to fight more independently from their parents, and often against their parents. That struggle results in a fourth period of seven years that can no longer be considered part of a person's 'upbringing'. It is in this fourth period that young people wage the fight for their own 'I'. Many questions arise: What should I do? With whom? What is my task on this earth?

A first identity in society is posited during this period. Later, many of the questions will come back on another level, but roughly between the twenty-first and twenty-eighth years the strength is mustered to lead a meaningful life. The free individual 'I', which is spiritual in nature, looks for a dwelling in a young man or woman. This individual core takes over the educational task of the parents, so that young people thereafter educate themselves.

Parents hope that children will succeed in becoming themselves so they can find their way in life. A healthy teenage period forms the bridge between a child who is happy to be led by someone else and a self-motivated adult who leads her or himself. This bridge is the narrow path I want discuss in this book: the bridge of the third period of growth – the teenage period.

The Development of the Soul

When children are born they have souls that are still open to all influences from outside. The soul does not yet have a 'skin' that can ward off or filter incoming influences, and the soul also has not yet formed a place or channel for all those influences. Just as rain soaks the soil, the soul is submerged in influences. These sink into a deeper soul layer and, held together by fitting images, form the soul content of the child. You can compare this early soul content with a kind of aquifer, a reservoir in the soul for times of drought.

Not until the teen years is there any direction in this aquifer, but now the water gathers between the banks of a channel and flows on in a particular direction. After the teen years, all emotions, ideas and behaviour have received their channel. In the personality of the human being you can encounter this channel; you can get to know the course of someone's soul life.

At the beginning of the teenage period, the young teen is full of thoughts, feelings and behaviour adopted from parents, teachers, or influences from society and the surroundings in general. All this content, which the young teen has received, and which resides in her or his soul, constitutes, properly viewed, gifts from the *past*.

Rarely do we stop to realise that all words and opinions, all material things, food, education, and so on, can exist only because others in the past have contributed to their existence. Just imagine a world without history, or imagine arriving immediately at the age of fourteen without any existing institutions or experience – with a clean slate – and living among animals in the field, far away from society, culture and family. You would not have to live through the teen period, because your soul would not have any influences from the past. But we do have these. In addition, young teens themselves bring much with them in the form of talents and predispositions, which likewise have their roots in previous times. At the beginning of the teen years we are full of fruits of the past, both of a personal and a more general nature.

As children grow up, their inner beings now and then sound a call. At first the call is very soft; as time goes on, it gains in strength. Then children become restless, irritable and lose their balance.

That call comes from the *future*. It arises from the spiritual core of the human being, the individual human spirit, the 'I'. This part of the human being calls for the formation of the future. It issues a challenge to liberate and let go of the past, and to strive valiantly for what is to come.

Before birth the human being lives in spiritual worlds. There, under spiritual guidance, an inner life question is formed that consists of a totality of intentions and tasks for the future life. This life question therefore embodies the key to a meaningful life. Those who manage to find this life question and go in search of answers live in accordance with the life goal they set themselves before birth.

This is not simple. For as soon as children come to earth they forget their life question. It is only in deep, unconscious layers of the soul that a clear awareness of the question is still alive, and there it works invisibly in what life brings us.

When they are approaching teenagehood, children experience emptiness and stagnation. Their former lust for life is gone. They are 'full' but they are not themselves. They have forgotten what they came on this earth to do. They become quiet or angry, depending on their character. They think of death, and have doubts as to their physical existence: are my parents really my true parents? Is there anyone who cares about me? These are strange questions for a child, and yet whoever knows what is bothering them in their inner being can place these questions. Movement seems to have stopped; after the building and extension in the first two periods, the ship seems to be strangely becalmed. In the year or two before puberty, many children also become physically heavy, unwieldy, awkward, or they show a strange apathy.

The Development of the 'I'

In every human being there lives an individual spirit core that guards our life question from the beginning, and places this question in front of us at the right moment.

For highly specialised tasks you need people and instruments that have highly specialised qualifications. A surgeon cannot operate with carpenter's tools and a grower of orchids needs to know different things from a regular farmer. Each human being has an assignment in life to become a specialist. What I mean by this is that we become a real individual, a person who can hear her or his own life question from within and can also respond to it. Once this has happened, we are free human beings who can also associate with others in a *profound* sense. For *superficial* contact we do not need an individuality. In fact, it can even be experienced as disturbing.

The individual 'I' is the 'inner master' who is always working during life. In the first two growth periods the 'I' still works on our own body and life forces. It has its hands full doing that, and is not yet available for real 'I' tasks, such as responsibilities, questions of conscience, chosen assignments or living in unconditional love with and for others. In these years, parents are still a kind of substitute 'I' for their children in such tasks. They make decisions and assume responsibility for their children; they give them love and warmth. That is a good foundation for growing children. Later, parents will transfer these tasks to their children bit by bit. That begins with taking care of feeding the cat and choosing their own clothes, and ends with the departure of young adults from the parental home to take their own place in society and assume the concomitant responsibilities themselves. And this includes thinking of their own further development and self-education.

That is how it is supposed to go, and yet there is this antithesis: children have the task of becoming unique, independent human beings, their own specialists if you will, *but* are at the same time still determined by the people bringing them up and educating them.

At the onset of teenagehood an inner tension will develop: no matter how well it is all intended, everything that is weaving and living there in the soul still came from other people. As a young teen you feel this lack of freedom; you walk around with a soul filled with influences from outside. At that point you don't really know how to handle this. You can only do something with what you have acquired as your own.

But then comes the call! The voice of the future! The individual 'I' in a way calls the young teen to her or his own essential being, to adulthood. In reality, this call is none other than a reminder: 'Remember who you are and what you came to do!'

Young teens do not understand that language, and can therefore find no answer. But the future keeps calling, and teens become restless. Their soul life begins to move; something needs to happen, but it is not clear what that will be. The inner movement increases, a storm starts to brew, inner balance evaporates and the anchor slips. A strange urge develops to reach and search for the future. Young teens want out, they want to do completely different things from before, especially things that are ahead of their age.

In all the confusion teenagers gradually feel one thing more and more distinctly: 'I am un-free.' Their inner life is still filled with everything that came from the past. Whether it is good or bad, acquired with great effort perhaps, it is from the past. And all those symbols of the past all around... parents...

At that point teenagers take up the struggle, the struggle for the future. Everything they have accumulated is thrown upside-down. New things and new people are tried out. It is like a raging spring clean of the soul in which much is thrown overboard. Even if not every teen shows it outwardly in behaviour and rejection, inwardly it can still be there. The fight for the future can be waged in many different ways.

As more and more gifts from the past are thrown overboard, the voice of the future will sound more and more distinctly. This tells the young person whether those ideas, feelings and things are perhaps still important for the future. Then the developing teen may fish them out of the water again, shine them up and put them on the wall as her or his own achievement.

In the midst of the chaos of these raging soul tempests, new patterns are gradually forming. In many areas new lines become visible that are the first indications of the growing personality. Tried and tested content is reinstated, and many newly acquired insights and habits fall into place. They form an individual soul structure, a completely personal inner network, just like the lines on our hands, but inside and invisible. At that point the search for the life question can begin consciously. Feeling their way, older teens can start on their paths into the future. Their souls have been liberated so that they can track down that one question which belongs to this life.

If the human 'I' can connect with the remodelled soul, if it can dwell and work there, then the bridge between past and future has been created and the young adult can perform her or his tasks. People who stand in life, guided inwardly by the wisdom of their own core beings and assisted by their own liberated souls, will have the capability to lead meaningful lives, and to help others find meaning in their lives.

THE RED THREAD OF MEANING IN LIFE

When the life of the soul has found its channel during the teen years, the essential core of the human being can express itself through the soul. The 'inner master' has then found a fitting instrument for its unique life task. The life question is inwardly heard and rises more and more into consciousness. The entelechy of the human being, that which wants to come into being and wants to bring itself to realisation, can then work in the world. The central impulse of the 'I' will then, when we look back, become visible in the biography: for when we look back we see a clear red thread of meaning running through life. In that red thread the design of our life lights up.

Life is felt and experienced on the basis of a profound connection with the essential core of another human being, with nature, with the world around us and with spiritual realities. In order to reach a point where this is possible, as it wouldn't be for a child, we need teenagehood: a storm that must destroy many things so as to arrive at a fitting dwelling for the soul and the 'I'.

Fully present adults whose souls are liberated and who are guided from their own core are an ideal that in reality will rarely be brought into being by the end of the teen years. In most cases there are soul regions that have been freed during teenagehood, while there are other areas that are not yet free. An example of an incomplete teenage journey, and incomplete inner freedom, will illustrate this.

A boy is growing up. His family is heavily focused on studying, career making and so on. The boy is a quick student and his parents are proud of him. But then as a teenager he often chucks his study and goes out with his friends. He fails his exams and is moved out of the university entrance streams in his school. Finally, he drops out of school and finds a job. He lives in a rented room. Around his twentieth year he looks for a school of adult education. Years later he finishes his studies with honours and builds a wonderful career.

From the parents' point of view this boy made an unnecessary detour, but that is not really true. By first throwing the ideas of his parents overboard, his soul was liberated from their influence. His soul was then open to the influences of the individual 'I', which results in a new choice that only in an external sense looks very much like the first tendency. This boy does not need to repeat teenagehood in his later life when he acquires new knowledge and skills. In this respect he is an adult.

But this same boy was greatly spoiled at home by his parents. He never needed to take responsibility for anything. He never had to do the laundry, wash the dishes or mow the lawn. Everything was always cleaned for him and taken care of. He always felt this was normal, and accepted it as such.

Once he was living on his own he entered into a relationship as soon as possible, and expected the same kind of things from his girlfriend. They often quarrelled about this, but the girlfriend would then run into his childlike, immature attitude. Afterwards, he would feel pathetic and complain about her incomprehensible nagging. We will return to this boy in a later section.

Incomplete Teenage Journeys

At the end of the teen years the channel of the soul has been dug, and it defines the structure of the soul life in the personality of the human being. Impressions, feelings, desires, urges, sympathies and antipathies, but also ways of thinking; in brief, everything that lives in the soul now has its fixed course and limitations.

Now the 'I' works on the goal of life. We look for lessons and experiences that enable us to realise this goal. We avoid experiences and feelings that lie outside this channel of the soul. If the soul has freely transformed itself on the basis of its own individual nature, the channel will have enough space to accommodate and work with the incoming experiences in its development. The human being then has the courage to be led by inspiration, by the inner master.

When, however, the soul structure does not fit, is not free and has simply been adopted from the experiences of youth, chances are that the adult will feel resistance in the soul. The experiences are going too far; perhaps they have to be admitted but the adult self blocks them. The adult continues to hold on to the old; dogma and prejudice reveal the narrowness of the inner foundation.

Or maybe it is not even a question of going too far in what the 'I' is asking for. Maybe the impulse cannot even come in, the idea never even enters the mind. Maybe the channel is not too narrow; rather, there is no channel at all for the red thread that tries to manifest.

In such a case there is an inner conflict. The 'I' refuses to accept this senseless situation. The inner master never gives up. The 'I' will try to dig a new or wider channel in order to make progress. This is often accompanied by vehement suffering in body and soul. The liberation is a necessity, but it is extremely painful. In such a case the need for a meaningful future plays havoc with the need for rest and security.

It can also be that the person feels within that their soul structure is not right. Then the tendency often rises in the soul for additional teenagehood. Much misery among people occurs when we expect adult behaviour in interactions with adults, and instead we are treated in an adolescent manner.

Sometimes you might see a father who, jealous of the youth of his son, starts to flirt with young girls after decades of happy married life. Or an adult woman who behaves like a teenager and, always complaining and moaning, asks for attention for every small act, or creates countless other imaginary problems.

Do we take the time to understand such behaviour and what it stems from? Or do we just condemn it? Giving in to it will merely lead to more of the same. But if we are able to give space to each other for a little catch-up teenagehood, and we invite each other to work on some inner transformation, then we create new adult potential.

LIMITS OF CHANGE FOLLOWING THE TEEN YEARS

As I have mentioned, after the teenage period the soul life has found its firm channel. I would call it a structure or form. You could also call it the soul body, within which the soul life is enacted.

After our physical growth we are limited by certain immutabilities of our body. After the teen years we are limited by certain immutabilities of the soul. In *content*, however, all change remains possible. When we really stop and think about this we will see that great differences may exist between soul *life* and soul *body*.

Later learning experiences can still lead to many new things. New insights, new feelings: everything that lives in our inner being opens – perhaps only through hard inner work – the possibility for change and expansion.

This flexibility, however, does not apply to the soul body. Once we are into our fourth seven-year phase the soul body is full-grown, and we are stuck with it for the rest of our lives. Realising this will be an especially painful experience for people who, after much inner wrestling and liberating, have developed a healthy content in their soul life, suitable for the realisation of their life's goal. That content must still function inside the soul body, with its shape set largely in the teen years.

The soul body consists of patterns of reaction, fixed habits that create inevitabilities. Even if we teach ourselves with the help of much self-control to behave differently, we still keep experiencing the same reactions. The habits that determine our actions are deeply anchored in our life forces. The habits of our feelings are similarly deeply anchored in our soul. The same inner reaction comes up again and again, even if we manage to avoid expressing it externally. An example will clarify this.

Let us return to the young man we described above who skipped his teenagehood as far as his physical care was concerned. He remained as he was, without ever having tried to be different. He could have resisted the loving care from his parents, for instance, by walking around the house unwashed, uncombed and in dirty sneakers, or by refusing the excellent meals they presented him with and eating fast food instead. He would have scandalised his parents, and perhaps they would have demanded that he clean up his mess. Maybe they would then have realised how they were spoiling him, and the young man would perhaps have been forced to find out for himself what was right for him. But nothing of the sort happened.

Finally, the young man reached the point in his life when he had run into the same problem with his third girlfriend as with the earlier ones. He did not want to lose her too, and was therefore willing to voice his problems in this area and discuss them with her. During their discussions and quarrels they arrived at a new insight. She understood why he was as he was, and he felt an inner resistance to his former habits. He understood that something had to change and made every effort to take more care of himself. Laboriously this young man conquered a new approach to his household chores. Through consciousness he was able to change his feelings and attitude.

And yet, his soul body remained as it was formed. Years later, he was liable to say: 'Could you make us a cup of coffee?' to his partner or co-worker when there was a visitor, and he caused irritation at his workplace because he never cleaned up after lunch. How are we to describe this? Did he really change? Or did it only look like it?

He may have made a real inner change and nevertheless have shown reactions that betrayed the old structure. It demands insight and trust in people to understand that essential changes in soul *content* are usually not accompanied by changes in soul *form* . Those who have developed the gift of inner honesty can observe patterns of reaction in themselves that the outside world has not noticed for dozens of years.

Occasionally, exceptionally, the soul form, the body of the soul also changes. This may happen if, during the teen years, the person hardly formed any soul body at all. Another exception can occur when people experience such great suffering, or such an immense series of trials, that they burst out of their soul skin. I have written about such cases in the past, and will not go into details here.

WHAT HAPPENS IF HUMANS DO NOT, OR NEARLY DO NOT, LIBERATE THEMSELVES IN THE TEEN YEARS?

If the soul just keeps growing from school child to young adult, and continues to use the same old norms and values it has adopted from the environment, the soul body will adapt to the situation. The adult develops a soul form that does not circumscribe its own inner life, but a form that circumscribes this adopted and imitated content.

Well, you might think, if the parents were sensible and good people, that is not so bad, is it? Yes, it is very bad. Because the 'I' finds no 'hearing' for its impulses in this soul and thus no hearing for the meaning it wants to give to this one human life. With such an 'adopted' soul we are in fact deaf and blind to what wants to come into being through us. You do not hear your own inner voice; you do not sense where your path is leading.

What happens then? You live a life based on expectations that do not come out of yourself. Even if you think that you have generated it all yourself, just examine yourself, listen closely and you will notice the difference. Did that career, that ambition, grow out of an inner need that arose from deep within you, or did the need arise in response to the expectations of your parents, your wife, your colleague, or perhaps even in response to ideas surrounding you socially – a vague general expectation? If your career is the result of others' expectations, your life is not based on your own unique life task. Without realising it, you are creating a phantom biography that hangs above your head like a balloon. Whoever dares to stick a pin in it will be roughly repulsed, for it is very scary when someone appeals to your true being, your true life path.

Over the course of years, the inner restlessness will grow. Nowhere do you find satisfaction, not at work nor at home. A vague fear, an unsettled state, and most of all an eternal lack of satisfaction will lead to a flight from facing your feelings – a flight into working even harder, to alcohol or other easy escapes until, sooner or later, such paths of denial are blocked and you must look into a mirror. Maybe you are laid off and suddenly have lots of time. Maybe an illness forces you to look in the mirror. It may also happen that your children reach their teenage years. Nothing will mirror the lack of freedom in your soul so mercilessly as a healthy teenager!

Will you now make a new beginning, or will you make a breach? Will it be hardening and rigidity for you, or a new life? At any rate, your teenage child will offer you every opportunity to examine your own soul life so you may feel where it is free and your own, and where it is still child-like and fettered to the past.

SIGNS IN ADULTS OF AN INCOMPLETE TEENAGEHOOD

If the teenage journey is not lived through in the years that have been given for it, it will sink down in the soul and live on in the darkness of the unconscious, until it comes to the surface again later. Before the teen period, children *cannot yet* free themselves in the soul; after the teen period adults *can no longer* free themselves in the soul. Adults can choose to behave in a manner that contradicts their soul structure but, as we have seen, this is a difficult path. Only teenagers have the opportunity to give form to their individuality in a natural way in their as-yet-flexible soul content.

Children who feel an inner demand for individuality and freedom of the soul express this in resistance to authority and in surprise and incomprehension in the face of things that are accepted facts for adults. An adult whose teenage impulse has sunk down in the soul because it has never been lived through will react with resistance and inner barriers to assigned tasks and duties. Whether these tasks are imposed by others or are self-imposed makes no difference. The resistance is felt and experienced, but is usually not expressed. It may become visible on the surface as *forgetfulness* or *impatience*. Those are the two poles of irritation, of hidden psychic allergy: impatience is the active irritation, and forgetting the passive one.

Here are some examples. The impatient father who has to yell at his kids every time he puts them to bed; the mother who insists that her children do the dishes in the same way and with the same speed as she does them; the father who forgets the visit of his children and keeps them waiting, or who can never remember his wedding anniversary; the mother who is always late picking up her child or forgets her promises. They all show signs of submerged, unconscious teenage behaviour.

Laziness, tardiness and sloppiness in adults can indicate sneaky ways in which the un-free soul is protesting. If a person really has such character traits they will be evident in everything that person does. But if they represent hidden resistance, secret teenage disturbances, then the behaviour becomes very unpredictable: in some things the person may be blessed with the patience of an angel, while in other respects the same person will be incredibly impatient. Someone may be a stickler for detail and remember those things they are attentive to with precision, while at the same time being sloppy and forgetful about other seemingly important things.

Hidden resistance like this shows an unpredictable picture. People who have missed their chance for a teenagehood keep rebelling without knowing it. Don't we all know people who choose the opposite point of view from the previous speaker in a meeting and refuse every compromise? Or those who are driven by their emotions and sensations rather than by conscious choices and responsibility?

Of course, adults who did go through a healthy teenagehood can still from time to time fall back into teenage behaviour, but that will be a temporary aberration. It may indicate a strong imprisonment of the soul in a particular situation. Perhaps things at work are very stressful, or a situation in the family is oppressing. In such instances the struggle for freedom comes up again.

But there can also be *favourable* circumstances to transform a remnant of inauthentic and un-free soul life into something more adult. People who assume responsibilities when still too young may well get the chance later to desert and rebel a bit. Every part of the soul that is still un-free forms a hindrance. When the 'I' of the human being wants and needs to manifest itself more strongly and accelerate progress towards the life task, the urge for freedom comes to the fore. The childlike part of the soul then obstructs growth and becomes troublesome ballast the adult wants to jettison. Inner teenagehood raises its head: rebellion, refusal, challenge, destruction. As adults we can become conscious of this tendency when we realise that we now hate things we had before accepted as self-evident. Or when we get irritated by people with whom we used to be good friends. Or when we no longer feel at home in situations that used to be completely comfortable. You feel estranged, everything becomes a problem, you lose interest, you are annoyed by people and things.

Then it is time to stop and take a look at yourself to discover where this evidence of lacking freedom is coming from. Insight into the reasons why you are not free opens the door to the ability to work with the problem. If you can become conscious of the un-free part of your soul, if you can understand it and substitute your own authentic content for it, the symptoms will disappear. Your soul will then be permeated with your own essential being and filled with strength and warmth. Older and wiser, you resume your path. If not, you may be stuck for years with a feeling of walking *beside* your life rather than *in* it.

THE HUMAN CAPACITY TO CHOOSE AND CHANGE

In my view, what we have learned indicates a number of unique human possibilities. When the soul has been formed in a firm pattern, it will be in our nature to behave accordingly. The liar messes around with truth, and the covetous person indulges in greed. But because of our 'I' we are able to be truly human and we have the ability to see to it that such fixed forms do not determine our life. We are able to put our consciousness, heart and willpower in the service of our true 'I', and can then make choices that transcend our nature. This demands great strength. But it does make us free individuals who are not formed by destiny and fate; rather we are able to recreate ourselves. Then the liar can serve truth better than anyone around, and the covetous one will show more restraint than the most modest among us.

Not out of fear or contortion, but from a free 'I'-choice we can inwardly change. Thus we can exhibit a behaviour that differs from what we would have done on the basis of our soul body.

These possibilities are purely human. No animal can live other than in the way dictated by its soul body. Viewed in this way, the teenage journey is indeed an immensely important event, but it does not have the last word. That is always reserved for the human spirit!

A Metaphor for Teenagehood: The lock in the river

Life can be compared with a river. Down from high mountains and from rain the water flows together into a river. The river has many twists and turns. Here the water flows fast, there it takes its time.

When a child is born it gets a little boat and sets out on the river of life. In the first periods of its life we are, as parents, still captain of this boat, but toward the teenage years we have to change functions. Instead of being captain we become lock keepers. The child continues on its own, until it suddenly comes to a lock in the river. The lock is an obstacle, but it also creates the possibility of safe further progress: it allows for a safe adjustment to a lower water level.

The lock is a picture of the teenage period. You will easily enter the lock, unless the doors are not opened. Once you are inside, the water level has to be brought to that of the river along which you will subsequently travel. Water flows in and causes the boat to rock. Once in the lock you are barred from return to the previous stretch of the river, and pretty soon the water level in the lock is different from that before.

But the water level in the river ahead is also different. There you are in your rocking boat, and you are supposed to trust that after a while the doors at the other end will be opened, and that by then your little boat will be at the right level so you can continue. Boats are tied up in a lock with a rope. As the water level then falls you have to be alert to let out the rope.

How can parents be good lock keepers?

◊ Is your child allowed to enter the lock of their teenage journey or are the doors not opened?

◊ Do we close the doors after the child has entered? Or do we keep interfering with the boat? Is the child being forced to keep sharing everything with us? Ask permission for everything? Do we keep making all the decisions?

◊ Do we tie the little boat securely to the side? Or do we just let it rock and drift so it bumps against the side and other boats? Do we continue to set boundaries and offer support? Or do we suddenly throw all rules and customs overboard?

◊ Do we notice when a young teenager needs more leeway and when she or he has too much? Do we understand when to be flexible and when to pull in the line? Or when we need to intervene and how?

◊ Do we know when the water in the lock has reached the same level as the river ahead? Do we recognise when our teenager is ready for independence? Do we keep looking for that moment?

◊ And will we remember to open the lock doors to the future when it is time? Imagine everything being ready and the doors remaining closed! Is the child allowed to leave the family? Or do we prevent any chance to leave home? 'Yes, my dear, you are now an adult, but it is cheaper and nicer and more practical...' and so on, and so on. In this way many lock doors unfortunately remain closed until the little boat does not even want to move on, even if you open the doors wide! Or until the little boat rams the lock doors in desperation and breaks out. The damage can then be serious on both sides.

If we keep this picture of the lock in mind, we can prevent many parenting problems in the teen years.

When the Teenage Journey is Missed

WHY IS THE TEENAGE JOURNEY NECESSARY?

In earlier historical eras it was important for a child to continue the values of their parents without testing or rejecting them. Instead of an individual goal in life, the child then lived out the goal of their group, family or folk.

In our time, people are born who want to realise an individual life task. They cannot do much with the soul life they have taken over from their parents. So a teenage journey is necessary and, as a result, our children mature much later into adults. In this way we grow into a community of conscious, individual human beings who collaborate out of their own 'I' and not, for instance, out of blood relationships. It simply takes more for a person to become an adult in our place and time.

Many of us still live in an in-between stage, between old times and the present. On the one hand we feel the need for that which is our own and, on the other hand, we experience that which is our own as a burden, and deny it.

CHILDREN WHO LOSE THEIR TEENAGEHOOD

Just as there are teenagers who are obviously and perhaps even crudely in that phase of their life, there are also those who create no problems at all. Their parents will later say: 'Highly exaggerated, all that talk about teenagers. I never noticed it much. My children just did their work, were nice at home, had nice friends and travelled together with us.' Such children never need counseling. They do not stand out, don't cause worries, pose no great demands. How can that be? *Why is it that some kids seem to hardly experience teenagehood?* Because they don't need it? Because they can't? Because the parents are too strong? Because they themselves are too weak? Because they don't take the time?

I think that all these answers can be right in different cases. The

35

trick is to ask the question of your particular situation, and then to wait and see what the right answer seems to be for your child. I will elaborate on each answer.

WHEN THE TEENAGE JOURNEY IS NOT NEEDED

Children with a strong 'I' can find a home for their impulses in the childlike soul sooner than most others. When such children have parents who have a sense for this and respect it, the children develop a soul content of their own right away, and have no need for an extended teenage journey.

In actual practice, such children do not exist, or do not exist in a perfect, complete state. We do see big differences in regard to the need for teenagehood. Children with a strong life goal will perhaps, in favorable circumstances, build up many soul areas as their own. Other children may be able to do that with a single soul area. In regard to these areas they indeed will have no need for a teenage journey. This is often the case with respect to particular talents and gifts they brought with them. Beethoven surely had no need for a teenage journey with his music. Such a talent is something that emerges in the soul out of the individual 'I' force; it is far ahead of its time. We call such children prodigies. The miracle here really consists in a degree of maturity and individuality at an age when this is usually not yet possible.

It is quite fascinating to try and see where the miracles are hiding in your own child. Not all children are little Beethovens, but everyone does have their own little miracle. On that point the child has no need, or hardly any need, to be educated. There are children who seem to know the subject already when the teacher is just opening it up. And there are children who have insight into the characters of people at a very young age, and also know how to work with that in a way that astonishes the parents. In such cases, the parents should hold back. The child simply has no need for them there.

Proud parents who boast about their children and pay much too much attention to their talents often do harm. Later, in the teen years for instance, the child may refuse the role of show pony and, unfortunately, they then often abandon their talent or lose it. It may come back in later years, but it is almost always damaged.

The child has no need of confirmation or encouragement in its little miracles. They will confirm themselves. The best thing to do is to give the child the opportunities it longs for out of these gifts with which it was born. Let the child study, meet people and things, or whatever is appropriate to its talents. Then the gift can unfold itself.

In addition, the miracles in children gives you as a parent the opportunity to love them even more, because their unique individuality emerges so soon. Thus you can have an encounter with the true 'I' of your child.

When the teenage journey is not possible

Why would the teenage journey not be possible? Young people don't think that way, do they? They certainly do. Teenagehood is a luxury – a necessary luxury, but a luxury all the same. Let us take a look at the conditions that are needed for a teenager to experience the luxury of the teen journey.

First of all, the child has to live in a society in which the primary necessities of life are taken care of as a matter of course. That may sound strange, but in places where there is hunger or war, the time and opportunity to reject things often does not exist. In most western countries this is not usually a problem: most people have food and drink, clothes and shelter. We live luxuriously indeed when compared with many other places in the world.

People who live their teen years during a war often find that the luxury of a teenage journey was denied them, especially if hunger and fear of death were daily companions. In countries with massive poverty or other heartbreaking circumstances, children have little chance to transform themselves in their souls into real individuals. The will life has often grown very strong: they have become real fighters. But the feeling life is poor and immature. They are often left with a new distress after the bad times have subsided. Even when hope has arisen after a time of misery, many people are left wrestling with the question of the meaning of their life. Why am I alive? What is the use? They have never had the chance to discover the red thread of meaning in their own existence.

Although in our society there is no war or hunger, yet here the luxury of teenage journeys is also sometimes lacking. Why? Perhaps because the young person has no parents. Or because one of them dies just in that period. Or because just in that period the parents are caught in a divorce full of fights and misery. In such circumstances, the parents may fall back into their own teen selves so badly that there is no room any more for their child.

Then there are children who are engaged in a fight for survival emotionally. Physically, things seem relatively all right, but emotionally, life is so empty and cold that it takes all their forces to survive in their inner life. Whatever is there in their soul, they hold onto it for dear life; something is better than nothing. They too are unable to afford the luxury of a teenage journey.

And finally, there are children with serious health problems. If you are a victim of AIDS or cancer, or of a car accident, you need all your forces to survive. Then there is no life energy left for teenage tricks.

WHEN THE PARENTS ARE TOO STRONG

Some parents keep the entire upbringing and education process in hand with iron willpower. With order and discipline, guilt and punishment, in a strict and often highly authoritarian way, they rule over the kingdom of the youth of their children. This has decided advantages. Everything rolls along smoothly, and the parents never need to be ashamed of the behaviour of their children. As a child you never dream of stepping out of the well-worn path, and if you have the temerity to try it, you get immediately taken by the scruff of the neck and resolutely put back in line. The threat is always there of total rejection of *who you are* if you don't obey your parents. It is not your behaviour that is rejected; you are rejected yourself.

Many children find a way to adapt in such a situation, and develop along the lines laid out by their parents. They pay for this later with a great lack of freedom in the soul. You could almost say that they will then need parents for as long as they live. The boss, the partner, acceptable ideas in society, everything and anything will function as a substitute for the domineering parents. *Inner* parenthood, listening to one's own 'I', has unfortunately not been conquered. Such people have lost their opportunity for a teenage journey.

The parents are often quite satisfied with themselves. They did a neat job in a responsible way and now enjoy their well-deserved rest. They indeed avoided many problems, but don't realise that they left a more serious deficiency behind.

There are also children in such situations who break out. Unfortunately this often happens almost literally, and then what is in fact a healthy reaction may well result in a very lonely road toward freedom and individuality. While used to having no freedom at all, the child then has to switch over to total freedom from one day to the next. Of course this has huge risks. The parents will predict that the child will go wrong, and they write that child off.

Some time ago there was an article in the newspaper about a girl who grew up in a family with exceptionally strong strictures on behaviour. The children were governed out of an extreme religious conviction. In another family in the neighbourhood the girl encountered a much freer and more tolerant atmosphere, and she began the struggle for her own freedom. When she lost the fight at home, she fled. She ended up in institutions; lawsuits followed, but she did not give in. In the end she won. She was not forced to return to the parental home, despite being a minor, but was allowed to grow up in a foster family.

This girl is an exception; most children do not have that kind of courage. Moreover, the pain of the breach with the parents keeps coming back through life, so that the child is really always the loser.

Parents who are too strong often effectively prevent the teenage journey of their child. Sometimes, because the soul is flexible, the son or daughter will have a good time being teenage once they go to college, far from home. As long as you make the grades you need, your parents need never know! I think that in such belated teen journeys, students still manage to free themselves of fetters in their soul, and that they can make the discovery of their identity successfully this way. It may take a few extra years, but for these young people it is better late than never.

Back to the domineering parents: many exemplary families evoke feelings of guilt and doubt in other parents whose children try out everything that is forbidden. But it would be better if the parents in the strict family had *their* doubts provoked by the fact that so much more happens in other families!

WHEN THE PARENTS ARE TOO WEAK

There are more and more parents who leave their teenagers free, spoil them and set no boundaries. But where there is nothing to resist, how does a teenager rebel? Teens need resistance; it is only in the encounter with the inner authenticity and strength of the parents that they discover their own strength in thinking and action.

It seems like a paradox, but extreme laxity and indolence in parents has the same effect as extreme strictness: it becomes impossible for the teenager to experience their journey within the safety of a healthy family structure. In cases like this, some teens also skip this phase, or they challenge teachers, the police and other adults so they can experience boundaries that aren't set at home.

WHEN THE CHILDREN THEMSELVES ARE TOO WEAK

What does that mean: a child is too weak? The child does not have a healthy 'soul skin'. Let me explain. As a result of the positive and negative experiences children have, an inner sympathy and antipathy for the world will grow in the soul, for people and for everything they can experience. A healthy soul skin is based on these forces of sympathy and antipathy. The forces of antipathy form a sort of separation between children's own feeling life and that of their surroundings. Sympathies, on the other hand, maintain the connection with the surroundings.

If these forces are both present and balanced, the soul skin can breathe: it serves to protect us and can also connect us with something or someone we encounter. In contrast, a child with a soul skin that is too thin feels everything around as if it were inside. Such children will not be able to bear any criticism or anger from their parents regarding their behaviour. They will do anything to make it up, and will try to avoid such confrontations in the future. Such children are too weak because they cannot distinguish between their own feelings and those of their parents.

It can also happen that some children have only a very thin thread connecting them with their own 'I'. They go through life wibbly-wobbly, vacillating and wavering. 'Mum, is this dress better, or that one?' 'Dad, did I do my maths okay?' Such children are not yet fully incarnated; their 'I' still stays too much in the background. Understanding parents will consciously stimulate the teenage journey of such a child. Give them a challenge, encourage them to form an opinion, seduce them gently into teenagehood, and let them feel that things won't blow up when there is a problem.

A child who is really, fundamentally too weak will skip their teen journey anyway and first try to find more strength. It may take many years before the questions of teenagehood then come back.

WHEN THE TEENAGER DOES NOT TAKE THE TIME

Yes, this is indeed possible! Ambitious teenagers, driven by demands at school and at home, sometimes throw themselves into performance with all their energy. They *will* get that certificate! Or they *will* become a professional football player. With almost grim determination they finish their program. No one and nothing can hold them back. They have absolutely no time for all the nonsense of their contemporaries. Going out is a waste of time, they will never miss school, and so on. Whatever the sport demands in the way of sacrifice, they will do. Some of these teens will admit later to feeling that they robbed themselves of their youth; in those cases there was clearly a certain self-imposed lack of freedom. But there are also children who do this kind of thing completely out of themselves. They are totally single-minded, and their need to perform will last until they have exhausted their energy. Then they develop an illness, or something goes wrong, and only then, from sheer necessity, is there time for an inner life.

> When children, for any reason whatsoever, lose the chance to go through their teen journey, they will carry the problems of that phase with them into the future, where sooner or later these problems will appear, at a much more difficult time and in much more complicated social circumstances.

DIFFERENCES IN THE NEED FOR A TEENAGE JOURNEY

As I mentioned before, there are parents who give their children as much opportunity as they can to discover for themselves how they can and want to develop their talents. These are the aspects in which the children will not need to go through a teenage journey. And if the red thread of meaning of the parents and the future red thread of the child are closely related, the impulses toward liberation will be less pronounced in the teen years. But when you pay close attention, you will yet see that the child still investigates every area, even if just briefly. When an area or subject subsequently quickly fits in with the individuality of the child, then such excursions are merely little bumps in the road that are taken without a scratch.

However, children with future life impulses that strongly deviate from where they grow up will have a lot of ballast to throw overboard. No matter how kindly and lovingly the influences of the parents were meant, when they are tested against the individual 'I', if they are found unfitting they have to be rejected.

Why then did those parents get the task of bringing up this child? Good question! It looks as if their work was all for nothing. And yet, that is not so. The efforts they put into the process and the content they generated will live as kernels in the soul of the child forever. Your child does not come to you for no reason. Even if she or he pulls out your influence root and branch, the essence of what you have given never disappears. It is like a still and patient seed lying deep in the soul of the child, until the moment comes when it is needed. And you can trust that everything your child was given in love and sincerity will one day germinate, grow and bear fruit. But it may well be that you will then no longer be there.

Difficult experiences and failures can also bring with them something your child badly needs later. It is therefore important not to be too quick in judging the way you are bringing up your child. Those who have sincerely tried to do the right thing can trust that in the end the intention of the upbringing will win over the upbringing itself.

1. Three Types of Teenager; Three Phases of Teenagehood

In principle, all teenagers are different from all others; nevertheless we can recognise some general categories. In this chapter I would like to describe three broad kinds of teenager.

◊   Thinking Teenagers
◊   Feeling Teenagers
◊   Doing Teenagers

Every child has to go through their teen years in all these three soul functions, but one of them often predominates. When we look at it over time, we can say that the first teen years most strongly call for growth of independence in thinking, subsequent years for growth in feeling, and the last phase for freeing the will.

For the Thinking Teenager, the one in whom the function of thinking predominates, the emphasis of the whole process will therefore be on the first few years, while for the Feeling Teenager the emphasis will be on the next few years, and for the Doing Teenager on the last years. Knowing what kind of teenagers your children are and which phases they are currently going through can be a great help in ensuring healthy time in the lock in the river.

Later in the book I will elaborate on these three soul functions in relation to sexuality.

The Thinking Teenager

In the first place we should realise that these teens are not necessarily intelligent intellectuals. We can find them anywhere teenagers study and work and play. What they all have in common, however, is that they express their restlessness and doubt through thinking. They have lost their way. They walk around with doubts in their heads and put question marks after everything. Out of the depth of their soul, influences of the awakening 'I' are surging up, striving for inner authenticity. For the Thinking Teenager these influences work in the head and are there experienced as strange thoughts. Some examples may help to show this.

◊ Am I a real girl?
◊ Why do I have to go to school?
◊ Why was I born here?
◊ Why is democracy a good thing? Is it really?
◊ Who causes my destiny?
◊ Do God and life after death exist?
◊ What do I want to become? Do I want to become anything?
◊ Who is this other person? Does this history teacher really like teaching?
◊ Is my friend herself?
◊ Does faithfulness between people exist?
◊ What is the point of it all?

Many of these questions are like those many adults ask themselves in some corner of their soul. Thinking Teenagers ask themselves more questions than many a professor has ever dared to do. They may cause problems because they not only carry these questions inside, they also want answers from the people around them, answers they will then critically examine and often reject as nonsense. They talk night and day with each other about all kinds of philosophical and concrete personal questions. Everything under the sun is interrogated.

Such teenagers are in search of themselves through all this thinking, talking and puzzling. They explore all these ideas and opinions, turn them upside down and inside out, and in the course of the years will try out a number of ideas that seem plausible to them. Some of them become Buddhists or immerse in the philosophy of southeast Asia. Others join a protest movement or look for a radical political party. More than anything else, though, they look for other young people with whom they can share their often contorted thoughts.

For parents of such teenagers the risks are that we may feel we can no longer understand them, and that we stop taking them seriously. Indeed, it is hard to reconcile when one day your teen says that the whole world is maya and you should not get attached to earthly possessions, then the next day loudly claims his or her allowance because it is already the second day of the month! In the meantime, practically all the ideas you have worked so hard to instill in your child, and which to you are authentic and of real value, have become the target of scorn and ridicule. All your thoughts and values are thrown out as retarded, behind the times and useless.

Try at all costs to be above such allegations. Don't act like a bull presented with a red flag!

What can you do?

◊   First of all, simply stay who you have been all along.
    Don't throw overboard the ideas you have used to
    bring up your teenager, for then you also throw his or
    her anchor, or security, overboard. Teenagers need a
    basic premise, and if you pull that away they will lose
    the ground under their feet. Standing firmly by your
    convictions is crucial.

◊   Further, it is incredibly important with the Thinking
    Teenager, as it is for all types of teenagers, to *stay
    with them!* For the thinkers this means: keep listening
    to their ideas and discoveries. Immerse yourself in

Buddhist wisdom, in that party platform, in the flyer of that movement, and listen to what your child and his or her friends have to say. That way you are unlikely to lose your child. But don't become a Buddhist yourself!

◊ Third, take the position – inwardly – that everything your child is saying that makes you feel hurt or angry, could possibly be true. It seems odd, but this does make your own thinking much more flexible; it is a first-class exercise for the spirit. Moreover, it prevents your immediate angry reaction, for if you first reflect on what was said, you give yourself some room and time. In most instances you will discover that what they said was not really true, but that it had a kernel of truth hidden somewhere. Something is living in those teenage words that is at least worth hearing and thinking about. In this way appreciation can grow for the motivation behind your son or daughter's destructive behaviour.

◊ Finally, do not get tempted into endless verbal aggression. There are families in which every meal is a battleground of words between parents and teenager. Who wins? Who is right? Most of the time it ends in quarrels, exasperated silence or painful taunts. Or someone walks away from the table and refuses to eat any more. These are endless and senseless word confrontations. People who would never physically fight with their children don't hesitate to fight to the death with words. Just give your teenagers the chance to say what they want, just let them demand to be right and celebrate their triumph with the machine gun of their words. Dads, mums: it is only teenagehood – and it will pass! Unless you behave like a teenager yourself! Unless you so urgently need to be right yourself, talk everything to pieces and terrorise everyone with your

sensible but domineering thoughts. Then there are
two teenagers at the table; the task of the older one is
to realise that his or her own behaviour is like that of
a teenager, and to strive for adulthood. And to realise
that his or her child needs room to go through this
phase of life.

Difficult, right? I don't mean for the teenager, but for that part of
your own soul that falls back into teenagehood. Teenagers are often
quite rough, unreasonable and untrue in their remarks. But at the
same time they are quite vulnerable and insecure, and they are
hungry for truth. And you yourself are just as vulnerable in that part
of the soul where you fall back into your teen years.

Imagine that you have worked very hard for twenty years and you
have succeeded so you now run your own factory making synthetic
fibres. As a child you had lived in poverty, never had enough clothes
and the clothes you had were so worn that you were always cold.
Your factory now makes fibres that are durable and inexpensive.
Then this fifteen- or sixteen-year-old brat tells you that all synthetic
fibres are worthless, and that it is your fault that the environment is
being destroyed. Despite you having always meticulously followed
all the rules of environmental legislation. You have worked hard for
your family and given your child everything so he or she has always
been well clothed and never known cold. It is enough to strangle
your teen, right?

Yes, that is totally understandable, but do try to quietly listen.
Just let your teen go on and on. If there are real questions you can
give answers, but if all your teen does is make statements, challenge
and taunt, don't react too much. If there are things in what he or she
says that are new or strange, you may wonder where the ideas come
from. Perhaps he or she is being singled out at school because of the
fibre factory? Or perhaps your teen is afraid of the future? Or does
he or she simply need your attention? Answer, not with fighting
but with listening. When your teen goes too far, just quietly and
determinedly put an end to it. 'We'll talk about it later.' Or 'Mike, I
get it, I'll think about it, but now I have to go.' And indeed, you must

come back to it so that in time dear son or daughter gets to hear how you think about it.

DANGERS FOR THINKING TEENAGERS

The forces of the intellect are actually death forces. They rob us of life energy, especially if they are abstract. Thinking Teenagers whose intellect is waking up in their thirteenth, fourteenth and fifteenth years often experience this. Death forces come into the soul; childhood, so full of vitality, is concluded.

These death forces can cause anxiety and concern for the teenager. Usually this goes away again, but there is a danger that children of that age harden in it and dry up. They can get lost in their own little world of thoughts.

They can also lose their way in the thought world of others. A closed system of ideas is the most dangerous thing for a teenager. Extreme religious groups, for instance, do not tolerate any freedom of thinking. Gurus and leaders of sects you would already be cautious about. But that very ambitious school where children are treated as a think-container that has to be filled? Or that domineering friend of yours who indoctrinates your daughter so strongly that she thinks that everything he says is right? Thinking Teenagers are most healthy when they are changing often, when everything is serious and urgent, but does not last long. Fixing the soul at an early stage inside another's thoughts, whether an individual or group, amounts to a lack of freedom. And the point of the teenage journey is precisely to gain inner freedom.

If you are still fanatical about something in your twenties, then you have become stuck as a teenager, and you have simply traded your upbringing for a different system. Children of authoritarian parents particularly run that risk, because they are used to the domination of a particular way of thinking. They often look for a replacement. But children who have been brought up in a thought-vacuum run the same risk: after all that nothing, all that lack of clarity, they are now looking for the one and only truth once and for all, at the expense of all else.

Examples of children who grow up in emptiness are those who are neglected, or who live in a family where everything is allowed and where no attention is paid to anything. They look for groups: youth groups, gangs, football teams, and similar organisations where everything is strictly determined. Groups in which how you behave and what you do is observed, judged and perhaps condemned. In gratitude, these children trade their individual freedom for the security they receive from the group, with all the consequences of that.

Instead of a peripheral group or subculture like this, some children go for the opposite. They don't look for the exception but for the rule. The biggest 'group' is society in general. These children will simply adopt the dominant, general, conventional ideas in society as their own, and strive for those things which are generally portrayed as worthy to strive for. They then live in accordance with generally accepted norms and values. Thus they try to become themselves and find their own red thread when they are hardly capable of questioning general values.

Such young people can look like the ideal person in society: they work hard, study hard, have sensible relationships, and so on. But all their security comes from the general notions they have blindly accepted. They sacrifice much freedom and the opportunity to become an individual by pursuing such 'security'.

All in all, it is important to understand from the foregoing that if we bring up children in an environment lacking ideas and convictions, we create a fertile soil for these wrong turns of teenagehood: joining a closed system of ideas or adopting broad norms as our own. The question to ask is: where did these teens' own individual inner calls go? When there is nothing to resist and reject, when there is nothing you have to free yourself from, you remain unfree.

Even if you realise that your ideas and beliefs are not infallible, use them anyway in the upbringing of your children. They will later throw overboard what does not fit in with them. If they have nothing to throw overboard, perhaps they will go overboard themselves!

The Feeling Teenager

Oh yes, those teary girls! Don't mind them, they'll get over it. Well, it isn't that simple. Both boys and girls can be Feeling Teenagers. It happens when the urge to freedom does not express itself in thoughts or deeds, but gets stuck in moods. This can be observed in every teenager, but here I want to limit myself to those in whom this form of teenagehood is predominant.

Where do these moods come from? The soul is filled with content that the child has absorbed from its surroundings. This capacity of absorption is based on the forces of sympathy in the child's soul. Not the kind of sympathy we usually mean, in the sense of being nice and understanding to others, but forces of sympathy in the sense of the capacity to join or go along with something, to connect with something. A child is born with an immense capacity for openness, for connection. This capacity keeps the soul open.

FORCES OF ANTIPATHY

The forces of antipathy, which are by nature foreign to the small child, come in when the child experiences trouble, is afraid, is disappointed or runs into resistance. These forces of antipathy form the soul skin. The child throws up a barrier between itself and the outside world. This barrier *must* come into being on the path to adulthood. We cannot stand in the world like a small child, we must be able to defend and manifest ourselves.

The soul body comes into being when the soul skin is finished. Actually, the soul body is nothing other than the birth of the formative forces of the soul as a result of the soul skin closing.

If a child has developed insufficient forces of antipathy, it has formed an inadequate soul skin. How can you give form to your own individuality and come to terms with the influences from your youth, if your own soul space is still much too open and exposed? That simply won't be possible. The soul pushes the urge toward completion of the soul skin upward in the form of a need for forces of antipathy. The 'I' awakens these forces in the soul and they manifest as moods such as sullenness. That 'filthy mood' is the outer indication of increasing forces of antipathy. The teenager expresses these feelings of antipathy and is then experienced as hostile or contrarian. Moody faces, peevish responses and negative looks evoke similar reactions from other people, with the result of some more hardening and fencing around the soul: the soul skin is tightening and thickening.

Of course, there is always the danger of too much withdrawal, of total negativity. So try to keep giving that moody face your love and warmth. This gives teenagers the opening to find their forces of sympathy again at some later moment. With a great wall around the soul no one is able to get to know themselves or others.

FORCES OF SYMPATHY

On the other hand, it can happen that by the teen years the forces of antipathy have grown too strong. Perhaps in children who have constantly had to defend themselves, or who were in situations where they had to hide their inner feelings. In these cases the dwelling of the soul can become too tight so it looks for more inner space. The 'I' in these teenagers will seek connections so forces of sympathy will have to be mobilised.

What does that look like? These extra forces of sympathy are expressed in excessive enthusiasm, love-sickness (often Platonic), sweet dreams, in melting away at a pretty song, a pretty guy or a pretty blouse. These ways of losing yourself in something outside the self are moments in which the soul opens itself completely.

The danger is, of course, that this degenerates into a kind of intoxication in which, because of all these forces of sympathy, the child does not have enough boundaries and protection. When the soul skin completely opens itself, teenagers surrender themselves like a small child to the object of adoration. When this object is an adult with bad intentions the teen will not recognise it. Without boundaries between inner and outer you are unable to distinguish between illusion and reality!

This situation looks very much like that of our early childhood. At that time, too, there was this openness of the soul, this surrender to the outside world. Thus, on the one hand Feeling Teenagers have a unique potential for openness and connection. On the other they risk losing themselves in something outside, without as yet having the capacity to find themselves again.

I think that the great motive behind these soul movements is the struggle to become yourself in the world of feelings. Strangely enough, this becomes visible when you lose yourself. The experience painfully gained in such soul movements will lead to a consciousness of your own soul or your own content, and of the necessity of being and remaining yourself.

Part of the picture of Feeling Teenagers is the experience of loneliness, disappointment, illusion and disillusion. Feeling Teenagers feel rejected, experience the totality of their own feelings, and make the painful discovery that the outside world does not recognise these feelings to the same extent and does not confirm them, let alone respond to them. This reveals to the teen the pain of consciousness, which brings into being in the soul that which is one's own, one's individuality. This pain may become so intense that the tender thread with one's own being is broken. Then the loneliness may turn into a desperate fear of the isolation caused by the process of becoming an adult. When that happens, teenagers may take refuge in distractions such as games or drugs, or in a rejection of themselves and of adulthood such as we see in anorexia. Or sometimes they exhibit a languid dullness in which they drag themselves along with a numb, lifeless soul.

WHAT CAN YOU DO?

◊   Most important is to have an *intimate* relationship with your child already, *before* the onset of the teen years. If you have nothing more than superficial contact with your child you lack a basis from which to work. Having a good relationship does not mean that there are no run-ins or conflicts. It is precisely the child with whom you have a deep inner bond who will rebel vehemently against you.

◊   Most of the time, parents do indeed have a deep bond with their children. This means that they are also connected with their child's soul life, which creates the possibility to act, you could say, as guarantor: if teenagers falter under the weight of a surging feeling life, their parents can provide the support they are not yet able to find in their own 'I'. Through this loving guarantor, the teenager can feel that there exists an inner self, that another person knows this and senses it, even at times when the teenager can't quite muster that inner strength alone.

◊   In practice, this means that you have to train yourself to find your child's own, individual content in everything he or she says and does, to find what is so characteristic of this child. When you affirm this you always, metaphorically speaking, put your child back in his or her own shoes. You learn to recognise many little anecdotes, such as the way the child always does some particular thing, his or her attitude to something or way of quarreling, and so on – little indications that give a picture of this one, unique child.

◊   In addition, there is value in *being seen*. You cannot take away the grief of your son or daughter's unrequited love – in most cases they cannot even stand it if you mention it – but when you do *see* it and they are aware of the fact that you are with them in their inner distress *in silence*, then the loneliness is no longer so deadly.

◊   Many teenagers who have a tendency to lose themselves in emotions totally identify with a social group or with kids in the neighbourhood. Or they do the complete opposite and withdraw into themselves behind heavy screens.

◊   If you manage to get them to participate in family events such as birthdays, a weekend camping trip or some

shopping together in town, then you can break through
these extremes of either living outside themselves or
being shut up inside themselves.

By looking for small openings you can create circumstances that
allow your child the opportunity so uniquely offered by the teenage
journey, while at the same time giving him or her as much protection
and accompaniment as possible.

In order to find these countless little openings you need two fac-
ulties. The first is *creativity*. This helps you find those small opportunities and, indeed, invent them. The second faculty is a *sense of
humour*. For this is what will be chronically lacking in teenagers who
are being pulled out of themselves or, conversely, are completely
wrapped up in themselves. There is no relativity, and therefore no
humour. If you manage in a situation to roll your eyes with a smile,
and also to share that with your teen, you have created a golden
moment.

It is crucial, though, never to fall into ridicule. Ridiculing
something achieves the opposite of humour. It makes children
lonelier than ever, and destroys the intimacy between parent and
child. For teenagers, all these emotions are realities, and if you can
be there with them without losing yourself in them, then this stage
in the river lock will end in a great liberation: the doors to the future
will open.

OVERWHELMED FEELING TEENAGERS

There are also teenagers who are completely submerged in the
waves of their soul life. They often have an enormously rich soul life.
They have much more soul content than the people around them,
so are constantly being inundated. All kinds of wild storm waves rise
up in their souls.

The idea is of course that they find a way to get a handle on
this wealth of soul life and dig their own channel for it, but in
most cases they can't manage to do that. These children have a
very rich soul life and are able to experience great heights and

depths in their feelings, but at the same time their 'I' is not strong enough. It is as if a little captain in a minuscule vessel has to make it across the ocean. The trick for them is not to drown in their inner tempests. They can inwardly feel the suffering of the whole world, but sometimes also explode in happiness and joy, and the next moment they are so aggressive that they don't know what to do with themselves.

If this is expressed in actions, then you are seeing the Doing Teenager. However, if it remains stuck in feeling, the problems may *seem* less difficult, but the teenager is consuming him or herself inwardly. Overwhelmed Feeling Teenagers can become very depressed and, in isolated cases, consider commit suicide without any apparent reason.

Alternatively, these teenagers may become very quiet. They are then so tired of the tempest that they lose all interest. They walk around in a daze. This has the great danger that they may then do something foolish, such as commit to living with some-one, or take a job wherever they can find one, as long as they can get out of 'it'. In a way they hang onto the first straw they see: not their inner straw but a temporary solution. Chances are that after some time this solution will fall through and they will be thrown back onto themselves, and have to yet again face a time of turbulence.

Some parents succeed in letting their own 'I', their own captain, travel with their teen on all excursions as a kind of guarantor. When that is possible, the soul of the teenager does not become so exhausted, and there may also be times of rest when the little captain can rise and take the rudder him or herself. Obviously, this is only possible with a strong basis of trust.

The Doing Teenager

This tendency demands a great deal of energy, both of the teenagers and of the parents. These teens look for their individuality not through consciousness but through direct experience, something we as parents have often forgotten how to do. We adults tend to want to change the world using our heads, rather than intervene in concrete reality. The latter method is much more difficult and comes with great risks. Maybe we dream of resigning from our job, selling the house and travelling around the world for a few years. Beautiful dreams – who doesn't have them sometimes? But rarely does anyone act on them. Do we lack the courage? Are we too attached to our possessions? What will your family say?

Then, suddenly, your teenager is doing it! He or she simply turns a dream of travel into reality. It may end with your prodigal teen returning after some time, without money and with their schooling incomplete. If so, the hope is that you will be able to get the train back on the rails again.

Doing Teenagehood is not always expressed as a grand drama. It usually starts with little things, such as clothing. The Doing Teenager will wear worn or dirty clothes, especially items you consider ugly or inappropriate. Are you able to count to ten and give yourself time to think, or do you immediately burst out with disapproval? If you are really honest, don't you agree your teen has courage? Would you have the guts yourself?

And, if you stop and consider, are you able to see the humour? These parents who spent loads of money on designer clothes for their little one... and now look at their teen in old jeans with holes! If you sit back and think about it, don't you feel a little chuckle emerging? Your well-presented child, now in torn jeans... And perhaps they are now listening to 'awful' music on their iPod, when they used to be so good with the violin!

After such minor external demonstrations, Doing Teenagers are ready for real experiments – look, the whole world is open to them! As a teenager, suddenly you can travel anywhere and do anything you want; you can earn money and there are so many fascinating things to spend it on. First alcohol, smoking and pot, then expressing your sexuality, dancing, parties with pills – the deeper into the night the better. Virtual reality has its own attractions. The world is full of games of speed and violence, so even moments spent alone indoors can be crammed with thrilling experiences and Doing Teenagers can have their kicks there too.

If you are lucky, your Doing Teenager will skip some of these things, but then, they may also start gambling or join a gang. All teenagers will look for their own things to explore. The adults around will keep telling them to think about what they are doing. But that is exactly what they don't do, and even if they did, it wouldn't keep them from experimenting. The restlessness and urge to freedom in their souls impels them to bravura and all these stunts. They form their individuality through experience and its consequences.

WHAT CAN YOU DO?

◊ Doing Teenagers demand total freedom of action, effective immediately. Don't give them their way. Give them every time *a little* more freedom of action. Don't say: 'From now on you are on your own.' Don't give everything at once, but also don't give nothing. A house is built one board or one brick at a time.

◊ Always remember that it is only *after* the experiment that the child understands what was good and bad about it. Preventing it won't work, and indoctrination doesn't work either. Try to manage it in such a way that they won't want to do every experiment at once. Open up a vista toward the freedoms they are going to get. Don't focus on all the things that are still not allowed. For instance: 'If you come away with us this year, you may go with your friends next year. Then you have time to save up for it.'

◊ Because Doing Teenagers can learn so much from their experiments, you can achieve a lot when everything goes awry. But never say, 'I told you so,' and don't despair when your teen causes a lot of commotion and trouble.

◊ Make use of the quiet after the storm to sit down with your child and put in perspective what happened and what can be learned from it. Why not ask what they have learned, and how things could have been done differently? This kind of sharing of the individual learning process creates warmth and a lasting solid ground. And you yourself are then staying part of it.

◊ With all this it is important that you, as parent, remain perfectly certain that the child will get through it all: everything will be all right. But aren't there also children in the world for whom everything does not turn out all right? Yes, that is true, but parents are worth their weight in gold if, in spite of everything, they hold onto the knowledge that their son or daughter will eventually make the step to adulthood. That gives great support to children. Time and again they will lose that confidence in themselves. Their parents' confidence is like a lifeline they can hold onto as they climb a sheer cliff.

◊ Doing Teenagers also require a lot of care. The parents have to be willing to pick up a lot of pieces, and also to create new opportunities even though the teenager has wasted earlier ones.

◊ *Be a person of action yourself.* Your child will then understand you. These teens don't even hear you when you talk to them, but what you *do* speaks to them. Then they experience who you are and that you will be true to them; that they may stumble but can also get up again.

Actually, the gap between the teenager and 'adult society' is not as wide as we sometimes think. Teenagers are more radical, more all or nothing, more authentic, courageous and ready for battle because of their age, but it is really just more of what the world around them carries in itself. In effect, young people experiment with a world created by adults.

Adults are often highly hypocritical. They disapprove of gambling, but always buy a lottery ticket. Sexual experiments for their teens are a no-no, but they themselves visit porn sites.

The Doing Teenager who does nothing

We also have the teenager who experiments by doing nothing at all. The overgrown child you can't get out of bed in the morning or into bed at night, who doesn't do homework and skips school. He or she never does anything in the house and is bored to death.

Dealing with such teenagers can be very difficult. And yet, a lot actually happens when a teen experiments this way. You always had to do all kinds of things, and now you are making yourself free and you simply do nothing. But then things are set in motion ... your parents start talking, fighting, beating, threatening, crying or they throw you out of the house. Or you get called for an interview with the principal or the counsellor at school. Or your girlfriend leaves you for someone else, or you lose your summer job, and so on. Doing nothing thus leads directly to a lot of experiences, a lot of learning.

What can you do?

◊ You will constantly have to set limits on this doing-nothing. And at the moment when things go awry, you can learn together. Most of all, you can try to find a little inner flame of your teen's 'I', which will have to give some indication of what it does really want to do.

◊ Among teenagers who do nothing there tend to be many who have been indulged. For them, doing nothing is a desperate attempt at conquering the consequences of being spoiled by their parents. Children who were indulged in their childhood years often have a weak will force. Everything has always been easy for them, they've never had to fight for attention, material things, good grades... Fighting for something is, however, a condition for an inner bond with the striving of the 'I'.

◊ If you always fight *against* something you often connect with the striving of your lower ego, your own arrogant little person. Egoism and a thought world that is too fully filled with oneself are characteristics of a human being who is too strongly determined by their own ego. Obviously, you need an ego to stand on your own feet and conquer your place in the world, but too much ego means that you are perennially fighting against things. Then there is no inner attitude of listening – listening to others, but also to one's own true being, the higher 'I'.

◊ Fighting *for* something proceeds from the strength that is the trailblazer for the true essence of the human being, the 'I'. Fighting for something is based on a connection that has come into being between something outside yourself and your own inner being. This demands openness of the inner being and prevents an excess of ego. Every child should have had to fight for something with fire and sword: for a friend, to learn to read, to go to bed later – it doesn't matter what, but the holy fire must have burned. If that does not happen, children will have, one could say, a will deficit. They will lack motivation.

◊ Because the teen years are also the time when children try to catch up with growth they have missed, such a child will, as a teen, create this doing-nothing. Then all that surrounds this teenager will start fighting for his or her life. The people around the Doing-nothing Teenager will change from indulging into demanding and confronting adults, at least if you are lucky. If you are unlucky, they will just let you be and turn away from you as a hopeless, indifferent good-for-nothing. The parents may say that they have taken such good care of you all these years and have given you everything your little heart desired, and now you have become a thankless and lazy bum and they will simply drop you. That *is* exactly what you are, but it would be better if they could understand that you are

> sitting there waiting for someone to light the holy fire in
> you. For inside you it is cold and empty.

An example of this is a son, an only child, of very successful parents who work day and night. The son had always had a life of luxury. According to the father, as a teen the boy had become a weakling, did nothing, accomplished nothing. He just hung out with some friends and threw away money. He was failing in everything he did, his grades were bad, he lost his jobs.

One day an adult became really interested in him. This adult made a connection with this boy and did not demean him. When the boy once again needed money he borrowed it from this adult, who did not have any to spare. The money disappeared of course. But the boy took this so seriously that he swore he would repay it. For the first time, he cared about something that had happened. The first little fire was lit. It took an extreme effort, but the boy did succeed in paying the money back. Little by little the fire grew; one by one things began to have value.

Of course, a boy like that has a long way to go, but at least there was a turn-around. The inner, loving 'I'-fire of the adult managed to light a small tentative flame in the boy. In this way his will power started growing so that in time he could become capable of more and more actual deeds.

The Transition from Feeling to Doing

Teenagehood begins with thinking, flows over into feeling and concludes with doing. Doing Teenagehood could also be called Will Teenagehood. Each period lasts around two years. Every teenager lives through all three but, depending on the child, they will experience one more intently than the others. The phase of Doing Teenagehood arrives at about the age of seventeen or eighteen. Emotionally these teens have quieted down a bit. Every great inner change is preceded by a calm before the storm.

The transition to Will Teenagehood demands a lot of energy;

it is a really high threshold. Beforehand it looks as if the inner engine is stalled. Teens lose energy, they lose courage and they lose connection with things that occupied them. Suddenly they drop all interest and don't know what they've been doing it all for. They tend toward apathy and . They often skip school, and let go of many things that had been important to them, both relationships and goals, both at school and at home. They don't know what to do with this feeling of 'slack lines'. It almost looks like menopause!

Usually this period does not last very long, but it can be extreme, and it is risky. People around teens in this stage often think that the worst is over, but precisely at this time young people can lose the red thread and drift away, or lose the way in their entelechy. Children who strongly lived their period of Feeling Teenagehood and always found a lot of energy in their souls may undergo this later soul experience as deeply shocking. They were carried by great impulses of a feeling nature, but these have stopped coming.

Impulses of will come from a very different direction and they have not yet arrived. Such experiences are the most baffling ones in the teen years; both parents and the children themselves are bewildered. People grumble about the teenagers because they don't seem to accomplish anything any more, because they walk around lethargic like morons. They are often so discouraged that they become depressed. Some of them have gone through high school without difficulties but right before final exams they drop out and refuse the final sprint.

WHAT CAN YOU DO?

◊ When an adult is able to make an appeal to the 'I' of the teenager out of genuine concern and involvement, and out of insight into what is taking place, the latter may receive that as a wake-up call, which may produce a breakthrough. Suddenly they are back, they are awake again. A spark flew across and they came into action – so their eighteenth year, or thereabouts, marks the beginning of a period of completion, decisions and doing things.

◊ In any case it is important that in this crisis 'the car keeps going'. The teenager on the threshold of the period of doing must continue with their life and commitments, even if they don't do well with them. They must not quit school and become unemployed. Being too nice to teens at this point may be interpreted as the door being wide open to desertion. Then they grandly sink back in the comfort of Feeling Teenagehood and will not cross the threshold. It is like an alibi for failing to move on in their growth. A way out of such desertion is often hard to find.

◊ In this period we sometimes see cases of glandular fever or mononucleosis, which means that the ill teenager is not allowed to do anything. This is a dangerous illness, not just physically, but also and especially for the inner being, for life then does indeed stand still and the risks mentioned above become reality. Sometimes the teenagers have finished one course of study but there is no room for them in the next one. They are stopped in their tracks.

◊ The treasury of youth is empty. Where then do teens at this late stage find the necessary energy? No longer from the past, but from the future! This future is as yet unborn, but it can direct its energy if the future 'I' lights the spark, for instance, when something touches a teenager in his or her inner being. It can be anything: a book, or something someone says, a trip or some other experience. Then the engine starts up again; new enthusiasm and new courage for life stream into the soul, and the future can be conquered.

◊ It is as if the teenager is sitting on a swing that is pushed hard in one direction. The swing's point of stillness at the top of the arc can be compared to this moment right before the period of Will Teenagehood. Teenagers must then start to move themselves, otherwise their swings will fall still, for no one is pushing them any more. At that point of stillness, it would perhaps help if the parents would loudly shout, 'Go!' so that their teen can wake up and not sleep through the moment. That demands great parental attention in a period when you had already started to step back. But it is definitely worth the effort!

2. The Body and the Relation between Soul and Body

As we have seen, the higher 'I' uses the soul as an instrument. The soul has eyes and ears for the impulses of the higher spiritual being that lives and works in us. The entire teen period serves the healthy development of the soul, and the 'I' will later make use of this.

But the 'I' and the soul are not the whole story. We human beings live on earth in a physical body, which is permeated by life forces. Everything we learn and all that belongs to the current development of humanity has to be worked through and lived through at the level of the physical and earthly. That which remains stuck at some other level is as yet unfinished, is not yet fully human.

A healthy soul becomes an instrument of the 'I', but also has to work down into the body. The soul communicates the impulses of the 'I' to the body. This may sound pretty theoretical, but it is happening all day long, often without our realising. Imagine that the 'I' has the impulse of making a work of art. The soul feels this as an inner urge, an idea, an inspiration. Then comes the moment when the soul responds to this urge and seeks to bring it into reality. The person may, for instance, want to go to work on a piece of wood. He or she sees the wood and picks it up. The soul now needs an influence that penetrates all the way to the tips of the fingers: an influence that permeates the muscles, the movements of fingers, hands and arms, even down into the heartbeat and breathing. The entire body comes into play.

What does the body do in return for the soul? The body has eyes and ears, and the soul uses these to observe the world around it. And the soul feels the world through the body's sense of touch. Just as, on the one hand, the soul listens to the 'I' internally, so, on the other hand, it listens to the world through the body.

> The soul connects our higher 'I' to the physical world and also connects the world around us to our higher 'I'.

One could say that the soul of the human being is one great open sense organ that is able to hear the high tones from the spiritual world and the dark tones from the physical world.

Although we may not be so conscious of this deeper task of listening, we are living with it all the time. For instance, at an interesting lecture the soul listens to the words and admits them into the life of feelings in order to know whether what is being said is enriching or not. When the soul has taken the words in, the human being can work with them emotionally and intellectually and with the will. But if the soul has not listened, has kept its ears closed during that lecture, nothing at all will happen: no new thinking, no new feelings, no new activity. Before impulses from the outside world can have effect, the soul must have perceived them. All our physical senses extend themselves into the soul and have their sequel there. In fact, it is the soul that perceives, through the medium of the body.

Perhaps that sounds strange. But we all know that when two people are in the same situation they often perceive different things. What is perceived depends on the nature of the soul's inner eyes and ears. When you take a country walk along with others, one of them will notice all the flowers and trees, another will hear all the birds and identify them from their songs. A third sees and hears everything, while another notices nothing. The difference is not in the eyes and ears, it is in the souls of these people.

Everything your soul has learned to listen to and look for, sensed or tasted, has become part of your life and experience. Things for which your soul has not developed a sense organ do not really exist for you. You do not live in them and so your 'I' impulses can't work with them.

In the teenage years, a child is in the process of developing the soul into something truly individual, so it is important that there is an open channel for 'I' impulses. And it is just as important that there be an open channel for physical impulses to the soul. The soul can then channel the essence of the observations made in the world to the 'I'. This bridging function of the soul is extremely important and is often underestimated.

The way from the 'I' (spirit, meaningful goal)
To the *soul* (feeling, thought, striving)
To the *physical body* (experience, deeds, movement, observation)
Is a kind of stepwise speaking.

The way back from the *physical body* (hearing, seeing, touching, experiencing)
To the *soul* (empathy, compassion, sympathy, antipathy)
To the 'I' (learning, understanding, acknowledging, recognising value, loving)
Is a kind of stepwise listening.

If the soul has no ear for a subject being taught at school, these children are unable to learn. At best they can adopt this subject by rote, through habit or tricks. But they will not enter into an understanding, and will not develop a feeling for the subject.

If the soul has no feeling for nature, the child will not become someone who is able to take care of the natural world and enjoy it.

If the soul has no eye for the bodies of other human beings and has no feeling for them, that person will not be able to interact with the body of the other in a living and loving way. If a person has no sense organs for the unique aspect of another person, he or she will not be able to have an encounter or relationship with that person.

The task of the teen years has, therefore, two parts. On the one hand, the soul must open itself to the higher 'I' so that it can find its direction in life. On the other hand, the soul must open itself to a genuine experience of the earth and fellow human beings so that the impressions it lives among can be handed on to the higher 'I'. These two functions of the soul are the basis for a meaningful life. In them, human beings make communication possible between spirit and earth, and between earth and spirit.

Opening the Teenage Soul to the Body: The vital role of movement

When children reach the age of puberty their bodies undergo great changes. They become men and women instead of children, at least as regards the body. Teenagers often wrestle with their physicality and suffer from it. They rarely feel young, beautiful and strong. Getting to know their own body as it manifests itself in physical reality and accepting their body are difficult tasks for many young people. The soul is unable to develop sense organs in those aspects of the body that a young person is not yet connected with. For the soul or 'inner' sense organs, acceptance of the body is an absolute condition.

However, it is not only one's own body that has to be accepted and known, but also the body of the earth, nature, animals and other people. We could say that the entire world in its physical appearance implores us to accept it. But in the post-industrial world, it seems as if the way in which we live closes even the soul sense organs our children bring with them, instead of helping them to open. Small children sometimes bring very bright soul sense organs with them from their life before birth. They may then experience a miracle when the first crocus opens after the winter. What their eyes see, their soul also sees.

Once, a farmer accepted the soil, the weather and his cows as they were, and because he did he was able to make a connection with them in his soul. The food was distinct, honest and recognisable, and the soul listened to all those impressions. Our youth grow up in cities, amid synthetics, with computers and television, with frozen dinners warmed up in microwave ovens, and they are kept warm in houses where fire is nowhere to be seen. The food is often produced by unnatural methods. Many impressions are in fact de-souled, unreal. Because of this unreality, the soul is prevented from developing inner sense organs for the world.

In consequence, people are inwardly deaf and blind to the world, which leads to vandalism and indifference in relation to food and everything else. We find it strange that young people cannot develop a feeling for the things around them. But they are unable to notice them: their observation does not reach beyond their physical senses because the soul experiences nothing. It doesn't mean a thing to them when the nice new bus shelter is broken again. For such a thing to hurt inwardly, the soul must perceive it. Then you have an inner connection with your physical eye: your soul eyes are opened.

Then love arises for what is perceived, for when the soul transmits the essence of an observation to the higher 'I', the reaction of the 'I' will be a force of love that radiates into the soul. This can be observed because it will result in loving words and deeds. We have then come full circle. Love, therefore, can only be learned on the basis of the soul being able to develop its bridge functions. Love means respect, healing instead of breaking – not because there are rules against breaking, but because a connection is forged in the soul.

Teenagers begin by observing their own bodies. We wish we could make clear to our kids that whatever they find there is all good, beautiful and true. But in their insecurity they look for examples. In a world filled with seductive pictures of men and women with 'ideal' outer appearances, this is often a discouraging experience. Most teenagers feel they do not measure up when compared with people on screen or in magazines. Thus they begin their struggle to live up to the ideal of being human *externally*. Energy that could otherwise be spent struggling to become a real, full human being in an *inner* sense is thus consumed to a greater or lesser degree by concern with the external. Some never even try the struggle for an external ideal, but develop feelings of inferiority, which they then hide in their behaviour.

Either way, concern with the external impedes the development of inner eyes and ears. They only see the physical muscles and only hear talk of physical beauty; all they are aware of are physical differences. Thus many teens look for affirmation and want to be appreciated on the basis of their physical appearance. Such affirmation, however, is flighty. It does not provide rest and confidence, because it is gone as quickly as it came. When the body is experienced and used in this way, what arises is a kind of soul deafness, not caused this time by an untrue world around the young people, but by estrangement from their own bodies.

But what is a true experience of the body? This can occur only when *the body moves*. When you feel how this exquisite instrument of your body serves movement, you experience it as a standing-in-the-world. When you work on a farm during a summer break, or when you paddle a canoe down rushing rapids, you develop a healthy feeling for the body. Then it is no longer about that one little pimple, or one unruly strand of hair, but about the body as an instrument for perception moving in the world, for the soul, too, is all movement. It is the most mobile thing we have. The soul expresses its mobility in the rhythms of heart and lungs. The soul is so mobile that it can only truly connect itself with the body when it senses that the body is going to move. Then the inner eyes and inner ears can grow.

It is no accident that the condition for making the soul quiet and still in meditation is keeping the body also quiet and still: not too much food, comfortable digestion, restful position. Buddhist or Hindu yogis quiet the body, quiet the soul, and are then able to withdraw into spiritual heights.

Teenagers need the opposite. Put the body into motion in sports and games, in work and in lively learning processes full of experiments and explorations. This will bring the soul into activity so that it can listen and learn and so, in turn, the spirit can connect with the soul enabling the 'I' to send its impulses.

Wise people are beginning to realise that shutting youthful delinquents up in prison cells is senseless. *It means imprisoning the body and therefore also the soul.* Given such impediment to soul development, we should not be surprised when teens come out of detention worse than they went in. Alternative penalties might include having young people clean up the walls they had covered with graffiti. Their outer, but also their inner eyes would be opened to what they are seeing. Challenging hiking trips can also work with young convicts, but because many young people have never known much exercise and movement of the body – and therefore of the soul – this kind of initiative is incredibly difficult. How do you keep them going? How do you stop them from sitting down, or hitchhiking back? And yet, for inner development, this is the solution.

Parents, keep your teenagers moving, physically moving, whether it be dancing, skating, team sports or climbing mountains! As long as they are in motion they will develop. Also keep the metabolism moving with regular meals of food the body needs to work on to digest. It doesn't matter if they snack on hot chips or French fries now and then, as long as most days they get regular, healthy food.

Sometimes when young people can't connect with their bodies, anorexia nervosa will develop. Those with anorexia don't accept their bodies; in their eyes their body is not right. They don't eat, so the metabolism is idle. When that happens, the soul cannot connect properly with body and life. Anorexic teens hear and see so little that the soul receives too few impressions, and in due course they may let go of the body and end up in hospital having intravenous feeding. They can also let go of the soul, which means they cannot make connections with friends, study or anything else. You could say that the 'I' is struck dumb and can find no way of sending impulses for meaningful activity into the soul.

Teenagers wrestle so hard with their bodies, with growing up and with bringing vitality into the soul – let us bring them into movement! I hope that many physical education teachers under-stand this. The point is not to get good grades, to win, or to master a particular exercise; it is of vital importance that all young people participate in movement. Moving all kinds of muscles that usually don't move much, and learning to move with joy are essential.

When we teach our children to cook or to paint the house we also organise movement for them. If at all possible, teenagers should be stimulated in this manner, although it takes a lot of humour and creativity. When body and soul interact in a healthy way you see this expressed in lively reactions. Just tell a class that they are going to get an extra field trip. You will see how the joy of their souls expresses itself in lively and enthusiastic reaction. When teenagers are having a long and boring lesson they will slump lower and lower in their seats. But when they are having an outdoor event that evening you immediately see the difference.

I must also acknowledge that physical exercise can be overdone, when we see, for example, an excessive need to exercise or team fanaticism. Many adults enjoy a game of volleyball or football, but many others become un-free in such games; sport becomes an obsession. Instead of enjoying experiences on the basis of soul movement, the experiences proceed from physical reactions and have the effect of suppressing soul experiences. Adrenaline generated through physical exercise gives a kick, but that is quite different from enjoying a hike in the mountains or a walk on the beach. Sporting fanaticism and the high following exertion can be addictive; this impoverishes the soul and its sense organs. The bicycle that never moves forward is a remarkable phenomenon in our culture. We cycle and move for fitness, but our eyes are on our watch and on the gauges and our ears are full of music. The connection between the sense organs of body and soul is then strained.

In summary, the soul develops inner eyes and ears by connecting itself in a healthy way with the body through the body's lively and meaningful movements.

THE BODY OF LIFE FORCES

Between the soul and the physical body we have the body of life forces. I did not mention this before because I wanted to avoid making things too complicated, but for the sake of completeness, it has to be said that a lack of life forces shows up directly in a lack of the urge to move. Often when teenagers are not really ill, they may be suffering from a drop in their life forces making them tired and lethargic. To restore these life forces they need to be outside a lot, and to get good food and rest. Excessive intellectual work and too much pressure have a negative impact on life forces.

People who are dead tired may do something with complete indifference something which they would normally never dream of doing. It's as if the act and its consequences simply don't get through to them. And that is literally true in such a case: it does not penetrate into the soul.

3. Seven Days of the Week: A key to teenagers' individuality

Every week has seven days, each of which gives a different colour to our lives. We can sense how those days are all different from each other. Birth, death, marriage and many other events carry the sign of the day of the week on which they occur. Not many people get married on Monday or Tuesday. Is that just for practical reasons, or is there more involved?

Growing children thrive when there is a recognisable rhythm to the days of the week. Staying up late on Saturday evening, a special breakfast on Sunday morning, Monday back to school, a particular day for sport or for the babysitter – this gives security. If anything can happen on any day, or if every day is the same as the previous one, children are not likely to be healthy.

Having no weekly rhythm also makes adults nervous or depressed. It is for good reason that prisoners shut off from the outside world will scratch signs into their walls to keep track of days and weeks. Astronauts also adhere strictly to daily and weekly schedules. People who have irregular work hours or who often have to work on weekends notice that having two weekdays off is not the same as having Saturday and Sunday off, irrespective of church attendance or other regular practices.

Every day has a different atmosphere, a different quality. Sunday is different from Monday or Wednesday. Through the centuries, people have been going to church on Sundays; there has to be a good reason for that. People who are sensitive to this sort of thing will feel that a walk or a difficult conversation on a Sunday morning has a different quality to the same activity on a different day.

We usually think that a day is different because we do different things that day. But then we confuse cause and effect. We do different things that day because the day is different! Travelling in Israel we discover that the Palestinian Muslims take their weekly day off on Friday, the orthodox Jews on Saturday and the Christians on Sunday. This is very practical, because there are always people willing to work on the weekend!

Still, it is interesting that Muslims, Jews and Christians experience a different day as the most important. In the Jewish religion, regular rituals are maintained with extreme precision. Some of these rituals are thousands of years old, such as the celebration of the liberation from Egyptian bondage. On Saturday the quality of the past can be felt most clearly. The Jewish religion experiences its individuality as closely related to that of Saturday.

We could give many more examples of the different qualities of the days of the week. You can go against this and act as if there are no differences, or you can learn to collaborate with them. If you pay attention to what is easy or more difficult on a particular day of the week, you will begin to observe the days' different qualities.

Why is this kind of experience so important in relation to teenagers? It is because in the teen years these seven qualities work strongly into the soul of the child. Younger children experience them in a more external way and are still dependent on the stable rhythm of their surroundings. Teenagers experience them more inwardly. The seven qualities that are active in the days of the week also come to life in the teenager's inner being. With every teenager the effects will be different because each one of them will have a different disposition relative to the 'colours' of the days.

When the individuality in the soul awakens, it is like a rainbow with seven colours in which some are vague and others very distinct. These differences come into being from the way the seven planetary spheres work into the soul before birth. This is also the reason why the days of the week are named after the seven traditional planets (including the sun).

The disharmony that exists between a teenager's own seven colours and those of people around him, the curriculum in school and culture in general causes the struggle that he or she experiences to grow up in a healthy way. For instance, take teenagers who are strong in the quality of Sunday. The golden radiance of their original individuality shines in their inner being. If all they are permitted to do in school is to repeat word for word what they are taught, then the predominant quality in school is that of Monday, the day dominated by the moon, not the sun. All that is demanded is a strict rhythm of taking things in and giving them out again unchanged, like high tide and low tide. A strong Sunday child is then likely to chuck it all, or to devise original actions during the lessons in school. Such behaviour will be called a disturbance, but the child is trying to find a connection between inner and outer. By allowing the sun to radiate into the lesson, the quality of Monday may be enriched, and a good teacher will be open to that. This demands great understanding and an awareness of the soul quality of the student.

When teaching a Tuesday teenager you need to give brief, forceful lessons and foster much learning by experience, whereas a Thursday student wants to have an overview and often digs more deeply into the subject than the teacher – but will be a stranger to detail. Details are what the Wednesday and Friday students are after. Being sensitive to such differences enables us to better observe, accept and appreciate young people in their own, deep-seated originality.

More and more we see labels slapped on young people on the basis of 'universal standards' and 'average deviations'. This turns them into dead dolls in a shop window. A living understanding of teenagers is achieved by sensing and recognising the way the seven colours are working in their souls.

The Seven Days and Dyslexia

Working with the differences in 'colour' we experience in the seven days of the week can throw light on the problem of dyslexia. Every educator knows that dyslexia is not just an inability to learn reading and writing. It means that the inner colours we have mentioned above show great differences. If we do not trap these children between performance demands and inabilities – as between a rock and a hard place – but accompany them within their characteristics, we can see their inner originality unfold.

Dyslexic children take many things literally. This means that their insight and memory are activated by observable connections, not by rote learning or abstractions. Dyslexic children will almost always forget to bring their raincoat back home after the sun has begun to shine. A dyslexic teenager who pays attention to clock time is an exception. Their rooms and book bags are disasters; so is their homework. But what looks like recalcitrant sloppiness is actually an incapacity that will have to be at least partly overcome by a great deal of patience and persistence. Great time pressure and stress increases the potential for dyslexics to overcome their difficulties, so they will have the natural tendency to wait with everything until the last minute. Girls tend to be a little better at compensating for these problems than boys, but they can also get caught up in their need to please and do things right. (Many adult dyslexics continue to show the same weaknesses.) It is important to keep remembering these characteristics, because this will help us accept and accompany a dyslexic teenager. Destructive criticism and reproaches will unnecessarily undermine self-confidence.

Dyslexic people are often Friday people – they like to meet others – and the playfulness of Wednesday shows up in them until deep into their teen years. The Saturday quality of order and precision is lacking. Saturday is a good day for cleaning up, for deciding what has to be kept in the garage and what should be thrown out. By nature, dyslexic children will say yes to everything, but that can also make them hesitating, insecure and vague. They don't know the difference between 'to lay' and 'to lie', and also have trouble distinguishing between keeping and letting go.

When relating to dyslexic teenagers, work from their own individuality and strength. These have the colours of Friday and Wednesday, full of the urge to meet people and of mobility. As well as encouraging these tendencies, it can of course be helpful to understand which characteristics are missing and how they might be stimulated.

Another characteristic of dyslexic teenagers is that they are late bloomers, remaining children much longer than their contemporaries. Their capacity for abstract thinking develops very late. They often master mathematical concepts much later than average. We must fight to keep the doors of average standards open until they have arrived, otherwise their capacities will grow when their schooling level has already been downgraded. Dyslexic teenagers need specifically customised educational methods, tailored to individual characteristics.

Like mathematics, learning to read music depends on the recognition of abstract signs and characters. This is just as difficult for dyslexics as reading and writing, so they need aural methods of music tuition. For them, abstraction is like a distant planet where their spaceship has not yet arrived.

Radiant Sunday children have a precious quality. If they are appreciated and protected they will, as dyslexic teenagers, become enthusiastic, joyful and social. Their thinking will be lively and especially imaginative, with original approaches to problem solving. For the school system and the teachers and parents who educate dyslexic children this demands careful observation and coaching. The fresco of the child's soul is all too easily painted over, so that it loses its original strength and colour.

Educators will succeed if they give dyslexic teenagers challenging, realistic problems that can be solved on different levels, instead of requiring them to absorb and regurgitate dry facts. Knowledge of the laws of physics, for instance, can be taken in and remembered by thirteen- or fourteen-year-old dyslexic teenagers if it is connected with experiments and examples from reality. A foreign language is no problem if they can spend time abroad among people who speak that language instead of being taught from a book. Whether these teens will ever write the foreign language without errors is most uncertain, but how important is that?

Because the seven inner qualities emerge and start working between the fourteenth and twenty-first year, much can be done for the understanding and health of growing young people. The future calls for custom-made approaches to raising and teaching teenagers. Indeed the exceptions have already become the rule. Thanks to Rudolf Steiner and the many teachers who grew up in Steiner-Waldorf schools, these seven qualities associated with the days of the week can once more come to consciousness. We must not let this extraordinary resource for understanding young people be lost again.

4. Soul Strength and the Inner Seeker

For a healthy development of the soul during the teen years it is important to know how much soul strength your child possesses, and how this soul strength is developing.

Soul strength – what is that? We are familiar with strength of spirit and body, but we rarely stop to realise that there is also something called soul strength. *'Soul strength' is my name for the quantity of soul energy a human being possesses and can bring into action.* Most of the time we don't become aware of soul strength until it is lacking – when the soul is exhausted and can no longer generate energy – just as the body and life forces can be exhausted so that we can no longer perform our physical tasks.

People differ from each other in soul strength just as much as they differ in physical strength. When one parent organises a birthday party it takes so much soul strength that he or she is totally empty when it is over. Another parent has children staying overnight after the party without any trouble whatsoever. It is often a difference in soul potential, available soul strength.

One person is overwhelmed by an ordinary sickness in their child, while another loses a child to cancer and manages to process that in his or her soul. For one it takes an extreme effort to bring up a child; another has so much energy that he or she has no trouble handling five children. One person always sees the humourous side of things, remains creative and inwardly able to make a new start, while another becomes rigid, stiff and dries up.

A child with sufficient soul strength will navigate a soul river that is broad and deep, and can accommodate the little ship of life so that it can always keep moving. However, if a child has too little soul strength, or is unable to use it, the soul body will only make a small, thin stream and adapt to its limitations. The danger is then that in times of drought, when there is little nourishment, the soul stream will run dry. The little ship of life then runs aground; it can go no further and the possibility of life stagnates, since without soul strength it can't go on. The soul is the great connector, and when it cannot do its work, life comes to an end. If the stream does not quickly get some new water, the soul will die and the human being will live on like a living corpse or will also physically die.

Should there still be water but too little, it will be necessary to build a lot of locks in the river to make sure that soul strength can be managed and preserved. The result is a frugal soul life with sand bars and rocks impeding navigation in the river. Resources are then limited and the potential for giving and living is restricted. If it is a question of limiting the celebration of carnival to one night instead of three, there is no problem. But if after two months on the job a teacher is sick of the children and constantly feels aggravated and empty, there is definitely something seriously wrong. Apparently the teacher did not have the soul strength that was needed for the job.

How Do You Get Soul Strength?

Soul strength arises from *inner* and *outer* causes. Inwardly, soul strength arises from *the quality of the seeker in the soul*. The seeker in the soul is a real, living being, part of who you are. The inner seeker works like a magnet, attracting what belongs and repulsing what does not. We hardly know our inner seeker, but we certainly recognise its magnetic effects:

◊ In our desires we see the shadow side of the seeker in our soul. The magnetism of what we want to have and possess is the 'uneducated' part of the inner seeker. This is very often the way our seeker brings us our homework in this life. We are asked to liberate these desires from egoism, and to transform them into a loving striving for something that benefits our fellow human beings. The shadow side can also be experienced in resistance, fear, aggression and antipathy.

◊ In the bright side of the inner seeker, love is already present, resulting in trust, acceptance and openness. The magnetism of the seeker works here in such a way that we can connect ourselves with someone or something: we can live them, experience them.

When the shadow side of the seeker dominates, you see that that which it is seeking becomes more important than the world. It simply insists on having the thing. The bright side of the seeker, however, allows the *importance* of the thing to predominate: what is best for the money, for that particular person, for that particular effort?

The relationship between these two sides of the seeker, the shadow side and the bright side, and the power of this inner magnetism, determine the soul strength of a person's inner being.

Aside from this inner cause there are also outer causes for the growth of soul strength. The inner seeker attracts a lot to himself, but the human being also receives much in his soul as gifts. We depend on this to such an extent that if no soul powers flow to us as gifts we will soon be doomed to death. I am not exaggerating. We can do without food and drink only to a very limited extent, but we can also do without being given soul strength only to a very limited extent. Soul strength is bestowed on us in three ways:

◊ The cosmos, the spiritual world, continually directs uninterrupted streams of love forces and wisdom to our souls, whether we are aware of it or not.

◊ Our fellow human beings, the souls of the people we meet and with whom we live, continually bestow on us inner and outer soul forces of all kinds, both positive and warming ones, but also negative and chilling ones.

◊ And finally, the earth bestows soul strength on us through stones, plants, animals and air.

INNER SEEKERS

It would be wonderful if parents could truly see the inner seeker in their child and know its strength and its bright and shadow sides. They would then not need to be ashamed of whatever is not yet under control in the child, for they would know who is working there.

All children bring their own inner seeker and, as parent, you can only wait and see what it may look like. A strong seeker will cause the child to connect with many things and to feel attracted to everything, whether out of passionate greed or in loving admiration.

Most of the time, the seeker will express itself both in its shadow and in its bright side. A child is born as a new human being, but he or she carries an old soul that has a long path of development behind it, a path of which we usually know nothing, and of which we may at best have some vague inkling. The result of this path of development is found in the seeker in the soul. Here, in this magnetic working in the centre of our soul, is concentrated the strength of all that preceded this life.

All we have already acquired and made human will emerge as bright strength in the soul. The child feels magically attracted to people, knowledge, or nature, and can immediately make such connections. He or she does not even need to seek these connections; they are already in existence. No wonder that the seeker quickly finds responses there. But the life lessons the child brought that have not yet been fulfilled emerge in the soul as desire, egoistic magnetism, or as resistance, repulsion – the opposite of magnetism. The child may, for instance, abhor arithmetic, weak people, or animals.

A weak seeker shows all of this with little power, while the power of a strong seeker may be almost overwhelming. And in between we will see all possible variations. As parents, there is nothing you can do about it. When you get to know your child in this regard, acceptance of the strength and colour of his or her soul life may grow. Such understanding and acceptance will help you in your interaction with the child.

How can we impart soul strength to our children?

The best opportunities to impart soul strength to our children arise before the teen years. We can protect them as much as possible from influences that close off the forces of a spiritual nature. We can ourselves bestow on them as much soul strength as we are able to. We can bring them in touch with the world through good food and through nature in all its many manifestations. That is the world that creates soul strength. On the other hand, an artificial world filled with inauthentic forms and objects has nothing positive to give to a child.

Everything we give to children enters into their still open soul and is collected there by the inner seeker. Combinations of similar experiences create corresponding images and become inner strength in the soul. Such direct gifts bestowed on children by their parents, and also indirect gifts such as a good education, are of the greatest importance.

Soul Strength in the Teen Years

During the teen years, the soul body is formed. The river of the content of the soul seeks and finds a channel for itself. During teenagehood it becomes increasingly difficult to impart soul strength to children. They are busy closing their soul skin and are facing the task of mastering our influences, testing them, throwing them out and, perhaps, retrieving them again. It is self-evident that in this period they will close themselves off from the gifts of the parents.

Parents, therefore, should not try to continue bestowing soul strength on them. It is counterproductive and, actually, it is also a bit unnatural. Gradually pull back your giving soul, so you do not compel your child to suddenly close the door in your face. Remain inwardly true to your child, but your love should now withdraw into a silent place. Just as you pull a small child onto your lap and experience how good that feels, similarly you can experience that it is good when you gradually put the teenager off your lap and let him or her go.

THE TEENAGER WITH LITTLE SOUL STRENGTH

A teenager with little soul strength may have received much, but if the inner seeker is weak, and therefore the magnetic power feeble, the child has not made much of what it has received. All that has been given does live as a memory in the soul, as a seed for later times, but it has not become genuine, useable soul strength.

It can also happen that children receive too little soul strength from their parents:

◊ If they grow up without reverence, without spiritual orientation, without celebrations, and in a superficial milieu in which what is hidden behind things is denied and reproved. That makes it impossible to remain open to gifts from the spiritual world.

◊ If they grow up with few soul connections with other people. Perhaps no one focused on them, and there was little warmth and attention. Or perhaps they grew up among people who had little soul strength themselves and were simply unable to give much.

◊ If they grow up in a stifling home without plants and animals in a polluted industrial town; if they went into the factory too young; if they were fed a lot of processed food and were often ill in bed.

In all such cases, and especially if they occurred simultaneously, the teenager will have absorbed insufficient soul strength.

The fact is, however, that teenagehood demands great soul strength. With insufficient soul strength, therefore, children are really unable to develop freely and fully during the teen years; they do not have the necessary energy. The danger then is great that they will skip the teenage journey in whole or in part.

What can you do?

Sometimes, in the first teen years, say until the age of fifteen or sixteen, you can still give nourishment through love and attention, interesting travel, starting a vegetable garden, visiting ancient churches with their special atmosphere, by studying the biography of someone admirable together, such as Martin Luther King. In things like the lives of people who overflowed with soul strength nourished out of the spirit, young teens can find something spiritual for themselves.

When a child no longer accepts this you can do something else. You can teach them to use their limited soul strength in a responsible way. If they waste their energy there will be little left over for their real soul tasks. It will then be difficult for the soul to develop into a good instrument for the higher 'I' and a good sense organ for the world and all that lives in it. If you consume all your strength by talking with everyone, sitting in cafés in busy streets, or by quarrelling and giving your emotions free reign, your soul strength will plummet and you will feel empty.

Try to coach your child in learning to cope with a shortage of reserve strength. Even if they don't follow your advice right away, show them how they can and must practice economy in this regard. If they don't do it, the notorious trait of indifference will raise its ugly head. Many young people who are not blessed with much soul strength waste the little they do have in drugs and alcohol, parties, sensation and sexual excitement. In the end, they can't get interested in anything any more. Their inner life has turned into a desert without a stream to water all that dryness.

Study Saps Soul Strength

Intellectual work of some significance destroys soul strength. If we want to make our thinking processes productive we have to bring them to life. We have to let them grow into imaginings with which we can make a connection and for which we can develop a feeling. This takes soul strength. The pace and the manner in which our conventional high schools impart knowledge to our teenagers amounts to a direct attack on soul strength.

When the teacher is inspired and knows how to en-soul the subject this will happen to a much lesser extent. Then this golden teacher bestows on the children what the process of acquiring knowledge takes away from them. It also makes a great difference if a lot of action and observation is incorporated in the lessons. Also the creative processing of what was learned is valuable, for instance, in a report or drawing. But simply absorbing knowledge through hearing and reading, and mechanically applying it, are soulless practices. They suck soul strength out of the child, and the knowledge remains dry and unfruitful.

A child with a lot of soul strength may well rebel against such scorched earth practices and refuse to invest much time and energy in study and school. When you think of it, it is really a healthy response, although of course it creates a whole range of new problems.

If a child has little soul strength and is also not very intelligent, there does not need to be much of a problem. It means that there will not be much schooling and a lot of practical work. As a result, the soul will not be robbed of the strength it does have.

However, a child with little soul strength and great intelligence may face a real trap. Out of its inner seeker, the child will feel magnetically attracted to knowledge and the professions study can lead to in later life. All soul strength will be focused and used in service of the learning process. The learning process will progress smoothly, but the child will in fact skip teenagehood because there is no energy left over. In this way, many really clever people never become free in their souls. They develop their intellectual talents at the expense of the soul task. We can see the result in the dry professor who is emotionally deprived and dependent but intellectually highly developed.

I ask that we give such talented but soul-deprived young people extra time. Extend their summer breaks to three months. Give them a year off so they can have time and energy to be teenagers. It may be expensive, but roaming free for a year can be of critical importance for their soul life. Do you have a zealous fifteen year old student? Let him or her skip school once in a while, or do something else for a year or so. What counts is to make room for the application of soul strength to the task of the teen journey.

Also, when your child has a friend who pulls them out of their fixation on school work, don't send the friend home right away. They may take some time away from study, but later it may prove to be so beneficial to have taken that time now and then to become adults in the soul. Besides, real students will do well no matter what – they don't give up easily! Many a young person who quits studies prematurely does this because he or she worked much too hard at it. The soul will then break out and look for its own opportunities to develop.

Wando

Once upon a time there was a young man who was born without legs. Because of his cheerful and courageous nature he always found a way to cope with his life. On a cart, on crutches or pushing himself on a smooth floor he managed to go everywhere he wanted.

His arms had become his strongest support. They were exercised and muscular, and had the strength of a bear. His hands were also strong, but they had slender, sensitive fingers. In the course of years the young man had learned to practice many trades with them. He had learned forging and welding from a blacksmith, had learned to paint from a great artist, and writing and arithmetic from a scholar. He had received these skills, and many more, because for everyone it was a joy to teach their trade to this young man.

His name was Wando. When he had reached adulthood he was asked about his plans for the future. What trade would he take on? Wando gave a strange answer. It was his dream to make a journey around the world. That was the goal to which he wanted to dedicate his life.

For the first time people laughed at him in his face. The fact that he had no legs had never seemed ridiculous to them, but now this plan for the future did! They talked and deliberated with the young man. They tried to convince him to let go of this foolish plan. He listened, nodded and agreed with all their objections. And then he started on his way.

Wando did not take much with him; carrying his body was already a job in itself. On two crutches he hobbled away from his birthplace, on his journey to the whole world. He travelled alone because no other travellers were happy with his company. He was much too slow and, besides, many people felt embarrassed by him. What a spectacle – a man without legs! Indeed, Wando was forced to take frequent and long rest periods along the way. As he was resting he would write in a big notebook everything he had seen and experienced. Nothing escaped his alert eyes and ears. Indeed, he needed to pay close attention, otherwise he would all too easily slip into the mud.

When finished with his writing he would take a sketchbook and make drawings of everything he had seen – trees, flowers, plants, little beetles, bunnies or a quick fox. But also dilapidated huts, castles and farms. And most of all the people he saw, old men and women, farmers, mothers, horsemen or children – everyone appeared on his pages. When Wando had finished this, he put everything back in his backpack and felt sufficiently rested to go further.

Thus days, weeks, months, even years went by. Many travellers passed him, and every one of them found a place in his sketchbook. His backpack filled itself with these sketchbooks and was very heavy, but he was strong and always kept going.

After travelling for seven years along all kinds of roads in all kinds of areas, Wando ran into someone he knew. It was a traveller who had passed him a long time ago. Wando asked him whether he had seen the end of the world. The traveller replied: 'No, no, the beginning and the end are lying right next to each other. If I had reached the end, I could have started at the beginning again, and I wouldn't have had to return the same way. I had to turn around because I was unable to cross the rainbow bridge. It is the only bridge across a wide river. When you want to go up that bridge you suddenly hear voices asking you about your journey, the things you have seen and heard and experienced. If you can answer them you may go on. But if you have forgotten something the bridge suddenly breaks and you fall down in the whirling water. Pretty soon, I did not remember the answers and thus I fell into the water. I was only just able to swim back to the riverbank and save my life. Now I am going back to my birthplace in order to start this journey again, but then without forgetting anything.'

Wando thought of his heavy backpack full of sketchbooks and

notebooks and nodded gravely. He wished the traveller all the best and went on. As can be expected, he now met more and more returning travellers who told him a similar story. He paid even more attention to his surroundings and forgot nothing of what he encountered along the way.

Thus, after long years, he also came to the rainbow bridge. It formed a high arch over the water. Wando pushed himself carefully up the arch. There sounded the first voice; it asked him about the flowers that had embellished his path. Wando told about the colours and fragrances and showed his books. Slowly he pushed himself further up the rainbow bridge while time and again he met with new questions, and he was able to answer them all. Every plant, every animal came to life before the eye of his spirit. He could describe every human face. Thus he almost reached the other side. But the last voice asked him whether he knew the questions that his fellow travellers had not been able to answer. He was silent: he could not answer – he had not asked the travellers. It had never occurred to him that he might be able to help them with all his books.

An eerie silence fell. Then, with an appalling crash, the rainbow bridge broke and Wando disappeared in the whirling water of the river. Desperately he beat around himself with his strong arms, for he could not swim. The water dragged him along and he would certainly have drowned if he had not been able to grab an overhanging branch. Hanging by his arms he managed to reach dry land. Now he had reached the other side! Exhausted he fell down in the tall grass, and was soon in a deep sleep.

After long, long hours Wando woke up and wanted to rub his eyes. A terrible shock awaited him. His arms! His arms were gone! In lieu of arms he had only two short stumps at his shoulders. Now he had four stumps. He cried and yelled and cursed like a madman, but nothing helped. There was no one there to see or hear him. He had reached the other side, but at what expense! He finally lay down as if dead.

Eventually his courageous, cheerful nature prevailed and he decided not to give up his journey. He tried rolling himself in the grass – that worked! He clenched his teeth and continued. Thus he rolled himself through dust and mud. Sometimes he had to go over a rock or a hill, and then all he could do was wait for a kind traveller to help him. He looked like a beggar, dirty and miserable, and he saw many people looking at him horrified, sneering and with hatred. In his pain and misery all these impressions were stamped deeply into his soul, and he forgot nothing. He was completely defenceless, anyone could do anything they wanted to him. Once in a while there was a compassionate face looking down on him, and then he was carried along for a way or received a good meal. Sometimes gentle hands washed him and put clean clothes on him. But most of the time he lived off the scraps left behind by passers-by, and he was clean only when it rained long enough at night.

After endlessly long years he was once more passed by the travellers who had been unable to cross the rainbow bridge and had started for the second time. This time they had crossed and carried backpacks full of notebooks. Wando, without arms and legs, asked them about their journey – he wanted to know everything that had happened to them, and kept every word in his heart. Thus time passed, and everyone hurried on until all of them had overtaken him. Wando grew old and tired, but did not give up. And after some time it happened that he met those same travellers again who were now, again, on their way back. They were walking with drooping shoulders, dragging themselves along with lifeless eyes.

Wando was surprised and asked them why they were returning this time. They replied that they had been stopped by a river of fire: 'You cannot go through it without being burned alive. No ship can go there. The only way to reach the other side is by asking the firebird to carry you on its back. It's a red and gold feathered bird that can take a traveller like a ferryman. With his powerful wing beat he flies high over the fire. But before he lets you climb on his back you have to throw all your possessions into the fire. All notebooks and backpacks are burned there. The firebird also asks a lot of questions, and if you don't know the answers he drops you right into the river of fire. We didn't dare give up our notebooks, so we had to go back again or give up our goal. The firebird said that we should imprint everything into our hearts. There it is safe from the fire!'

The man without arms and legs then asked them to return to the river of fire and take him along. For Wando carried all the answers in his heart. Thus they all went with him, taking turns to carry him on their backs. During this long trek Wando told them everything he had stored in his heart so that they too could fill their hearts with it.

When they approached the river of fire, the firebird jubilated high in the sky and soon landed in front of them. One by one he carried them across and let them off on the other side. They knew every answer. Last of all he carried Wando. Wando had no arms and legs to hold on to the bird, but the firebird was big and strong and protected Wando with his wings. On the other side he gently let him slide off his back into the grass. He gave him four feathers from his wings and laid these on Wando's stumps, and a moment later he got back his arms and even legs, which had never been there before. The other travellers were shouting for joy. They rested for a time and then continued on in groups, longing for the end of their journey.

Only Wando did not go with them. He stayed on the bank of the river of fire and built a house for himself and for the firebird, who came there to rest every night. Wando felt deep love and gratitude to the bird who had cured him.

The days went by, one after the other, until one day the firebird spoke to Wando. He told him to travel on, for the time had come. He gave him a little box of stone with fire from the river, fire than could not go out. Wando silently nodded thanks, embraced his saviour and departed with the precious fire. His step was fast and strong and, as was his custom, he saw and heard everything and inscribed it deeply into his heart.

One day he saw in the distance a high white castle, and his former travelling companions were sitting on the ground right in front of it. They looked exhausted, more dead than alive. An icy wind blew out of the castle, and the castle itself had frozen windows and thick snow on its roofs. No smoke came out of the chimneys.

Wando felt how this icy cold gripped him and how everything in him seemed to go rigid and stiff. But his hands found the little stone box in his pocket, and with stiff, cold fingers he opened it. The bright fire leaped out of it to the great doors of the castle, which opened with a creaking, grating sound. All the travellers got to their feet and followed Wando who was going with the fire, which was happily dancing through the castle from fireplace to fireplace and lighted a warming fire everywhere. Logs were lying in place everywhere as if waiting for the fire. Pretty soon it was nice and warm in all the rooms so that the ice melted on the windows and light radiated through them from the outside.

Finally, they arrived in a kind of great hall. Here the fire stayed in the fireplace – its work was done. The travellers stood around it and warmed their numb bodies. Suddenly, a door behind them opened and light figures entered the hall. 'The journey is accomplished,' spoke the first one, and he silently stood behind Wando. Every other figure chose one of the other travellers, and when each had his companion, a deep silence fell in the hall. Wando felt young as a child and wise as a greybeard. All he had experienced and encountered lived in his heart and his head, and he felt himself coming home.

After a while they all departed from the castle, the travellers and their companions. Each one returned to his place of birth; they had finished travelling. Each one built a house, including Wando and his companion. People were astonished at his strong wisdom and asked his advice about plants, animals and human beings – about everything they encountered in their lives and everything they experienced.

PART 2

ISSUES IN THE TEEN YEARS

The lock in the river

The doors wide open,
Inviting to enter, unsuspecting.

Doors closing on childhood times,
Lost past and unknown future.

Trapped within the walls, caught,
Not knowing what's you, what's me.

Churning water, rising, falling,
Always adrift, unsure.

Water surface quiet now:
Gather steam, power.
Slowly the sight of moving streams
Emerges from past riddle dreams.

Leaving the lock, new and strong,
See the future beckon, smiles?
Wave to those there on the banks.
Did they foresee it all along?

5. Excesses

Which teenager doesn't take things to excess at some time, in some way? According to most adults, everything about teenagers is excessive. Maybe that is true, and maybe it is normal, as the inner master is not yet really in charge. But much of what adults call excesses are transgressions against the norms and values of the society in which the teenagers happen to live. I don't want to call such transgressions excesses. In my view, excesses can be defined as follows:

◊ Behaviour that is out of proportion with its consequences;
◊ Thoughts that lack all basis and all relation to reality; and
◊ Feelings that do not arise from inner or outer causes and have no basis.

Excessive Behaviour

What does excessive behaviour look like? Crimes without reason, a person acting like a robot? Drunk or drugged-up carousing or running riot? There are also teenagers who experience such ecstasy when, for example, watching a soccer game, that they go on a raging rampage with all the attendant consequences. They display behaviour that is out of all proportion with its consequences.

It is always a question of a kind of intoxication, a state of lowered consciousness in which the inner master is overwhelmed and the 'I' cannot exercise its function. When the 'I' is really present and fulfils its task in the soul, the soul forces are kept under control and you remain conscious of what you are doing. But a young person is still working on forging a strong connection with this 'I'. Not until adulthood is the inner master capable of keeping you consistently awake and aware.

Excessive Thoughts

Excesses of thinking are thoughts that lack all foundation and have lost all relation to reality. Examples of this are best sought in psychiatry, rather than in crime. If I think that I am Napoleon, or if I am perfectly convinced that the whole of humanity is conspiring to murder me today, everyone will recognise that I am having uncontrolled, rampant thoughts. But in the case of a teenager it is likely to be less conspicuous.

An example is the skinny girl who is convinced that she looks fat and unattractive. Teenagers are especially prone to having excessive thoughts about their appearance.

There are also young people who are certain that everyone hates them, even though much warmth is exhibited around them. There are teenagers who consider themselves exceptionally sharp and intelligent, even though they never achieve anything. Some children develop the most bizarre thoughts about their parents and teachers, and hold these to be God-given truth – they lose contact with reality on that particular issue. These are examples of thoughts that lack all basis in reality.

When the life of the mind is replaced by a fictitious life in computer games we also see thoughts that are not genuine, that tend to excess. Thinking is then completely obsessive, and constrained by the limits of the game, its action and characters.

Excessive Feelings

It can be difficult to grasp what excessive feelings – feelings without basis – means in the abstract. Yet we know this phenomenon very well through screen and stage acting. Actors are able to evoke emotions in themselves that have no genuine trigger in their lives. A capacity for instantly creating and expressing any random emotion is useful if you need it in your profession, but deploying it in the course of real everyday life is quite another story.

Teenagers... everything is going fine and the family is having a good time together, but all of a sudden the expression on the face of your teen changes. She runs up to her room and throws herself on her bed sobbing violently. Is something really bothering her? She may have a reason. But it could also be that she is on a feeling rampage and just felt like being depressed for a moment. Or to be aggressive, or to put on a show.

Such excesses are based on inauthenticity. They occur in children who do not have a rich soul life. They just dream up things, and express anything. And while you as the parent are busy bringing all your reactions under control so you can say the right thing, you might notice that they don't know any more what you are talking about. They have completely forgotten it, because *it really was nothing*. It was just a momentary feeling game. When the family around the teenager is genuinely concerned, this may all result in a nice row, for they then feel the teen has made fools of them.

For most of us, certain occasions can produce emotions that outwardly seem to be connected with reality but in actuality are unperceived excesses of feeling. For instance, on New Year's Eve I start crying because I am a divorced mother and there is no partner to celebrate with me. Or when I hear a particular piece of music I fall completely in love.

Such emotions are like birthday cards. On the occasion of an event, you send an emotion up to the surface. There is indeed an occasion but, really, you could also turn the music off. And you could also just go to bed on New Year's Eve.

We allow ourselves such occasions, and that is why, in my view, they belong to the category of rampant feelings. We are unfree in these kinds of responses. We let ourselves be submerged in a feeling, and completely forget that we could just as well not have done so. When we do not make choices in this area we continue to behave like a teenager. The soul is then not the follower of the 'I' but the ruler.

Aren't we all familiar with the family party where the same story from old times has to be told again, or the same joke, so that we will all laugh to order? Or the feeling of 'we-love-our-grandma-so-much' on her birthday, after which we forget her again until the next occasion?

The media are very clever in the way they play into these occasion-based emotions. Just think of the publicity around national memorial days, Valentine's Day or Mother's Day. These are friendly forms of compulsion on the soul, which are accepted by most people. But it is not out of free, conscious involvement that the feelings arise in the soul, it is in reaction to an occasion that is magnified by others, hopefully with the best of intentions.

Children are better served by parents who are able to give actual form to real feelings and needs, who can participate socially in care and offer help with regularity and in a well-considered manner. By parents who, rather than shedding bucketfuls of tears for all the suffering in the world, quietly and inconspicuously roll up their sleeves to do something that is needed. Such examples will cure the tendency toward rampant feelings in a teenager.

Do teenagers with rampant feelings realise what they are doing when they play the same song over and over again and thus creates one depressive mood after another? Or are their emotions so excessive that they must create an inner morass? Even without any grief in your life, some music can make you very sad! Without any anger with something or someone, some music can still make you feel aggressive. The same is true for some foods, parties and other stimuli.

The danger of falsifying the feeling life has been greatly increased by the countless possibilities for connecting your own feelings with personalities who do not really exist. When we identify with the people who act in a soap opera we are well on the way to such fal-sification. The artificial identity you can create online falsifies your own feeling life because both your own and the other identities you meet in the virtual world are nothing but false appearance. An overweight and shy teenager is able to hide his problems behind a slender muscular hero in a 'second life'. This falsification of the self is an excess of the feeling life that is very difficult to combat. At first sight the teenager in front of his screen has no problem whatsoever. In reality that teen is estranging himself from his own problems and does nothing to solve them.

WHAT CAN YOU DO?

When weeds choke everything in your garden, what can you do? You had better roll up your sleeves, for there is real work to be done. It is the same with rampant soul tendencies. There are many things in teenagers with which it is better not to get overly involved. It is better to follow them inwardly and try to understand them. But with these excesses you may (and perhaps must) do something. Some things simply have to be forbidden, at least, as long as that is possible. No matter how democratic you are, do not hesitate to issue an order or prohibition now and then. Many young people who stopped listening to Mum and Dad long ago, and have reached an age when they decide for themselves what is done or not done, will still be perfectly able and willing to listen to a parental intervention when it is a question of excess. We are often too quick to think that this won't work any more. Inwardly the child distinctly senses that he or she will benefit from this particular parental intervention.

Such intervention does have to be based on the 'I' strength of the parent, never ever on an impulse of his or her temper. Otherwise you aggravate the situation and add your own excess to it. Only a decision made in a balanced state of mind, and which is communicated full of certainty and without passion, has a chance of succeeding.

There are girls who try out everything that is forbidden, but who acquiesce to their parents' financial guardianship. There are boys who move out of the house and become independent at an early age, but accept that their parents forbid them having anything to do with a certain sect. Obviously, they will put up resistance, but if it does not degenerate into a power struggle and is simply a given, it often does not raise a problem; the young person quietly follows the parental decisions.

When children are still young it is good for them to know that boundaries will always be set on excesses. To the extent they are incapable of doing that themselves, the adults will have to do it. It gives them security, and they have a kind of guarantor who, in the period when their own 'I' is not yet able to be their lord and master, guards their boundaries for them. What good fortune when a child receives such boundaries and can kick against them without them falling to pieces!

6. Lying and Stealing

Fibs and Lies

Young children cannot lie; rather than tell the truth, they substitute a 'truth' that fits better. This better-fitting truth is a fantasy that they need, for instance, when they are afraid. If your parents become extremely upset because you kicked the ball through the window, you are likely to say that the other boy did it, aren't you?

When children are neglected they will also often do this. If they need attention and don't get any, they have a stomach-ache. And if children think they are too small, they can become very creative. 'My father has already killed seven lions with his hands,' a little boy once told me. In many cases young children do not clearly distinguish the real from the unreal. They really do feel a stomach ache. Or they begin to believe the story of their father and the lions after they have told it three times.

I do not call this kind of untruth 'lying', but 'telling fibs'. I consider lying to be the fully conscious deceiving of a fellow human being by telling an untruth when it was possible to tell the truth. Small children are not fully conscious; they often do not sufficiently distinguish truth from fibs, and they often lack the ability to hold to the truth when they are afraid. Not until the higher 'I' becomes master of the soul can a human being be held responsible for a lie. In the meantime the conscience of the adult 'I' calls the young person to account. The voice of conscience can then sound in the soul of the other. Only then does the possibility exist of a free choice for the truth or for a lie.

The reason that children don't tell fibs much more often than they actually do is that we can't stand it. Our reactions are so ugly that they don't dare. Also, there are always children who already possess a strong, inborn sense of justice at a very young age. It is a living power in their soul: they cannot tell an untruth – in fact, they don't really have a choice because they just about suffocate in the conflict of conscience that then arises in their soul.

The best method for parents is to give children as little reason as possible to say something that is not true. Then the children can let reality be as it presents itself.

For children of primary school age who tell untruths and have fantasies, a good solution is the 'pretty stories book'. Buy a nice notebook and agree with these children that they will write all the stories *they have made themselves* in it – don't use the words 'fibs' or 'lies'. Children will begin to see the difference between their stories and truth as they go along. Then, should you suspect that a child is telling you a fib, you can ask whether or not this was meant for the pretty stories book. This is a very simple method that can be of great help; I have seen it prove its value many times. It helps a child make conscious distinctions between reality and invention.

Around age ten, when children become more conscious of themselves, you can carefully ask that they put the untruth away and look for the truth. If you are then too moral and strict, you will push the tendency toward untruth to the bottom of the child's soul, where it will become food for a false attitude to life later. In actual fact, strict treatment forces a child into accepting the obligation to lie.

Here is an example. At one time I knew a highly respected father. Integrity was his motto. His youngest son displayed a tendency to tell untruths, even a tendency to untruth in the deed: stealing. For this father that was intolerable, and he went to work on his son with hard words and iron consequences. Only it did not get better.

When I told the father that the son felt weak and became progressively weaker due to the strict methods, this father was very surprised. I asked him to place himself *behind* his son instead of *confronting* him. Then the son would be able to feel himself strong with his father. The father agreed to a trial period. Together with his son he was going to overcome this error. The two of them began a project: using every free hour to build a boat. The father made a close connection of trust with his son, whose courage and self-confidence grew by leaps and bounds. Untruth and stealing were soon forgotten; they were old instruments the boy no longer needed. The father was able to be proud of his son.

This example clearly shows that lying is a result of weakness, and that therefore it is necessary to work on strengthening the child. Such children have a need of fairy tales and stories in which the good and moral are victorious. The Grimm's *Snow White* and Hans Christian Andersen's *The Wild Swans* are good examples.

TEENAGERS CAN INDEED LIE

In the teen years the 'I' begins to light up in the soul to a greater or lesser extent, and the child then becomes capable of choosing to lie or tell the truth. Most teenagers will at some point try out a lie to serve their interests. The parent's reaction to this is very important. If you continue to treat the teenager as a child ('The poor thing was frightened of detention, so of course she told a little lie...'), what you in fact communicate is: 'In my view you do not yet have an "I" of your own that can exercise any mastery in the soul. For me, you are not yet capable of being responsible.'

This is not a strengthening message for the teenager. Teens who meet such a reaction will withdraw into a childish way of behaving that precisely fits the picture their parents have of them. With this reinforcement of the childlike, the influence of the 'I' declines, and the function of conscience cannot properly unfold.

WHAT CAN YOU DO?

Assuming that a growing child has a well-formed conscience is like wanting to pick apples in the spring. You can pick apples only in the autumn, when they are fully grown and ripe. They need good soil, a lot of sun warmth, enough rain, protection from infestations, and a competent gardener who takes care of the tree and knows when the apples are ready.

Consider this picture of the apple tree – it clarifies a lot. You could say that in our children's teen years, we as parents are the gardeners of the 'I' that is growing in each of them like a young tree. When teenagers lie, they are asking for overtime from the gardener. If we are able to tie the stem of the young apple tree to a post so that it can grow straight – which is like placing our own 'I' beside the child as a silent support – then we are good gardeners. Being a silent support means first of all that you look to make a connection with the 'I' of your teen. If you don't recognise what is happening for the tree, you cannot give it what it needs.

Even with young children it is possible to seek a connection with the as yet unborn 'I'. There are five ways in which parents can develop their experience of the 'I' of the child:

◊ Note the phases of the child's development and look for those points when a breakthrough of the 'I' lights up, for instance in the period of obstinacy, or during the crisis of the ninth year.

◊ Observe moments when the child shows extraordinary individual strength.

◊ Notice physical growth in which the working of the 'I' becomes visible.

◊ Work as parents on our own entelechy, on the task of our own development; this will enable us also to experience the task of the 'I' of the child.

◊ It can be a great help to seek a connection with the angel who accompanies your child.

In the teen years the important point is always to be aware of the 'I' and to affirm it in its *forms of manifestation*. We should not only sense it in our inner being, but also recognise how it emerges outwardly in words and deeds. The 'I' comes to the fore in moral impulses, idealism, creativity, in forceful self-willed choices, and in accepting responsibility with its consequences. In brief, in the emergence of true adulthood. It is like the appearance of molehills in the garden: it is perfectly clear that there must be a mole living and working below the surface, but it is still invisible and you can only know it is there by the little heaps of earth.

A small child still acts without commitment. But when the 'I' takes possession of the soul, this open-endedness disappears. Words, choices, behaviour, even thoughts, then carry self-chosen responsibility with them, not because of fear, dogma or imitation, but out of the person's own human will. Parents can learn to observe every new little molehill and affirm it. This provides inner support and strength to the young person, it gives courage and it is a testament to parental loyalty.

Lying means that the 'I' is going *underground*. Giving the lie too much attention amounts to focusing on the wrong thing. Make sure the young person clearly realises that you know the truth and that the lie was heard or seen. This is already a great relief to him or her, because then they know that lying has no purpose any more. An attentive parent prevents many lies, because the teenager realises that lies are of no use. That does not mean you should check up on everything, for no one can stand the atmosphere of a police state. It is also unnecessary: time spent and interest shown will give you much more insight into the life of your child, without an annoying attitude of wanting to know every detail.

Rather than focusing on the lie, make sure you also notice every little manifestation of the 'I' of the child. Affirm it very concretely. This will fan the little flame. For instance, take children who tend to be quiet, but who suddenly voice an opinion. Usually they are immediately silenced by differing, stronger opinions and arguments. Instead, listen to such children, emphasise the importance of them voicing their opinion, no matter what the content was. This encourages growth. A reaction like, 'Ah, I am glad you said that; I had never looked at it that way,' has a completely different effect to, 'What a stupid remark; don't you see that's totally impossible?' On the other hand, it is also important that growing young people who are very strong at home and at school be kept in check. That helps them learn to also be quiet and think about what other people say.

A teenager who lies often needs more affirmation of genuine expressions of his or her own individuality. Opportunities for affirmation arise when teenagers have earned their own money for something, or when they have chosen 'different' clothes, or developed their own travel plans. No matter how strange their choices may look to us – 'things could be much better, more efficient, cheaper, and so on' – the trick with these steps towards independence is to hold back critical opinion, and affirm their originality. In the course of years – naturally not right away – this has a strengthening effect on the teenager, with the result that dishonesty disappears because it was an expression of weakness that has been overcome by inner strength.

Stealing

Lying and stealing are like brother and sister. Stealing is lying through a deed; both cases are violations of truth. The causes of stealing are therefore similar to those of lying, and the same is true for the way we need to handle it. When a toddler takes something it is not yet really stealing. Just as for a small child there are not yet clear boundaries between its own soul life and that of others, the difference between yours and mine is also still vague.

When a small child has had a wonderful time playing with an object in school, the toy feels as if it belongs to him or her, and sometimes disappears into a pocket. If the parents tell the child to return it, or ask if it may be borrowed for a while, there is no problem. Pouring out a stream of holy indignation over the child will only create fear and encourage sneaky behaviour. Consistently and quietly returning things suffices at a young age. Normally, this helps children build up an awareness of their own property and that of others, while at the same time forming their soul skin.

Unfortunately, however, stealing is quite common among teenagers. It is for good reason that high schools often feel more like secure storage lock-ups than schools. Students each have their own locker, there are keys everywhere and much emphasis on security. Why is there so much theft? What is going on with teens?

First of all, this is not preeminently a phenomenon of teenagehood. It is a phenomenon of our time and pervades all of society, which includes the world of young people. Western materialism teaches people to enrich themselves with many things that exceed their direct needs. Possessing and consuming luxuries is widespread, and children learn to want these things from their earliest years. Just look at all the things that are on sale to new parents for a baby's room! It is astonishing.

Children grow up, see all this stuff and want it too. Not all parents can satisfy such wants. And, indeed, the wants are insatiable in all of us – we desire more and more all the time. Adults who are millionaires tell you with great conviction that a million does not amount to so very much today, and that they therefore have to make still more.

If there are no means to buy for teenagers all that their hearts desire, this does not need to be a problem. A teen can get a job and work hard, so with will power, energy and patience he or she will earn what is needed. This way all is above board and legitimate.

Should there be insufficient will power or no patience, or if temptation has the soul in its grip, or indeed if there are no job opportunities, then things may become more difficult. As has been pointed out, the 'I' forms the conscience, but this is a work in progress during the teen years. Weaker teenagers, who have little will power, feel the urge to belong and participate even more than most teenagers. They are scared of being left out. There are countless norms and codes among young people, starting as early as primary school. Clothes and shoes have to be specific brands, and you are supposed to have the latest smartphone or whatever else is in at the time.

In this way we see that desires often arise not from physical needs but out of social anxiety. Kids want to belong, and parents are often unwilling to satisfy the – in their eyes – ridiculous demands. I have regularly met teenagers who have stolen money to treat their friends to drinks in a bar. What they are in fact trying to buy is their place in the group.

Just as with lying, in theft the much-desired thing is obtained in the wrong way through weakness.

WHAT CAN YOU DO?

The tasks are to support where there is weakness, and to awaken the 'I' force. Obviously, bad behaviour has to be strongly and explicitly rejected, but never reject teens themselves in the process. That will weaken them further, and the risk of repeat offences will grow.

As well as helping these teens bring to consciousness a profound respect for that which is materially 'my own,' we must also provide sexual education. A strong sense of respect for the possessions of another, and for your own, will be apparent later on in sexual behaviour. Without such respect for ownership, sexuality can all too easily degenerate into theft of the body. Those who are weak do not realise the value of their own body, and are not able to protect it adequately.

THE POWER OF GIVING

The diametric opposite of stealing is giving. Instead of fighting a teenager's stealing, much can be achieved by developing the gesture of giving. A real gift is a deed full of strength and choice. You are giving away something of yourself, which is only possible on the basis of *inner richness*, of warmth for and involvement with the other. You lose something to the other, and in doing so you find yourself in the other. Giving is therefore a vulnerable encounter, in which both parties can grow.

But let us understand each other here. Giving has to be distinguished from unconsciously letting everything flow out of oneself into others. That is not a gift, but a loss of individuality. In this way there is no real encounter with the other. In sexuality the act of truly giving oneself to the other is a gesture of strength and love.

Just as giving is a genuine *encounter* with the other, in the same way stealing is the *avoidance* of the other. As a result, it creates emptiness and loneliness on both sides, the victim as well as the perpetrator.

The other is not recognised, not looked for, but denied. Things that belong to the other are taken away, which is a violation of the individuality of the other. But the thief also loses individuality; one could say that thieves falsify their own personalities. And thus we find ourselves in a vicious cycle, for stealing comes from weakness and inner poverty. But they who enrich themselves outwardly with the possessions of others weaken their own souls, and thus cause, inwardly, even worse poverty.

Strength and inner richness are conditions for giving. Those who set the example of giving for their children from their earliest childhood build a solid foundation that will offer a counterweight to all the temptations approaching the child in the teen years. Rather than the easy store-bought present, presents selected with love and care, or those that are handmade and personal, are of the greatest value. It is a long way to go from the first toddler's drawing given to a parent or grandparent, to a warm, giving adult soul, but this is the route along which the necessary inner strength is developed.

There have been experiments in which thieves were brought into contact with their victims so that the gap might be bridged and an encounter could take place. The discovery of the suffering and inconvenience of the victims is experienced as shocking by the perpetrators, and often inspires a wish to repair the damage. In descriptions of such experiments we can clearly see the necessity of an encounter with the other as the counterpart of theft, for theft achieves the opposite.

STEALING AND ADDICTION

Many thefts are committed by people with addictions to drugs, including alcohol. Ron Dunselman wrote an enlightening book about addiction, which, for good reason, he gave the title, *In Place of the Self* (Hawthorne Press, 2007). He describes how drugs affect a person's consciousness and connection with the core of his or her being, the 'I'. This weakening of the 'I' is the perfect preparation for theft. Addicts need money fast, often and in large quantities. In addition, their weakened souls are no longer capable of giving, only of taking, socially and materially. Parents, friends and others then have the experience of being sucked dry and consumed or, worse, their soul strength is stolen.

It is interesting to take a look at those who are able to break their addictions and why. Have they perhaps found a person in their life to whom they want to give? Be that as it may, anyone working or coping with an addict will have to be conscious of the dualism stealing/giving, because behind it hides the dualism impotence/strength.

Teens with a Soul Disability

Unfortunately, there are also children in whom good and evil are in such a struggle with each other that the 'I' is not able to light up in the soul in a normal way. Are we here perhaps dealing with lessons they have brought with them? Are these children still struggling with 'homework' from previous lives? Are they taking in lessons from their surroundings? If you are not clairvoyant, you can only guess at these things. But still, it is important not to give up on these children, who are living between light and shadow.

Sometimes you can see them lie in complete consciousness and with great pleasure; they enjoy the power this gives over their surroundings. Their conscience is not working properly. As an adult, do not forget that these are expressions of poverty, for if you possess true strength of heart – a true 'I' force – you have no need of surrogate forces, and you don't show that mean side. Evil is born from poverty of soul and spirit. The pain inflicted on others by untruth and power is a consequence of handicaps in the perpetrator's soul.

In such situations the parents are asked to give as much and as long as possible so as to combat the evil and overcome the inner poverty. How much can the parents give? That depends on their own inner riches. If the adult succumbs under the weight, it is not a gift. That will only be an extra burden on the child – something you don't want to be responsible for. Everything they can give such children is good, as long as it is warm, genuine and honest. These children can't unlearn their lying straight away. In a way it is in their bones. In this respect they are so deficient that they fall back all the time.

In such cases – these are exceptions – we are dealing with a soul disability. Just as a great deal is expected of parents of a child with Down's Syndrome, but not that they change their child into a highly intellectual person, much is also expected of parents of a child with a soul disability, but not that they change their child into a saint.

The lives of these (courageous) children are characterised by a mountain of homework they have brought with them. That took courage: so much homework in one life! As adults we have a task here. The more you can do, the better, but don't feel guilty about the things you are no longer able to do. After you, the parents, life itself becomes the great educator. In the biography of these children, destiny ensures that they will be given their homework in increasing quantity and intensity. Accepting such a pre-birth path of development can be a great burden. As parents, don't be misled. Even if your child becomes a difficult person – for him or herself and for others – perhaps he or she will lead a more meaningful life than the virtuous child of your neighbour.

Who do we think we are to make judgments in such cases? What counts is that we do what we can, and that we have confidence in the individual inner task that children brings within themselves when they are born. One school is tougher than another... Even for the children I call disabled in soul, it is a blessing if the parents approach them in the way outlined above. But the results will not be as clearly visible as in other cases; the parents will often have to be content with very small improvements.

Here I would like to say something on behalf of the parents and teachers who accompany these children. Let us stop our cheap and unsolicited advice; let us stop proclaiming that the parents are making a mess of it and that we know better. We must not be backseat drivers! Let us support them and appreciate them whenever possible. Let us not judge, bother, or avoid them, and most of all, let us not leave them to manage alone.

7. The Contemporary Family

Gender Identity

Most teenagers in our societies live in small families with two or three children. A large number of young people also live with only one of their parents, usually their mother, most often because of divorce.

In the past thirty years many changes have taken place in family situations. Not only are most families smaller than before and subject to more divorces, but the emphasis on family life has also significantly diminished. In many cases both parents work, so neither parent has a complete focus on the family. Through technology, many household tasks have moved from a primary to a secondary place: cooking, washing and cleaning have fallen into the category of that-also-has-to-be-done, rather than being anyone's central concern.

As children grow older, the most important activities of the family occur outside the house. The parents have their work, the children go to school and the car enables the family to go anywhere in its leisure time. Whether for sport, family visits or holidays, the fact is that we are often on the road.

The first generation of people who grew up in this way now have small children of their own. It is too early to know the long-term effects of this changing family culture. Many people look back nostalgically to the warm nest of former times, with a mother who was always there enveloping everything in her warmth. It seems to me that this too easily evokes a distorted, romanticised image. I am sure mothers were often exhausted, there was extensive financial need and women were much less independent – and that this was all most cruelly revealed if the father died or did not treat his wife with respect.

Teenagers are now more often alone, simply because there are fewer people at home. This means that they have to build their own social life at an early age. The importance of friendships, hobbies and sports has greatly increased.

Girls and boys both have to find a place for themselves in society where they can earn their own livelihood. Qualities that girls formerly had to develop in their inner world, they must now also display externally. While once the woman was the pivotal point of the family because of her inner involvement, her intense soul life and endless household chores, today she is called to realise her capacities outside the house as well, under the critical eye of society. Girls now succeed in completing their school and further study more often than boys. Having children is often postponed until women are well into their thirties.

Because of the changing nature of the family, boys are not able to build their future identity as easily as they once did. They still need to conquer a place for themselves in society from which they can provide for themselves, but girls also do that. While pregnancy and breastfeeding children remains women's work, there is not much specifically men's work left. Has it therefore become more difficult for boys to build up their identity as boys? What do they have left with which to prove themselves as men?

I think this insecurity leads to many teenage boys' noisy, laddish behaviour, especially when they are together in a group. The masculine values demanded of them are more inward in nature, more those of an individual human being, rather than overtly masculine outer behaviour. For many men this change is a real liberation, but for teenage boys it can complicate the path to adulthood. In the past there was a certain masculine significance in wearing long pants, or in earning money, but that is all gone. Only the body still shows signs of approaching male adulthood: with the appearance of facial hair and the voice breaking people will note that a boy is growing into a man. But this in itself leads to no particular expectations or conclusions.

Inner courage, steadfastness, loyalty and strength, persistence and identity are traits boys must now acquire for themselves; in our culture they no longer find rituals or customs to help them with this. Knights are expected to knight themselves, and damsels set out to change the world themselves!

Girls must manifest inner qualities in the outside world as well as in their inner life, and boys are required to build outer qualities in their inner world as well as in their public life. A mother or father can support their child to find their own contemporary, adult identity based on both masculine and feminine qualities.

Parents as Examples

When parents dislike their work outside the house, they convey a clear message. Without words they are saying: 'I need the job for the money, but that is unpleasant and un-free.' Or, in the case when a mother or father detests household work, they are saying: 'Those eternal household chores are so useless and boring. I would much rather be out of the house where I could earn status and income.' Such messages penetrate deeply into growing children. They often refuse to do what we ourselves dislike doing. Since they are more honest in their reactions, they will show in outer behaviour what adults experience as inner resistance.

If a teenager has no outer ambition at all, it can help if the parents talk about how much they are enjoying their work. If a parent is not employed at the moment but once was, she or he can share good memories with their child. This kind of conversation may be particularly influential with the parent of the same sex as the teenager.

If we think household work is inferior, but then expect our children to participate in it, we should not be surprised if they refuse or make a mess of it. They must clean their rooms, prepare meals once in a while, and so on. Caring for your own home is part of life.

Parents who are continually nervous about being laid off and who fanatically insure themselves against every possible financial risk will cause fear in their children instead of self-confidence in regard to their future place in society. Parents who work with eagerness and pleasure in the outside world are a support for their children, not because of what they say, but because of their own way of life.

Examples create their opposites where there is fanaticism. It makes no difference whether it is the father or the mother, housework or outside work, parents who exaggerate make things difficult for their children and often achieve the opposite of their own demands. Don't we all know the workaholic with a lazy son or daughter, the fanatically clean parent with the sloppy teenager? Too much leads to rejection. Young people see right through our perfect exterior and observe the lack of freedom that is hiding inside. Perhaps they get discouraged, because they'll never be as neat or as successful as their mother or father.

If we want to be a good example for our teenagers we only need to act normally. Not in the extreme, not perfect. There is nothing wrong with an occasional grumble, failing, disliking or being laid off, as long as our basic attitude to our tasks in the outside world and in the house is healthy.

The values of the parents are absorbed by young people with everything that happens in the home, at breakfast, dinner, or just pottering about. Every time they meet each other, this fructification takes place. And this brings us to that important part of the day for teenagers, leisure time.

8. Leisure Time

Teenagers' leisure time is filled with homework, paid jobs, hanging out, social encounters, sport, going out, music, television, computers, social networking and games, falling in and out of love, gossiping and deep conversation, eating and drinking – the list is endless.

Homework

In many families homework is a source of conflict. The kids just slouch by the television or at their computers, but don't do their homework. Or they are supposedly doing homework but are really just dreaming away. Why is homework such a problem? Largely because it has to be done on teenagers' own time. That is the biggest obstacle for the teen: they have been sitting in school all day and now that they are home they have to turn to it all again.

There are schools that offer homework classes. The kids can do their homework there after school so that they are finished when they come home and are then really free. For many children that is a good solution. It may also work for families where no one is at home to keep an eye on things, or where homework causes too many conflicts.

However, there are many advantages to doing homework at home: you learn to work independently. When there is no teacher or parent to constantly keep an eye on you, you will have to muster the will power needed to stay with it. By trial and error you learn to work in the manner and at the pace that are right for you. You learn to take yourself in hand and make yourself do the homework. It is also good practice for your self-control and perseverance. When you are quietly in your own room you learn to concentrate in silence all by yourself. Or at least, you are in a position to learn that!

The second advantage of doing homework at home is that you can talk about it more. Your parents will see you sweating over it and know what you are doing.

And finally, you have the opportunity to be yourself: the floor scattered with books and things, or perhaps everything neatly organised on the desk. You can choose to do homework before dinner in the evening or early in the morning. You have the opportunity to work in a much more individual way.

It is obvious that homework has to be done, but what if the child is not managing very well? Does it then become the task of the parents? There are indeed parents who might just as well put their child's high school diploma in their own pocket, for they have supervised and tested every step and all the homework. Is that an enormous achievement? Is it really?

In my opinion, a child should not be burdened with homework too young, certainly not before the tenth year. Young children of six or seven are often forced to practice reading at home every day. They often develop an intense dislike of it. Reading is then charged with negative feelings with the result that they will be able to read but will not read. Towards the end of primary or grade school children can be given some homework in order to prepare them for middle or high school.

When children start getting significant amounts of homework they will need help with allocating their time and energy and with learning how to study. School and parents can then assist in the development of good and regular study habits. This should really take place before the fourteenth or fifteenth year, before teenage life gets going in earnest and it becomes much too difficult for teens to allow themselves to be directed in this way.

Later, parents can still give their children a little push here and there: just send them to their room to do their work, to help them across a little threshold so they get started. They can see to it that the atmosphere in the house is quiet – a lot of visitors, activity or music often breaks the thin thread of concentration. When parents themselves simply accept and do their own work in the house they will stimulate the children. If the living room is always full of people, or you are continually slouching in front of the TV while not getting around to responding to your email, it will be difficult to get your children to do their homework!

Checking up on homework, and every other task for that matter, is something I don't believe in. Teenagers will find ways to fool you, or resist you, or they will study to the limits of their parents' checking capacities, which means that they do not develop themselves. Showing interest, in contrast, is much healthier. Reading their book reports, or letting them explain what they have been studying, are much more stimulating. Children who do their homework badly are often weak in their will or emotionally out of balance; they may also have disturbances in their power of concentration. It is much better to work on such things in collaboration with the school than to turn parenthood into a police state.

My Room

It is common for teenagers to have a room of their own these days. They can therefore choose to be alone at any time. There is always a space to read, write or do homework undisturbed, to do nothing or to be together with a friend without other people around. They have their own computer and can entertain themselves endlessly. Wonderful, isn't it, that room? The walls are hung with posters and photos, and the floor is usually covered in highly important things that look like junk to others.

It is a good thing that growing young people have such privacy; it is a good thing that they have their own little realm. But there is also a shadow side. We can observe more and more that a teenager's room is a complete life situation. They live on their own, as if in a rented room. The single family house is split up into several smaller private units while the refrigerator, washing machine, microwave oven and bathrooms are common. There is no problem with that as long as the children are old enough for it.

When is the moment that a teenager is ready to move out and rent their own room somewhere else? Of course, that depends on the person, but it is certain that many children who live at home 'in a rented room' in this way are much too young to leave the nest and live on their own. A teenager who always lives in his or her own room, works, sleeps, plays with the computer and enjoys hobbies there, may also become too isolated. People then do not share their lives with each other, they are polite to each other and communicate only when necessary. What then is your function as parent in your child's teenagehood? Why not let her or him move out into rental accommodation already when they are thirteen or fourteen? Are you held back only by practicalities?

A healthy balance between being openly together and being left in privacy is required for a meaningful sojourn in the lock in the river. Sometimes a young person has more need of seclusion than at other times. No standard rules are possible here, it varies for each teenager. But we do have to be alert that the scale remains in balance. Similarly, instead of *always* being in your room, it is also possible *never* to be in your room, never to want to be alone. That is also out of balance.

In the course of the teen years, the need for seclusion grows. It is very important that every member of the family not violate the others' need for privacy. Listening in, checking emails and iphone, borrowing stuff without asking and not returning it – all this kind of thing betrays a lack of respect for the individuality of the other.

I would not be surprised if many conflicts in later life are based on a lack of respect of this kind experienced in the home. People who have received respect at home and were required to give it will later sense the boundary between their own world and that of others in their relations with other people. It can make teenagers furious when their boundaries are not taken seriously – and in my view that is justified. Their own room is a symbol of this, organised and decorated in their own way with their own precious stuff. Naturally, in the course of the years, the care of this room falls on the shoulders of the young person too. At some point in the process they will learn that owning things also involves caring for them.

Going Out

For many young people going out is the most important thing they do in their leisure time. It begins on Friday afternoon when they head for the city or get together in each other's homes. Then there are clubs, bars and gigs.

Going out is an issue that crosses the generations. Every teenager wants more than they are permitted, a later curfew than usual. In every generation most parents are worried and tend to view this part of their children's lives with distrust. Why?

When young people go out, they literally go 'out'. It is exactly the right word. At home they are still the children of their parents, and at school they are still the students of their teachers. This brings dependence and lack of freedom. It also brings care and protection, but teenagers are not so interested in that – that is the parents' concern, not theirs. When they go 'out', they leave the safe situation of youth and enter into an adult situation: there is no one watching them, no one to whom they are responsible, no one telling them what to do. They can be free and let themselves go. Of course they also have their own responsibilities, they run more risks, and so on, but, again, that is really a parental point-of-view!

In going out, teenagers get a brief taste of adulthood, but mostly adulthood as a dream. They can be free, independent and attractive, they can meet nice people, and most of all they can be happy. Adulthood will be like a flush of liberation: going *out*!

No wonder they spare no pain or expense to look whatever way is on trend. Going out has codes. Most important among these: they must not look like children. Before the startled eyes of their parents, young girls change into seductive young women and young guys into self-assured young men. Nothing hurts more than getting your age underestimated, for then you may not be admitted to the bar or may not be served alcohol. When a fifteen year old is accepted as eighteen, he has achieved something. It boosts his ego and thus his self-confidence.

Naturally, parties have to begin later and later at night, for you don't really feel you are 'out' when your parents have not yet gone to bed. And since, at the weekend, most parents also go to bed a little later, a young person can't very well start partying until midnight.

Naturally, going out is a great time for experiments, not only with soft drugs, liquor, pills and loud music, but especially with moods of the soul. You can literally see the kids impersonate and indulge every soul mood – all their inner feelings 'go out'. They go wild with the music, they are totally beside themselves. Or they become completely depressed in the atmosphere or because of what is going on with a friend. There is provocative, seductive behaviour, or the opposite, an excessive turning inward – everything extreme. If you want to encounter open displays of every human emotion, a disco for teenagers is the place to go.

When they are not able to really let themselves go there are always alcohol and drugs to help a little. And that is the danger. Those who easily turn inside out do not need such help, but those who don't dare to do that use artificial courage. We are all familiar with the reserved colleague who, after Friday evening cocktails or at an office party, suddenly proves to possess great extrovert qualities and entertains everyone freely with jokes. Alcohol and drugs, and the whole atmosphere of going out, have the same effect on young people. The soul freely indulges in it, away from the restrictions of age and personality.

I think that if we understand this urge to go 'out', we are in a better place to care for our teenagers. They want to go out when they want to loosen themselves from the nest. It is one of the signals of the approaching individuality of the soul and of the longing for adulthood. In fact, it is simply part of the package and is therefore a healthy thing in your teenager.

What can you do?

◊ Earlier in this book I spoke of the lock in the river as representing the period of the teen years, and of the importance of the lock keepers not cutting the lines all at once but easing them out bit by bit until the water inside the lock has reached the right level. This certainly applies to going out. In this world of apparent adulthood, young people run into many highly adult tasks. Managing their impulses and desires, such as those they experience through liquor and sex, the temptations of drugs and gambling – this is no child's play.

◊ When we take seriously a young person who wants to go out and we understand this need for freedom, we will not prohibit it but gradually give permission. Every time they can do a little more, keeping pace with the age of the child. There is no one-size-fits-all; upbringing has to be made to measure. Parents who know how to set the right pace with an early teen are worth their weight in gold; parents who continually block their teenager will eventually lose their connection with the child.

◊ The anxiety the parents feel here has to be squarely faced, because their stomach cramps are never helpful and will cause many conflicts between them and their child. One of the best ways to fight this parental fear is to remember what your own parents said when you wanted to go out as a teenager. All their worries – were they necessary? I am sure you remember the risks you took but, most of all, you will remember that nothing much ever happened. Modern times appear to bring more risks, but these days our children are no longer as naïve as those of earlier generations, with the result that the risk factor really has not increased. The farm girl who went to the fair a hundred years ago ran the same risks as our daughter who goes to a music festival.

◊ Going out is not for young children. They should remain in the protection of responsible parents, and this also applies when there is a party for twelve or thirteen year olds. Alcohol and party drugs have no place there. If in society we all agree that young people of fourteen or fifteen are not allowed to buy alcohol, why would we then accept that they drink it at private parties? It is already difficult enough for parents to maintain limits on alcohol use. Young teenagers who live with group codes are easy victims of addiction, long before their own 'I' is able to master such temptations.

◊ Regarding drugs, you might be interested in Raoul Goldberg's *Addictive Behavious in Children and Young Adults: The Struggle for Freedom* (Floris Books).

CONSIDERING RISK

Young people of seventeen or eighteen who go out are behaving in a way that is healthy and appropriate for their age. But because they are experimenting with adult behaviour and are throwing their soul life out into the world, this entails risks. Their own 'I' is not yet able to rein the soul in, especially when they are going out.

And yet, the risks associated with *never going out* are at least as great. The adventure of the transition from child to adult, the phase of teenagehood, is a narrow path that is easy to lose. But it is better to risk that narrow path than to land in an adult body with a soul that is still childlike, for in that case it will be even more difficult to find your life path.

When, despite all your attention and coaching and everything you have tried, your child still loses this narrow path, it does not mean the end of the world. Then there is work to do. There are possibilities to clean up the mess, start again and move on. Nothing ventured, nothing gained; but not every trial becomes a gain. Many problems your child carried deep within now become visible. The bullied child turns into a pretty girl, and now she will get every boy she wants; finally it is her turn. Or the reserved, shy boy can finally step on the gas and drink, because it seems to give him the key to his soul.

Parents who are loyal, who stay with it, often survive this period with their children. But when kids get into it too young and without any supervision the risks are much greater. True parental loyalty is precious and difficult, because a teenager is capable of putting out every little flame of love, and then it is up to you as the adult to find a way to light it again.

All in all, the risks are real, but even if your child takes a detour, or falls back temporarily, she or he can still grow into an adult, and perhaps be even better because of it!

9. The Digital Age

Teenagers need familiarity with the instruments and tools that are present in our culture. We are not living in the Stone Age, but in the digital age. This means that we use digital tools. Just as a small child learns to walk, ride a bike, use a knife and fork, and play a musical instrument, a young person must learn to use a keyboard, a touchscreen, the internet, social media and digital communication.

Because we have a tendency to treat computers, smartphones, tablets and other digital tools as extensions of ourselves, we often exhibit rather strange behaviour in relation to these kinds of impersonal apparatus. We talk to them, yell at them or praise them, and sometimes we throw them into a corner in frustration. This happens because often in practice it is hard to distinguish between human personality and the 'impersonality' of the machine. Which one of us never talks to a computer and never blames a programme for a bad result? This is something particular to our relationship with interactive digital media. We would not talk in the same way to our washing machine or breadmaker.

The complexity of today's communication technology makes it seem like magic. But the more we know how these things work, the more we are able to see the actual difference between what is personal and what is impersonal. These are instruments that do not have the ability to address a person's sense of 'I'. A machine has no 'I', no matter what is being suggested in movies and games. We have all seen the computers in *Star Wars* moving around like awkward, autonomous beings – you almost want to hug them! But that is science fiction. In reality, a supposedly living relationship with a machine is actually a nightmare, because human emotions and reactions are being imputed to dead things.

Some would have us believe that complex digital possibilities can replace people and take on a human aspect. In actuality, however, all one can expect when things are left up to machines is inhumanity. Take the case of computer-generated overdue notices or statements of account that continue to be sent out even after an organisation has been informed of someone's death. A human being would not pursue the estate of a deceased person for a tiny amount – a computer is indifferent to circumstances.

Teenagers need to know how computers work. They should also learn the history of digital technology and of the internet. They also need good training and practice in using digital technologies. We all know the frustration of having to do something on a computer that we don't really know how to do. This feeling of powerlessness soon turns into negativity directed at the screen, or at yourself or, in the worst case, at fellow human beings. Competence in using digital technologies and an understanding of what they can make possible is vital, as are lessons in distinguishing relevant information from irrelevant or unreliable material. But in the education of teenagers, computers will never be able to replace living teachers. Computers and the internet can add to education, but teenagers need personal interaction.

The teen years of young people ask for development of the soul. Inner feelings and experiences are transformed into firm soul content, and the soul skin will enclose these, a process that will have implications for later behaviour. When you look at soul development while a person is fully engaged by a screen you will see something very strange: an intense experience in the feeling life caused by a dead thing. The feelings of triumph or frustration are based solely on her or his own performance at the keyboard. There is no real encounter. The soul merely dances around itself in the hope of satisfying itself.

This is the polar opposite of the task of teenagehood, which asks for real soul encounters and experiences in relation to the surrounding world.

The point is that there has to be balance – balance between

isolation from others and doing things together with others. On one thing I want to be clear: the normal use of the computer, something very familiar to every teenager, is just part of our everyday life. It is the perfect instrument for doing a school assignment and many other projects. Used in this way it is just a tool like any other tool. No issues arise unless using it becomes a goal in itself.

WHAT CAN YOU DO?

◊   I want to voice a plea to parents to protect their children from the anti-social tendency associated with computer use. If your child takes an avid interest in digital technology but also has a lively soul, many friends, and likes playing football or some other sport, she or he probably has a healthy state of balance. But if your child spends most of her or his time at the computer, and is a bit of an introvert anyway, then it is important that parents put some limits on this.

◊   If as a parent you have an interest in computing, it may well be possible to talk about this with an older teen, even to develop a programme or an app together. This kind of interaction may help break the child's tendency to be shut up alone with the computer.

Exploitation Online

It can be hard to search the internet without being tempted into all kinds of irrelevant sidetracks. This brings us back to the question of whether a teenager's 'I' has the wherewithal to guide all the impulses working in the soul. Young people badly need opportunities to practice this guidance. While temptation used to come from places outside the house, today staying at home with all the digital media can evoke similar questions to going out. When going out, young people have to try – while still having fun with friends – to stick to their own intentions in a world full of pitfalls and traps. The same is now true in their own rooms at home. Undesirable intimacies and addictions are constant temptations on the screen. Games you play for fun with others may lead to dependence as much as addiction to drugs.

Encounters with undesirable characters is as possible online as out in a bar. Schoolgirls can fall head over heels in love with a married internet-lover, who is dozens of years older than they are and who may keep them imprisoned in their teenage souls for years. In such a case the narrow path to freedom has turned into a digital prison. The impossibility of such an online relationship remains hidden for a much longer time than it would be if formed in the real world, where it would have to stand up to all the influences of contemporaries and parents. Yet letting go of such a relationship may be experienced as breaking a deep connection.

Then there is the question of time. Parents will give their teenage children a time when they have to come home. Of course, the kids will do what they can to stretch the curfew, but concerned parents will notice when they come home late and ask for explanations. Yet how many teenagers are chained to their computers at night while their parents are asleep? The parents are not worried, because they think of their child as being safe at home. Modern parents have a double task now that 'going out' is just as much of a temptation inside the house as outside it.

Many parents deny access to porn sites and violent games on children's computers, tablets and phones – and this is indeed important. For when children do key in *sex* on an unprotected computer, they are often deeply upset by what they see. Witnessing perversion and violence is often something they are unable to deal with at a young age. Who would feed hard liquor or poisonous plants to a child that had just learned to eat? Similarly you don't feed children of twelve, thirteen or fourteen, who are just beginning to feel the first hormones playing in their bodies, sadism and horror. That would be in bad taste, to put it mildly. But realism also tells us that children surfing the internet cannot be totally protected from inappropriate images, especially when they grow a little older. Denying access is only possible in part. Images we as parents would never want to show them are readily accessible. Moreover, more modern paedophiles await them on the internet than in a city park.

Young teens are beginning to loosen the bonds with their parents, and thus to carry their own little secrets. They look for different tastes and different behavioural patterns. This makes them sensitive to new contacts and behaviours online. They quickly develop a digital life of their own, without having insight into the consequences of their actions.

The senses of hearing, speech, thinking and 'I' are our spiritual senses, but these are not yet fully developed in young teens, so it is difficult for them to tell whether a person is suspicious or is a nice friend down the street. On a screen it is even harder than usual to assess other people – to evaluate what they say, how they listen and what they are thinking. Young teens are still unable to experience their own 'I' as a grown-up reality in themselves, and feel the urge to experiment on their own. Any creep can enter into sweet relationships via a screen and webcam, and many do.

WHAT CAN YOU DO?

◊ Parents who take care to keep an eye on their teenager are not old-fashioned, but rather as modern as can be. They are conscious of the power of digital violence. As parents we need to be alert to what our children are doing, and with whom, on the internet. Yet today's parents were not themselves educated in these relationships. The average parent of a teenager is at least forty years old, so grew up in the 1980s, perhaps with Nintendo, but without the internet. It is a challenge for all educators and parents to stay alert in matters where they have had no experience during their own youth.

◊ Such supervision intrudes on the privacy of teenagers just when they are beginning to resist such intrusion. That is a real problem. The best way to approach it is for the parents to be clear from day one that some supervision and interference are necessary in relation to computer use. If they indicate from the start that they will not leave their children under sixteen unprotected in this regard, supervision need not become a source of serious conflict. Young people will accept clear arrangements if these are made explicitly and ahead of time. But people who let their teenagers do what they want as long as they don't cause any trouble and then later try to impose rules and supervision can expect major difficulties.

Twelve Senses

To fully understand what goes on inside a teenager playing computer games, we need to consider the twelve senses.

We all possess twelve senses. Five of them are well known to everyone, but the other seven are not so obvious. The senses we all know are: hearing, sight, smell, taste and touch. But there are more gates we can discern between inner world and outer world. We can subdivide the twelve senses into three groups, as follows.

Body	Soul	Spirit
touch	sight	hearing
movement	smell	thought
balance	taste	speech/language
life	warmth	'I'/ego

Babies need the first four senses as they learn to use their bodies. Through touch they begin to feel what can be experienced outside the womb. Babies develop by always moving and by seeking balance during those movements. In this way they learn to crawl, stand and walk. The sense of life tells a baby whether everything is functioning properly. When this is not the case, the baby will make this known loudly and clearly! Hunger and thirst are perceived through this sense of life. Using these body senses children gradually make connections with the reality of the world and their own bodies.

The soul senses serve our inner experiences. What we see, smell and taste tells us whether or not we like our food. We enjoy things through these senses, and we experience this enjoyment as pleasing warmth. In moments when our soul is numbed by an overly strong emotion, much will escape our perception: while seeing we appear blind, and all foods will taste the same to us. That is because the soul senses, which have the function of enabling us to experience the outside world, have shut down.

The spiritual senses enable us to be human beings among human beings. This requires a sense for language, since through listening to the language of someone we learn what kind of person she or he is. We receive the words a person speaks in a much deeper place than we usually realise. Words are able to form another person, but can also distort her or him. We can make or break each other merely by words. Without some form of inner language we would be unable to form thoughts. In this way the sense of thinking stands on the sense of speech and develops it further. And when we want to meet someone as an 'I' being, we need to be able to look into that person's eyes. Only then can we find the reliability and inner truth of the other. The sense of 'I' endows us with a sort of radar that enables us to see through the eyes of the other into her or his inner world.

If a child grows up in a healthy way, the twelve senses will develop well. This means that every gate of the senses can then be used for its proper purpose. You could say that together they comprise a person's unique toolbox.

The discussion and awareness of all these senses is important for developing a good understanding of the

> consequences of the changes taking place with lightning speed in the area of digital technology and its many applications.
>
> Readers who would like to become better informed about the twelve senses are referred to *The Twelve Senses* by Albert Soesman and also *The First Seven Years* by Edmond Schoorel.

Games Addiction and Obsessive Computer Use

The risks of the digital world have become very visible in computer games. Games are played either alone or with others and are highly competitive – you can win, and that is exciting.

How can we understand clearly what a computer game is doing in a teenager? A teenager is a human being who must remodel soul content copied from parents into soul content that is self-developed. This is a process that goes in fits and starts, especially in boys. Because everything that was nice and attractive to the young child has now become out of date and deadly boring, the world of the child has sunk into the depths. That creates emptiness, and many a teen has a feeling of living in no man's land. In addition, the uneven effects of developing hormonal activity create an unbalanced feeling life which is expressed in all kinds of unspecific questions without satisfactory answers – questions such as; 'What do others think of me, my body, my behaviour, my accomplishments? What am I supposed to say to someone I'm attracted to?' Teens try to find guidance by looking to the most popular kids, or at ideals presented on screens.

The sense of balance, through which the child learned to walk long ago, is out of kilter. The sense of speech, which used to be the natural gate between the child and its surroundings, seems to be numbed and closed. Teenagers often no longer understand or speak the language of the people around them.

This is a picture of stagnation and insecurity. No one and nothing is interesting any more. And that is the vacuum the makers of computer games are filling! Suddenly there is life, sensation, excitement. Adrenaline courses through the body and all boredom is chased away. A pimply adolescent can now identify with a self-made, attractive, strong, muscular body on the screen, and can be a match for others in situations of life and death.

In a computer game you can create your own personality, your own life and world. You get to do things that ordinary life does not permit. A kind of second life full of situations, encounters and experiences that pull you high above regular life is very attractive. The insecure ones who are caught in stagnation and isolation are served like kings while riding safely and speedily across the screen.

Games even address the unconscious need for spiritual challenges. The goals include spiritual ideals that must be conquered with great effort. Many games are loaded with secret enemies of darkness who have extraordinary capacities and skills. In the midst of fights with magical weapons and forces, the teenager in a comfortable seat becomes an idealist who changes and liberates the world. Why are many of these computer games so full of spiritual, esoteric and super-sensory elements? Such spiritual purpose wells up as a longing in the hearts of young people. But while people in the Middle East are fighting their dictators, and Russians and Chinese people are fighting corruption, and Africans are fighting hunger and illness, our young people are fighting with all their spirit in these computer games.

After a while even the most exciting game has been played to death and becomes a bore, no matter how hard its makers try to keep up with the most addicted and intelligent kids by putting out new versions and updates. But after the enjoyable overexcitement and sensation of the game, the silence and emptiness in the soul of the teenager is worse than before. And then we see the same pattern as with every other stimulant: they can't do without it any more, and the enjoyment turns into addiction.

Computer games have become an addiction that is spreading among teenagers, especially boys. The newer online games for multiple players are interesting much longer than the earlier generation of games. Younger teens are especially easily chained to the screen by these games, because they offer so many possibilities for playing with or against other people. You become known in the game; you play together in a team and you get the feeling that they can't do without you in that world. In the big multiplayer games such as *World of Warcraft*, *Assassin's Creed Revelations* or *Call of Duty – Modern Warfare 3* you choose and create your own personality. These games exert social pressure: if you don't play, your group may lose and you may be blamed. They demand the utmost in ambition from the young players.

Fighting together with your own team against a hostile group is something you also do when playing football. But after an hour or two of football, the body feels happy and tired. Computer games can be played for many hours on end. Then at school and in the family, the teenager's consciousness continues to revolve around strategy in the game.

This whole process kills impulses of youth and can all too easily prevent the emergence of the 'I'. When game addicts finally decommission their game personality, they may feel like they have committed a kind of suicide, which is experienced as terribly real. All thinking, all spirit had been completely dominated by the game, often for years. After this, life appears senseless and empty, because the real struggle of the teen years was never fought. The companies developing games are not interested in what growing young people actually need. All that counts is profit for the billion dollar entertainment industry. The industry needs young teen players, but the young teens do not need the industry.

Boys in Feeling Teenagehood – young teens – who have low self-esteem are especially vulnerable to game addiction. This often includes highly intelligent boys. At first, they will covertly play at night, but in due course, the rhythm of day and night disappears. Eating becomes a disagreeable interruption of the game just as every conversation, task or encounter becomes an unbearable disturbance. The rhythm and togetherness in family life is then more and more undermined. The second life has turned into the first life.

The senses of the body – the senses of life, touch, balance and movement – are violated because they are used in situations that have nothing to do with the body. And new technical possibilities are being invented all the time to make the entire body communicate with what is taking place on the screen.

But also the quick reactions you have to display so that your assassin can destroy the hired killer of someone else, to perform on a racetrack at 200 miles an hour, to deal with an exploding stinking robot – all such scenes bring totally foreign situations into the player, as if his body were actually involved. You really do have to use your sense of balance in such games, and suppress your sense of life when you are in the midst of a ritual fight. But your adrenaline is pumping for real! Although in the world of digital technology you barely touch anything, you still experience everything. Seeing and hearing the game deceives the true senses of sight and hearing, and the sense of speech is numbed. Thinking is limited by the framework of the game and your own role. Using the sense of 'I' to perceive the other players is an utter impossibility, for this requires that one comes eye to eye with the other human being.

A young computer game addict will begin to neglect himself. Eating, drinking, sleeping, washing and going out happen less and less, until all that remains of the war hero of the screen is a mere shadow of himself. Kicking the habit generates the same phenomena as drug withdrawal because the brain gets used to the dopamine and adrenaline.

As well as being addicted to games, teens can become obsessively involved in hacking and computer piracy. Power in the digital world brings a great feeling of triumph. The challenge is to master the thought process of the one who designed the programme or created the firewall. This produces a kick: it is sensational but only very briefly satisfying – you need to be able to do more and more with it, otherwise it is no longer fun. This is the nature of an addiction. You are not using the digital world for its functionality in your own projects, but for the inner excitement it evokes.

WHAT CAN YOU DO?

◊ It doesn't matter if your children call you old-fashioned or complain that all their friends are allowed to do or have so much more than they are. Remember, though, you can try to make agreements with the parents of your children's friends, so that your child does not feel left out. Most parents suffer too much from social fears. Consider what you are fighting for as parent: nothing less than the inner freedom of your child.

◊ As a parent, always investigate what an interactive game is about, and do not be content with checking that the recommended age is appropriate for your child. Just as not every film rated PG-13 can be tolerated by every fifteen year old, you cannot depend on the age indications on games. Of course, games that are clearly marked for age eighteen and older are often eagerly sought by sixteen year olds. Whatever can be said about games in a book like this will be out of date before the ink is dry. Parents need to do research for themselves – thoroughly and repeatedly. For instance, Wikipedia has an extensive article describing every aspect of *World of Warcraft*.

◊ Why not play the new game together with your sixteen year old and discuss it? Keep up with the times!

Parents should understand that playing screen games is all right for sixteen year olds and older, provided it is done in moderation, just like watching television. But be especially alert to the kind of games your teens play and the place the games take on in their lives. If you don't pay attention, you can easily lose your son, and also your daughter, to this world.

And then there are plenty of games to play on the little screens of ipads and tablets, so that many a teen thumbs his nose at his parents!

Social Media

Digital novelties are appearing with the speed of light. There are so many interesting and exciting new apps: Facebook and LinkedIn are supplanting texting and emailing, but the principal role of social media is still to supplement earlier methods of communication. We no longer have mail once a day, but a whole lot of mailboxes where we post and collect mail all the time. Receiving and sending mail is something people always enjoy. The social media now enable us to get messages and visits all the time, and to constantly affirm that we are being seen and heard.

Being in contact with everything and everyone, and knowing immediately what is happening where, is an absolute necessity for teenagers. It is as if they live every hour of the day in a sort of party; their communications have that tone. 'Where are you? What are you doing? Who is with you?' Naturally everything is illustrated with fun pictures, amusing reactions, or insistence on watching this or that YouTube film clip or reading this or that piece of gossip. Whoever has the most friends and gets the most visits receives the highest social score. This form of communication has a high 'foam content', meaning that the exchange of information is of an artificial and superficial social nature; it is like the foam on the tops of waves that is blown off by the wind.

The social profile is being remade all day long. Interminable nonsense stories form a sort of public diary, which challenges the humour, creativity, speed and alertness of the user. Why does a teenager want to tell all his contacts that his train is late, his mother impossible and his homework s..t? Because it gives her or him a feeling of not being forgotten. Thanks to social media you don't need to feel alone and isolated. Of course this is an illusion and has its shadow side. Trouble online accompanied by bullying and threats has also spread far and wide. Being always accessible to the threats and nastiness of others is part of the ever-present layer of foam in the Twitter world.

Social media offer sources of excitement and sensation for the bored teenage soul between childhood and adulthood. They can give life the appearance of being full of seething activity and speed. Here the girls are a big part of the scene with their chatter, their looks and their giggles with and at each other. Of course, teenagers have always done this with each other, only now they are able to do it endlessly, everywhere and with everyone.

No doubt, the makers of social media know all about teenagers. After all, Facebook came out of the student brain of Mark Zuckerberg. He started it at Harvard University with a system through which he could place pictures of female students on the screens of his male student friends, with the possibility of rating them. Facebook is therefore a literal name: it came from the idea of attaching a value judgment to faces.

I have seen the headline in a newspaper: 'Facebook + Twitter + LinkedIn = Power score'. That is a reality for many people. How full is my digital mailbox? Are people following me? Many young people live with the question: How important am I online? There are even specialised websites that calculate how high you are ranking on the social media ladder.

We could say that the social world has migrated from the fluid element to the airy one. The river with its locks through which the water of life flows is the place where the teenage soul belongs. But this is also an experience of shoals, floods and running aground. Often the young person is inwardly still adrift and has not yet developed sea legs on the sea of inner soul experiences. Sympathy and antipathy are surging up and down, dragging the teenage soul with them. Finding and maintaining their own course is no easy matter.

It is as if teenagers are using the busyness of social media to dissolve and evaporate all the disturbances in the troubled waters of their soul. They can transform the delay of the train, the impossible mother or the tough homework into fun messages. A picture of the angry mother or of the train delay announcement will complete the message. If everyone reacts with a joke and adds some predicament of their own, teenagers have no need to stop and undergo what they experience deep in their soul. Experiencing depth can be a real confrontation, and escaping it is a temptation for every human being, certainly for teens.

In this way life evaporates into the volatility and fleetingness of air. Depth is harder and harder to find, and people who look for it are soon estranged from social networks. Everything flashes on and off like little LED lights, but rarely does this communication stand firmly with its two feet on the ground. You could say that teenagers can be everywhere and nowhere in this world. This is why norms and values can easily be broken when using social media. Things are said and done there that some attentive consideration would have prevented.

In regard to the senses it is as though teens on social media are using antennas rather than touching. Movement becomes restlessness, and the sense of warmth depends on the score in the social media. Life is like a dance without a director. The 'I' may be able to give impulses, but they will rarely be followed.

As the feeling life becomes more active and profound, and lasting relationships are developed in the life of the young person, the airy foam once again returns to fluidity. A deep relationship permeated by a true connection with another person, with work and the teenager's own life path will make all superficiality superfluous. When the 'I' takes possession of the soul and of the direction of life, the feet will start to move again instead of just the fingertips.

For the parent or educator, the task is always to get teenagers involved in real encounters, not only with other people, but also with insights, awareness to physical reality and conversations. Then they come to earth so they can connect with reality again. The maintenance of a deep connection with your child even when she or he moves in realms where you can't follow demands much love, loyalty and attention. These are three gifts that make an appeal to young people to come back to themselves. Until that happens, all the social fluttering hither and thither produces a kind of nervous network that minimises the potential for attention, concentration and listening capacity. Young people talk online incessantly, but are at the same time incapable of having a really good conversation. As parents and educators you can always be on the lookout for moments and places when this is still possible – late in the evening, perhaps in the car, or on a walk. It is of prime importance for adults not to fall back into superficiality themselves, but to live and work full of attention for each other and the world. Sooner or later, examples become reality for teenagers.

The search for the value of your personality makes a person vulnerable. When we receive attention and responses from good educators and adults who care for us, we have the chance to develop a feeling of self-worth and self-confidence. In our society with its addiction to scores and ratings, the confirmation of the personality of a child is displaced from the family to the school and also to what they look like physically. Growing human beings are no longer measured by who they are themselves, but how they fit in relation to standards and averages. In effect, the adult world says: 'The child has to develop a socially desirable profile.' The world of statistics, averages and the steadily increasing control and demand in the area of school performance all create social estrangement. We see this estrangement mirrored in the behaviour of our teenagers. Reverence and respect for children's own inner being gives them the opportunity to seek and find themselves in the depths of their life and life tasks. The foam content of social media then becomes of secondary importance, and they will not so easily become dependent on them.

If the fighting spirit, stamina, thinking power, feeling life and imagination that are now exhibited in relation to a virtual world, are committed to the real world, teenagers will grow up to become healthy human beings. Then they will be able to bring to realisation that for which they have come into this life. Adults who interact with them can help by truly seeking and walking the same path. In addition, protection against overuse of digital media will remain a necessary and troublesome job for parents for a number of years. The challenge of the future is the connection of all of humanity with each other and with the spiritual world. Social media and relationships within the make-believe world of virtual connections are the narcotics of this challenge. Educators and parents are being asked to see through and resist these temptations.

10. Sexuality

Background

In the deepest layers of the human soul lives a primal pain. We have become separated from an original spiritual unity, we have lost our natural connections. In the deepest sense, the human being has a spiritual nature and origin. Every people has its mythology that tells the story of how, in the beginning of earthly humanity, a division occurred between a spiritual world and the human world. We carry this knowledge with us as a deep pain in our soul. This disconnection from the spirit also causes disconnection between human beings, because they are no longer able to experience each other's deepest essence.

Sexuality, which is built into the physicality of human beings, is perhaps the most powerful way to connect beyond the separated self. When sexuality is the expression of mature love between two people, an inspiration radiates from the spiritual world down into the body. There is then a spiritual connection, although an unconscious one. It is for good reason that this is the moment when a new – as yet spiritual – being can incarnate. It is the moment when fructification takes place, not only physically but also spiritually.

Every person is either a man or a woman; there is a duality among us. This duality arose because part of the purpose of humanity, of the earthly existence of human beings, is that we should need our fellow human being to enable us to continue to exist. Quite literally.

Every difference among people may degenerate into a difference in power, and that is also true between men and women.

Power difference becomes a barrier. But relationships of equality enable us to build a bridge between man and woman, a bridge in the realm of feeling, but also down into the depths of the body, into sexuality. Just like the deep pain of spiritual loneliness, that of human social loneliness lies at the very bottom of the soul. It leads us to search for the other, a striving that is expressed in the forming of relationships, and finally in sexuality. Physically we cannot approach each other more closely than in sexuality. Man and woman, with their widely differing talents and strengths, can then flow together.

Rudolf Steiner taught that the body of life forces of the man is feminine and that of the woman masculine. When we think deeply about this we recognise that man and woman can be each other's completion. When they join in love and soul relationships, they can now and then lose the deep ground of pain in the soul. This closeness, this response, is what we seek in sexuality. Sexuality can give us a momentary feeling of being whole, of human reconciliation. Sexuality offers the potential to experience ourselves – just briefly – not in loneliness but in togetherness.

Like everything else, sexuality also has its shadow side. There the exact opposite occurs: there it can degenerate into the deepest possible human loneliness, or into an animal urge without the engagement of the person, further removed from a spiritual connection than one can possibly imagine.

It is the task of the human being to enable sexuality to be an instrument of the human capacity for connecting, for relieving each other of the primal soul pain. Sexuality is able to do that, at least for a moment. After that, we fall back into our separateness. We are thrown back on our own. To bear this we are in dire need of our own spiritual core, because right then we often experience the pain of humanity even worse than before. Somehow we have to be able to endure that. This requires maturity.

Teenagers and Sexuality

In the teen years, the sexual aspect of relationships usually starts from impulses other than or combined with physical desire, such as wanting to belong, or to appear a big man, or not wanting to be rejected, or the hope of binding a boy or girlfriend to you. Sexuality is then the outcome of such needs and is not caused by desire itself.

By 'sexuality', I mean not so much the first tentative tender gestures and kisses, but the adult sexual deed during the teen years. Sexuality is a bit like Sleeping Beauty: once she is awake she wants to marry the prince, wake everyone up, and certainly not fall asleep again! When these forces come to life in the thoughts, feelings and will of a young person, they force him or her into adulthood. Dealing with this demands much, so much that teenagers will struggle to keep their 'I' on a sure footing in the midst of their own violent emotions and those of the other. Responsibility, desire, pain, extreme pleasure, you name it, suddenly it is all there and they have to live within it. This often means the end of the period of soul freedom.

When a child reaches puberty, the body is soon fully grown. Teenagers are capable of generating new life. They move up a rung on the ladder of physical life. And on the rung below they have made room for a new human child. Doesn't that mean that it is high time for them to loosen themselves from their parents and become independent? All the hormonal changes, all the changes in the body send this message into the inner being of the child. Intuitively, the answer is a wholehearted yes, and the striving for independence begins.

Sexuality has many functions. One of these functions is in service of procreation; another in service of our lower passions. Sometimes it is just a question of the satisfaction of desire, but also human needs for intimacy, tenderness and closeness can be satisfied in this way. In addition, sex can satisfy our need for identity as man or woman. As we have already seen, it can also take away the primal pain of the separated human being.

Sexuality is an interaction between body and soul. The soul is intimately connected with what goes on in the body in passion, intimacy or tenderness. In order to handle this, when the soul connects itself so deeply with the body it is important to be able to find the way back. I mean that the soul must also be able to loosen itself somewhat from the body. It is a matter of connecting and disconnecting again.

While the soul is not yet fully formed and enveloped by the soul skin, danger lurks in the soul and body trying to connect and disconnect. This is what you have to deal with in the teen years: the soul has not yet become an individuality and has not yet completed its skin. In this situation it can easily happen that the soul that connects itself with the body in sex is unable to loosen itself again and therefore loses inner freedom. The result can be that a teenager becomes the slave of his or her body.

Evidence of this might be the urge to experience sexuality continually. Or the development of other addictions. You could say that the soul becomes *glued* to the body, and is compelled to identify exclusively with the physical, and with the bodily sensations this can produce.

Many young people suffer from this kind of imprisonment. When the soul is still free it can indulge in dreaming and falling in love and fantasising. For the feeling life, the sky is the limit. But when the soul is imprisoned in the body, it is as if the sea is not allowed to be the sea, but as if it loses its high and low tides, its currents and waves, and is bound still and powerless like a reservoir held in check by stone and steel, with walls around it and a bottom of concrete.

While it is wonderful to fantasise about your dearly beloved, and to text and twitter with him or her; while kissing and petting can be a great experience, for teenagers, sex with the beloved often results in the end of youth. And it is often an end that comes too soon, not because it violates some norm of behaviour, but because the soul is not ready for it.

And there is more. Since sexuality is experienced together with someone else, it is not only a question of becoming glued to your own body, but also of becoming *tied up with the physicality of the other person*. That happens because the life forces, the etheric forces, of both are mingled together. The bodies unite and take the souls with them. But when the soul cannot loosen itself, it will be imprisoned in the other, so that it loses its freedom and independence.

When the couple then splits up, or one of them starts seeing someone else, the pain will go very deep. The other now possesses part of your soul, and carries that along in his or her life forces. Almost literally, a part of the one is living in the other. When those two are together they are 'whole' again in that moment, but as soon as they are separate they feel incomplete. If such a split occurs it can deteriorate into despair about the loss of a part of oneself, even though this is experienced as the loss of the other. These are real death experiences that threaten the inner, and sometimes even the outer, life.

Many teenagers are then left with the possibilities of numbing the experience, replacing it or hardening. Alcohol or drugs numb the experience. It can be replaced by throwing yourself into the arms of a new girlfriend or boyfriend, for it is too painful to be free or alone any longer now that a little death has entered your life. Hardening is closing yourself to any others so that it can't happen again. You don't engage your soul in relationships any more. In this latter case, you can go to bed with anyone without losing even more of yourself. It doesn't matter whom, where or how, as long as you can satisfy your physical needs. That this is accompanied with a total lack of love for the other is obvious. For in fact this hardening is another case of soul deafness: the inner soul senses are not participating.

If the hardened person then seeks sexual intercourse with a younger partner who has not had any sexual experience and who is too young to have closed his or her soul skin, this younger person will suffer in turn. There is also a power imbalance in such cases. Hardened ones remain free, because they shut the door to their souls to protect themselves from further soul amputation. Not so for the new boy or girlfriend, who loses part of his or her soul to the other. Then we see a one-sided dependency. He or she not only loses part of the soul but also life forces, and because of the loss of these life forces the soul becomes un-free.

If the younger person can stand firmly in his or her shoes, he or she will get over this, but a deep scar will remain. Something is lost, something that was part of you. Weaker personalities will feel themselves like a slave imprisoned by the other. No matter how they are cheated and mistreated and not given love, they still keep running after the other. This can escalate to an extreme with the Don Juan type, who knows how to make young girls so dependent on his own hardened soul that they can be abused like slaves.

We can also encounter such situations with adults, because while the body fully reaches adulthood, the soul often does so only to a much lesser extent. In such a case the adult man or woman is just as incapable of ending a disastrous relationship. And when it is a question of divorce, the partners will experience how difficult it is for the life forces, which were intermingled, to separate from each other. This is a death process that demands much mourning.

If it is so difficult for an adult, how difficult must it be for a teenager? If it has been a long-term relationship that was also lived sexually, the split-up will be no easier than a divorce.

Then there is the situation in which two young people, both of whom have not yet closed their soul skin, come into sexual contact with each other. If they have really met their one true love they are in luck; in that case, after their fourteenth or fifteenth year, no one else will come into their lives and they become *mutually dependent* – they live deeply in each other's life forces. And yet, this involves a sacrifice of the time to experience things alone in the soul, youth time, development time, time to reflect whether you want any relationship or want that particular relationship. But if these children really belong together, it is a done deal. Sometimes this is something very special, because in such an early bond they get to know each other's inner life better than anyone else. They really creep into each other's soul skin. In such exceptional cases a lifelong relationship may grow in which they live very easily together and understand each other perfectly, provided that sooner or later they develop inner independence.

More often though, we see that after being together for a few years, two young people develop the feeling that they would like to meet someone else, or that the other does not really prove to be the one who belongs to them, or perhaps that they have simply grown apart. Can they then let each other go? Or do they split up – and yet I can't live without you, so let's get together again, and so on. It becomes a case of *they can't live with each other but they can't live without each other* – great loss of freedom, caused by the loss of part of the soul, which is glued to the body of life forces of the other.

Some people repeat this pattern over and over. There are young people who time and again fail to form their soul body properly, and then lose part of themselves in the arms of someone else every time. They search and search to find themselves again, and they find less and less of themselves. Even if they have the ability to let each other go, a first relationship of this kind leaves deep tracks. Freely looking around and falling in love and having relationships at a young age is only possible if there is no adult sexuality.

The all-important goal of teenagehood is freeing oneself from the influences of one's surroundings and finding one's own content. That is the basis on which individuality and freedom can grow. When you consider the lack of freedom resulting from sex at too early an age, and you set next to it the goal of teenagehood, they reveal themselves as almost polar opposites. The child shakes off the parents, but becomes un-free in relation to someone else. Or the child feels a necessity to harden and close off the soul, but while in this case sexuality ceases to be a problem, it also ceases to enrich the person's life. And closing off the outside also always means a closing off on the inside. The person who is not able to have good relationships with fellow humans, is no longer able to form good relations with his own 'I' either – with what gives meaning to life. If that happens, teenagehood cannot perform its function. Instead of the primal pain in the soul being lifted through sexuality, it will be aggravated and experienced even more deeply.

What can you do?

Prevention is better than cure...

In my opinion, much too little attention is given to the question of how to handle sexuality during the teen years. Today's children are not forced to bear a child prematurely: they are educated about sex at an early age and can easily obtain contraceptives. Many a girl who does become pregnant in her fourteenth or fifteenth year has an abortion. That this intervention ends the life of a child is something we know. The fact that, in addition, it ends the youth of the mother is something that escapes many people. 'Solutions' like abortion create the appearance that the physical consequences of teen sexuality have been brought under control.

If the danger of AIDS raises its head, we all pay attention again, because that is something against which we have little physical defence. So we have shifted as a society from a focus on how to prevent premature pregnancy to a focus on how to prevent sexually transmitted diseases.

Naturally, these are important questions. But is this all that our care for our children's wellbeing amounts to? It seems to me that we need to think and look further. What we certainly no longer need to do is brood on the *correct norm*. It does not exist any more, if it ever did. Out of the inner human being, his or her own conscience must emerge as the guide, rather than social convention. That is something you can work on: the awakening of the inner conscience, the voice that rises up out of the true 'I' of the human being. You can immerse yourself in the question of a correct view of life through insight and deep thinking. Guidance so created is known out of our inmost depths. That is the basis on which we can work with our sons and daughters.

If you try to teach your teenage children what is done and not done, you are putting the cart before the horse. You have to do this kind of teaching before the teen years, because teenagers throw all those rules overboard. All those stories about how to behave may be totally justified and understandable, but they have only one function: they are wonderfully satisfying for the parents! If you want to teach standards of behaviour to teens, there is only one rule: live in accordance with your own values, consistently and wholeheartedly, in thought, word and deed. Come to grips with your own compromises, and don't cheat.

This effort can become an inner experience for your child; it may resonate in him or her. Imperceptibly his or her soul will move in harmony, so that if you can avoid evoking resistance, something can still be communicated by sheer example.

How can you coach your child in such a way as to reduce the likelihood he or she will explore the world of sexuality before the soul skin is completed and the soul body has reached its individual form? Here are some rules of thumb:

◊ Try to impart respect for the human body to your children from early childhood, by taking good care of it, appreciating it and accepting it as it is, in gratefulness for what it is able to do.

◊ Allow children to experience pleasure and enjoyment; that should be part of life. But do set some boundaries. Devouring a whole box of cookies is ultimately not a pleasure, unlike finding a freshly baked piece of cake in your school lunch. Treats now and then are not the same as endless indulgence.

◊ The freedom of one person ends when that of another is violated. Experimenting is fine, but not across the boundary of the other, whether it is the boundary of the mother or of the father. This takes a lot of practice. Many quarrels among children reflect their testing of each other's boundaries. If you succeed in showing your child that there is a boundary that has to be respected, you have created a sound basis for dealing with boundaries in the teen years and in sexuality.

◊ As an adult man or woman, treat someone of the opposite sex with regard and appreciation. Treat your husband or wife with respect, in word and deed. Lewd remarks or porn sites betray the fact that you consider the other largely as an object of lust. A child who is blessed with parents who love and respect each other stands on a solid foundation for its later life.

◊ Divorced parents must avoid criticising their former partner. Don't sow disdain for the other parent.

Respect your former partner, and process your grief or aggression without involving your children. If you can't manage that, say to them that you made a mistake, and tell them about former times and what was good between you and their other parent. If you are honest and look for it, you can always find something good. The boy or girl who grows to despise or even hate one of their parents is not well prepared for later interaction with the opposite sex. But a nice, positive photograph of your ex with your child or with you can say something very important.

◊   Teach your children that being pretty and healthy is precious, because it enables you to *do* more, not to *be* more. Who and what you really are is something that lives in your inner being, and it is not confirmed by people who say that you are pretty. If parents always treats one of their children as the 'ugly duckling', that child will look everywhere for confirmation of his or her appearance. He or she will reject his or her own body in the same way that the parents reject it, and at the same time search for people who do appreciate it. Some of these children pay a high price... On the other hand, giving exaggerated attention and extolling the attractive aspects of the body fosters a one-sided development. As so often, it is balance that fosters strength and health.

◊   It is important that children are often touched physically. Cuddle them, romp with them – don't think they are too old for a loving stroke over the head. People who have experienced little physical tenderness often look for that later in sexuality, and often in vain.

◊   Show respect for the child's own space. I mean not only that other children should not be allowed to use your child's desk or put on your child's clothes without asking, no, I mean *show respect for your child's private space yourself*. Don't open their mail, even if they are only six years old. They are perfectly capable of opening

envelopes themselves, and then they will freely ask you
to read the letter to them. And when they have grown
up a few years, stay out of their diary and out of their
clothes cupboard. Remember, email, text messages and
other communications are not public property. When
children learn that every person is entitled to his or
her private space, they will develop a natural feeling for
the defense and respect of privacy. Let them have their
secret conversations with their friends; parents don't
need to intrude everywhere, physically or otherwise. If
your child no longer wants to kiss you goodnight, that's
fine. Do they want to lock the bathroom door? Fine, just
wait your turn. Don't laugh at them, don't force them,
stay alert. You also don't need to accept that your own
clothes might suddenly disappear from your wardrobe,
or that your desk is stacked high with your child's stuff.
Ask for respect for your own boundaries as well.

◊   Our society is chock full of ideas and influences in the
area of men, women and sexuality that convey the polar
opposite of healthy mutual relationships: films full
of sex, ideals of beauty that you will never be able to
achieve, commercials filled with exaggerated seductive
scenes, and so on. While your children are small, you
can keep that away from such material if you want.
When they grow a little older, show them your own
values first, before they stumble over all these things
in the outside world. If nothing is ever said, then what
the outside world shows is the first influence they
encounter. Inform them yourself, before their friends
tell them that Santa Claus does not exist, or how that
baby got into mum's belly. Find beautiful, warm and
genuine pictures to inform your child. If they already
know everything as 'beautiful', they are better protected
against 'ugly' knowing. When they know already about
the warm little house in mum's belly where they were
living before they were born, the sensational story

told by the little boy down the street will make no impression at all. They knew it all along, and much better!

Should your teenage child already be involved in a sexual relationship, in this case, too, don't give total freedom right away. Freedom that is given with creativity and grows gradually is much better. It is important to open your house and show hospitality, but if this goes too far and your son or daughter's friend is allowed to stay overnight as often as they want, you will run the risk of having a fifteen- or sixteen-year-old couple in your home. If that is your choice and you know how to deal with it there may not be a problem, but most of the time this turns into a source of irritation in the family. Going back on freedom once given, however, is virtually impossible. Even if a teenager has the appearance of being resigned to the loss of freedoms, that is usually just exterior compliance. Think ahead, before opening the door too wide! If they can simply be together in the living room, and you withdraw now and then, there won't be a one-sided interest in each other's bodies quite so soon. Perhaps it is possible to open up the subject of sex, not to condemn it, but with an open ear. It may be that overly tempting situations can be avoided through open conversation.

When children enter into fixed relationships early, they will tend to have sex sooner. Naturally, if there has been a long-lasting friendship for years, sex is a very different story than a teenager who has one-night stands or experiments with many partners. In the latter case you can still effectively intervene. Let your child know that he or she has gone too far and express your opinion. That is better than putting your head in the sand for fear of losing the child.

If you see that your child is losing his or her soul freedom in a relationship and is becoming fixated on the other, you may well feel powerless. And yet, you continue to have a very important place in the soul of your child, even if it is hardly noticeable at that moment. This makes it possible for you to stay close to your child during teenagehood. For children in this situation, keep faith in them so they know that they are being seen. Perhaps they will then find the way back to their own individuality. When they have the courage to end the relationship they often fall into a pit, the pit of losing part of themselves. That is the moment when you can do something for them: you can open your arms to them, give them attention, spoil them a little. Distract them with a trip somewhere, or stimulate them to do something new. That will help them overcome this shaky period and get back on their feet. Parents have a special relationship with the life forces of their children. That was the basis from which the children started out in life and were nurtured all those years, so that now perhaps they can retrieve this channel, and the parents can reach and nurture the child again in his or her difficult time.

If your child starts to harden and you run into the consequences of this every day, it is a difficult but crucial question whether you can be a softening influence. Maybe you know of someone with little children who your hard teen can babysit – children may warm him or her up a bit. Maybe you can make a hiking trek through the mountains where nature could open a door again. He or she might want to go back to their musical instrument, or try a new one. Or you might find a wise old man or woman who is willing to talk with them from time to time. Seek and wrestle, but never give up! During teenagehood much can still change; later it will be much more difficult.

Healthy sexuality is something a teenager sniffs around and tastes, but which is better not eaten as long as the soul body does not yet have a firm form. It is hard to say when the soul body does develop a firm form; it all depends on the personal development of the young person. It differs per child and per situation.

One girl starts her period at eleven, another at fifteen. With such big physical differences there are matching differences in soul development. A parent who knows his or her child well will have a good feel for what stage the child has reached, and whether he or she is strong enough to stand up to the seductive forces of sexuality. Restrictions don't work, but coaching and understanding are vital.

In former times there were standard rules, which often had what look to us like ridiculous consequences. We have thrown these ridiculous consequences overboard, and that is a great relief, but the problem itself asks us for a solution nonetheless. A custom-made solution, which works for one child but maybe not for another, is the challenge faced by educators in our time, now that nothing is imposed any more and everything is allowed.

Sexuality and the Three Soul Functions

In the chapter entitled 'Three Types of Teenager, Three Phases of Teenagehood' I have considered teenagers as exhibiting a tendency towards one of the three soul functions, so we can distinguish Thinking Teenagers, Feeling Teenagers and Doing Teenagers. The age of the child also makes a difference:

◊ During the first teen years, our thinking is made independent – we learn abstract thought.

◊ In the middle teen years, the feeling life becomes free, resulting in violent moods.

◊ In the later teen years, the will becomes free, and many decisions have to be made; much has to be done in work and exams.

◊ It will be clear that a Thinking Teenager will be most confrontational and difficult to handle in the first teen years, a Feeling Teenager in the middle years, and a Doing Teenager in the final teen years.

◊ While the idea of these tendencies can be used in many areas, I will apply it here to the realm of sexuality.

SEXUALITY AND THE REALM OF THINKING

Thinking is free, it creates no commitments and is a private affair. It is part of the first phase of forming relationships, of falling in love. When there is too much thinking, the child may be introverted and shy. When a lot of thinking is mixed with strong feelings, the result will be deep conversations but also moods of depression: thinking

162

in circles fruitlessly with negative feelings creates depression. When there is a lot of thinking combined with a strong will, the likely result will be calculating behaviour and a certain hardening. Rigid concepts can fill the soul. When there is not much thinking but a strong will, there won't be much careful consideration; every emotion will quickly lead to a deed. Recklessness and the dictatorship of desire will easily take over.

When teenagers put sufficient thinking into their sexual growth, there will be time to experience in their own still, inner worlds what is filling their minds. This will create the opportunity to choose whether or not to go on. When teenagers think too much, they may have to be seduced into further experiments even after having had a relationship for years.

Thinking Teenagers will have a strong curiosity. They will want to know everything, and healthy sexual education makes that information available.

SEXUALITY AND THE REALM OF FEELING

Thinking does not lead to commitments, but feeling is not quite so free. Feeling can leave us a certain freedom, depending on whether the other soul functions are doing their work properly. People inspire especially strong feelings. The encounter with the other, the contrast with the other, reveals what we feel and thus forms, little by little, our self-image.

People who live strongly in their feelings may fluctuate from elation to depression – exactly what we often see with children in the middle teen years. They can easily lose themselves in excesses. People who do not live in their feelings, or whose feelings are not strong, don't tune in to the inner world of the other, or even to their own inner world. They will always cross boundaries without being aware of it. People without feeling remain cold and hard, and their consciences do not grow properly. In social respects, these people become 'stupid'. A strong feeling life combined with a strong will may be experienced as inner compulsion, like an uncontrollable urge to satisfy desire. Thinking is then needed to keep this in check.

Feeling is part of the second phase of forming a relationship:

the encounter, being together, talking together and looking for each other. It is obvious that a lack in the feeling realm can lead to great problems in sexuality, for instance those who satisfy desire by using another without really taking them into account, or those who remain ice-cold and fail to appreciate the approach of another. It can also lead to very shaky relationships: today your girlfriend is everything, tomorrow you don't even notice her.

SEXUALITY AND THE REALM OF THE WILL

In this area we can see a lot of real compulsion. Since the will leads to action, to performing deeds, it is obvious that commitments and obligations arise here. The will lives in outer reality. Through the will we place ourselves in the outside world and make lasting impressions. If this area strongly predominates for a teenager, it can run them into big trouble. Where there is no reflection (thinking) and no attuning (feeling), the person acts in thoughtless and inconsiderate ways. If there is a shortage of the will, people achieve nothing and remain teenagers forever. They belong to the floaters and dreamers in the kingdom of the sin of non-committal, the realm of saying yes and doing nothing.

In sexuality the realm of the will is that of physical contact. Here what is felt and thought is put into deed. The words express it: the sex *act*. It is no accident that the emphasis on the development of the will life, of doing, falls in the last teenage years. The act puts an end to the freedom of the young person, which is why this development occurs at the threshold to adulthood.

Sexual Abuse of Children

What happens in the soul of a child who is brought into contact with sexuality at a young age? The soul forces are then still unprotected, there is no soul skin as yet, or perhaps just the first beginning of one. All impressions and influences from outside flow freely into the soul and are experienced by children as their own. This characteristic of the soul is what makes children so defenceless. Only after fear and pain and fright can they begin to close off their soul prematurely. They are not able to do this ahead of time. They must first undergo and experience things before they will develop an urge to protect themselves.

Sexuality is still asleep in a young child. Of course – because it does not yet have a function. Physically a child is still unable to have children; the whole area of fertility lies dormant until the child reaches puberty. Like an inner Sleeping Beauty, sexuality and the feelings that go with it are waiting until they are awakened by the kiss of the handsome prince. A thick hedge of thorns protects Sleeping Beauty from intruders who could wake her up prematurely.

When children are sexually abused, it is as if someone chops a hole in the hedge with a dull axe and Sleeping Beauty is woken roughly and too soon. Now the child's soul is invaded by passionate forces that satisfy themselves without any regard for the child. The person who brings these forces to the child – in whom they are still asleep – is unable to master them. The adult who surprises a child with adult passion, even if only once and without violence, sows a highly poisonous message in the child's soul. The message is: 'Sexual passions escape the human 'I'. They take possession of you, and you have to let them control you. Conscience and the inner master are not present here.'

Because this message is experienced in the soul life of the child as his or her own, it becomes part of his or her soul content. It is received in total innocence. Even if the soul later closes itself strongly and prematurely because of pain and misery, this poisonous little plant will keep spreading inside. This is the cause of the powerlessness felt by many victims of abuse. They cannot defend themselves if this message is living in their inner world. The message continually tells them that mastery over these forces is not possible, neither for themselves, nor for the person abusing them. In this way the abuse may go on and on, which is something outsiders find hard to comprehend. Abuse creates powerlessness regarding abuse.

When children become teenagers, they attempt to test the soul content they have absorbed in order to discover to what extent it is their own. Thus when children being abused reach their teen years they will feel the urge to rid themselves of this intrusion by putting an end to it or by telling someone about it who may be able to end it. Such – often weak – efforts in the early teen years are frequently not really heard or taken seriously. Please let us listen to them! Many a survivor remembers this impulse years later and how he or she tried to do something with it, but was not understood or heard, or was rejected.

Many abused children and teenagers look old for their age and come across that way – they are not as playful as their peers. Or, in their despair, they may fall back into an earlier, unburdened phase of their life, and then they act as little children and seem behind in their development. In both cases we experience a thick soul skin: in the first case because the child comes across as so grown-up, and is able to listen and react sensibly, no longer with childlike spontaneity and directness. In the second case the child hides behind the wall of the premature soul skin and tries to relive his or her lost early youth.

When children suffering sexual abuse progress further into the teen years they are continually hampered in the true task of teenagehood. For the task is to search for individuality, to throw overboard whatever is foreign to you, to connect with your inner 'I' and to follow your own red thread: to find the other human being and the world through your 'I' and your red thread, and commit all your soul strength to this search. But if someone continually intrudes into your body, your room, your intimacy – if you are continually abused – how, for heaven's sake, can you possibly fulfill that task?

When eventually the abuse has come to an end, the young person faces a huge undertaking. Sure, process everything, people will say: crying, overcoming aggression, consoling, coaching, and then slowly getting on your feet again. But how do you get rid of that poisonous little plant? How do you find yourself, and how do you put your own inner master in the driver's seat?

If these questions are not resolved, the lives of sexual abuse survivors will often show the same pattern over and over again. New people come and sense that this soul is not free but permeated by that poisonous inner message. The survivor marries someone who treats him or her in the same way. A divorce follows. Is the poison then pulled out root and branch? If not, the survivor remains a plaything of those passionate forces: only the names in his or her life will change, not the experiences.

And there is something more. A person who continues to carry that poisonous little plant in the soul not only becomes a victim time and again, *but also runs the risk of making victims time and again.* A victim of abuse will not very easily commit abuse physically. But there is no natural feeling of reticence. In fact, the soul carries the seed of the exact opposite. It may then happen that when these children become parents, they completely lack the ability to respect their children's individuality. They may read their diaries or interfere with their friendships. They are unaware of the fact that they are now committing psychic abuse, caused by the poison that continues to work unnoticed in their souls.

There are teenagers who have such a father or mother. If the parents are able to discuss it and help each other with it, the parent who is the abuse survivor may be able to learn reticence through the voice of the growing child. Healthy teenagers will protest loudly against parents who continually look over their shoulder.

Teenagers who are not healthy may accept and even want this intrusion by a parent into their soul life. A symbiotic relationship will then grow, in which both parties are un-free. They know everything of each other and cannot be without each other. They experience their mutual dependency and lack of freedom as natural. The injured parent who was the abuse victim becomes attached to his or her children as a child, you could say, instead of as the 'I' who is ready to seek the 'I' of the children in order to stimulate them and set them free. No, in this case the poor parents soul attaches itself to its own child purely out of the soul forces that are nourished by the urge to possess, usurp and penetrate. *What you have not developed in yourself you are unable to recognise and coach in your children.*

As long as such parents are unable to rid themselves of their poison and find a way to their own 'I', they will be unable to deal with the free, true and essential being of their children. It is not a question of guilt, but an incapacity, and it is extremely important that these parents, and their children, receive good assistance and coaching.

MUTUAL CHILD SEXUALITY

What is mutual child sexuality? Children play games of getting-to-know-the-body with each other. They play doctor, father and mother, examiner – and that is then what they are. They examine. This natural childlike tendency to discover what everything looks like is very common and innocent. It passes when they have discovered enough. It is normal.

But our society is full of un-childlike suggestions. Through advertising, television and the computer, ever younger children are confronted with sexuality. Yes, perhaps they want to give it a try! If it is a case of two children of roughly the same age and strength, nothing much is likely to happen. They will soon find that it is not very exciting and go back to their baseball game. But if one is much stronger than the other, things may be different. If two strapping young boys start exploring the shy little girl or boy down the street, it is time to intervene. The danger that they would confront the little one with unwanted rough treatment is certainly not imaginary. Physically smaller or weaker children can be violated by exploration.

And then there is age difference. Teenagers often want everyone to believe they are big, strong and superior. When such a teenager starts a relationship with a much younger boy or girl and pushes experiments on them, they can cause great harm. Such mutual sexual activities may degenerate into what I call 'mutual abuse', and can have all the consequences of abuse. Here prevention is better than cure – caring parents need to watch that there is balance in their children's relationships. If children cannot hold their own, they are at risk.

Children who suffer from this type of mutual obsession often exhibit all kinds of complaints. Nightmares, anxieties, bedwetting, stomach-aches – these may all be signals that something is not right.

If you realise it at an early stage, the consequences will usually not be serious and the symptoms will soon disappear. Without being conspicuous about it, keep an eye on what is going on with your child. One child is more vulnerable than another, simply because a child with an open soul, who looks into the world full of confidence and trust, does not possess the same defences as another. Know your child, and be awake.

11. School

Schooling and the Three Phases of Teenagehood

As we have discussed in the section called 'Three Types of Teenager, Three Phases of Teenagehood', the teen years follow a sequence of soul functions: thinking, feeling and doing. In the first years of high school, students acquire knowledge of a general nature. This coincides with Thinking Teenagehood when thought strives to become an independent inner activity. These teens are curious. They want to know how something is put together, because then they can start working with it themselves. Understanding the system of mathematics or grammar gives a feeling of liberation; it enables us to deal with the subject through our own thinking. We don't need to parrot the teacher any longer.

Children of twelve are not yet real teenagers no matter how difficult they may be. The years of school when they are twelve or thirteen tends to be fairly quiet; good habits can be formed. But at age fourteen, we see a big change. Many later behavioural difficulties rear their head at the age of fourteen or fifteen. It demands skill to be awake to the difference between normal teenage behaviour and an intense cry for help.

The years when children are twelve and thirteen generate the fewest number of problems. You could say that the development of teenagers, and that which society offers them, are still attuned to each other. New knowledge and skill are a challenge. The children want to learn, and they are fond of teachers who know a lot and can explain things well. Teachers often find this young class the easiest. This is not because the kids are good and obedient, but because they feel at home in this way of receiving knowledge.

By the time the second phase of the teen years begins – Feeling Teenagehood – many more problems raise their heads. What counts now is the encounter with others. Classmates feel more important than the subject of the lesson. Encounters in their own time, relationships and falling in love, gossip and endlessly fluctuating moods determine the teenagers' inner worlds. When their classes are in this phase, teachers will succeed if they can present knowledge full of emotion and human participation. When they bring the great explorers to life in Geography, or describe events from the viewpoint of an era's leaders in History, they will fascinate their audience.

In other subjects it may be more difficult, but everything depends on the love a teacher has, on the one hand, for the subject and, on the other hand, for those restless teenagers in front of her or him. When young people experience inner engagement on the part of their teacher, they are able to connect with what they have to learn.

I believe that at this phase of teenagehood, a teacher who dislikes the way young people are today, or who recites the subject like a recording, constitutes a real disaster for the students. At this age, teens look for adults who are personally involved in what they say, and if they find someone like that they can be reached and will respond. If they have such a teacher in one year they will get high grades and do all their homework. If the next year they get a teacher who is tired and just recites classes, the grades will plummet and the school will complain about the kids' commitment. These teenagers are still unable to sustain their interest in the subject out of their own inner forces. They need the soul strength of the teacher.

In the third phase of the teen years, Doing Teenagehood, young people start to differentiate. They have to make choices. What kind of work do they want to do later? What kind of college do they want to go to? They frequently don't really know which profession they want, and end up choosing specialised subjects on emotional grounds. Such specialisation, in my opinion, does not belong in high school but in college or university.

The Purpose of Education in the Teen Years

Relationships between young teenagers are formed out in the street, on the sports field and, most of all, in school. Imperceptibly, all kinds of exercises are practiced there in social relationships between individuals and in groups.

The roles teenagers take on in high school are often continuations of their roles in primary school. The joker remains the joker, the bullied child continues to be bullied, the shy child remains a spectator, the choleric child becomes a hothead. Roles among people have a much longer life than their original causes. When you observe relationships among adult brothers and sisters and their parents, you often see patterns repeating themselves from decades before, although they have lost all relevance. Some teenagers are the exceptions, who do not continue in their earlier role but take on an opposite one. The obvious example of this is teenage bullies who used to be bullied themselves when they were smaller children.

For young people to find the narrow path to inner freedom, they need schoolteachers who are able to form new and healthy social patterns among groups of teens between twelve and sixteen years old. Teachers have the potential to break through patterns that have arisen in the past, so that teens can free themselves from their former set roles. Students at this stage do not need to distance themselves from their teachers the way they feel they must from their parents. The conversations teachers have with students about bullying and its consequences, or about taking responsibility in relationships, are of great importance, especially if these subjects are not approached in the abstract, but in a lively lesson filled with examples and questions from practical daily life. If teachers are able to find a good form for this, they can make a group of students socially healthy. At this age, the experiences in a healthy, cohesive group in which each student feels safe and permitted to participate with his own characteristic nature, have enormous significance for the future.

Sexual education is getting a lot of attention today. Yet education concerning relationships is far more important. For you may know

173

exactly when to use a condom, but if you have not learned how to indicate your boundaries, you can still end up in trouble with teenage sexuality. Sexual education is meaningful only if it is embedded in the education about and practice of relationships. Between twelve and eighteen is the time when teenagers learn most quickly how to handle trust and jealousy, and how to respect other people while, at the same time, daring to set their own boundaries. Unhealthy patterns and roles can disappear or be prevented.

If such education is done well, respect for people of a different sexual orientation, for example, becomes a matter of course. Discrimination against gay people is the result of a failure to form a group with healthy inner relationships.

But it is only in explicit conversations that a class of students has the opportunity to practice mutual relationships. For instance, learning to listen to each other's class presentations is related to learning to listen to each other's boundaries and privacy. In this way you learn whether you have understood the other and treated him or her with respect. Students are often tested on their schoolwork using multiple-choice questions. When they don't know the right answer they pick one of the choices and have at least a chance of being correct. It does not work that way between people. If you have not really listened so that you understood the other, you cannot just take a chance on the answer. In relationships, life does not offer multiple-choice options.

If you take a close look at the subjects taught in high school, relationships play a role in all of them. This means that, consciously or unconsciously, every teacher is involved in the creation or destruction of relationships in the lessons he or she presents. For instance, parsing a sentence is nothing other than an exercise in becoming conscious of mutual relationships and dealing with these. In every meeting someone is the subject and, unfortunately, all too often there is also an object. Grammar is the form that orders a language so that words become intelligible and misunderstandings are avoided. Only the human being has language in its countless variations and forms.

In my experience of images and symbols, I have observed that a young person keeps making the language mistakes that are an analogy, a picture, of his or her inner weaknesses. For a weak personality, the mere writing of his or her name in clear, large letters is already a problem. That is logical as soon as we realise that human language and schooling in a language cannot be separated from each other. Mistakes and weaknesses in school show what the teenager still needs to develop. Language mistakes and relationship problems demonstrate the same kinds of weaknesses.

Certain aspects of mathematics are based on spatial insight. Images of relationships are at work here as well. It is not coincidental that we have the expression 'give me some space'. And when two people are considering having a child, they are in fact considering whether they will transform their two lines into a triangle by inviting the line of the child into their picture. This creates a space within the triangle. In ordinary language it is called the family, formed when the life situation changes from two adults into parents with a child.

A healthy group in school will have much fewer drop-outs than other groups. The mentor and other teachers may strengthen the group with tasks that foster consciousness and good impulses in relationships. Such a group may come to a firm decision, such as, 'In our class there is no bullying and no exclusion,' or 'If I want something from someone else I have to ask for it, and it is only okay after I have had a *yes* answer; if the other does not reply it means *no*.'

Lessons in economics can strengthen consciousness of money, the power of advertising and one's own buying habits. Do fifteen year olds know ahead of time how they want to spend their self-earned money, or are they seduced by every impulse, a seduction that becomes stronger and stronger in our age of online shopping? Consciousness of economics can help prevent addiction when it strengthens the awareness of the person's own 'I' in relation to the temptations it faces. This means that teachers of economics must keep in mind that even their subject can have a big impact in the realm of relationships. If understanding of economics results in insights that grow deep roots in the inner world of the teenagers, they will become diligent and autonomous.

We may have to get used to thinking about school subjects in these terms, for this can liberate school, teacher and student from the spiral of superficiality and disinterest that occurs when the only important thing is performance on the next test.

During history the students are acquainted with exploitation, slavery and genocide. Those were, and are, the extreme consequences of the loss of respect for the freedom and free will of the individual. It is a challenge to give students such an experience of history that they inwardly draw their own conclusions in ways that guarantee their socially responsible behaviour.

Sooner or later, any rule imposed from the outside will be shrugged off or broken. Self-regulation through firm, self-made decisions of a moral nature can guide human beings through their entire life. They are the building blocks of a healthy future in relationships. In my work with many people I have become impressed with the depth of decisions made in youth. They frequently continue to work through a person's entire life.

One day I met a man who, when he was a boy, had beaten up another boy so badly that the victim had to be taken to hospital. He was so frightened by the encounter with his own aggression that he came to an inner decision never to hurt anyone. This resolve sank down into a deep layer of his unconscious, but it had far-reaching consequences. As an adult, this man, who in every respect was a strong personality, behaved like an extreme introvert and was incapable of standing his ground and of setting boundaries. The decision in his youth had grown into a blockage that made balanced relationships impossible. It took much effort for him to recognise the blockage and gradually to overcome it. In this case the youthful decision had been too strong and unbalanced, but it demonstrates how resolutions made at a young age can work their way deeply into the personality.

When teachers know that impossible and egocentric teenagers are, in essence, human beings who are trying to find their innate, spiritual impulses in the reality of their lives, they can help foster healthy relationships between those teenagers and others, and indeed those teenagers' healthy relationships with themselves. In Steiner-Waldorf schools we can still see the influences of Rudolf Steiner's insights into growing children in the early 1920s. Steiner showed how the content of school lessons, full of culture and living wisdom, can be transformed so that the content itself has the potential to affect the development of young people.

By contrast, our culture and society form and force growing young people into a desired model of performance. This mode of force is portrayed as necessary for the young people themselves in their later professions and for the functioning of society in general. Yet these teenagers will only develop into healthy adults if lessons can be taught so that the students can really make the content their own – so that they recognise themselves in it. In such lessons, students learn fast and will have a good connection with their work and fellow human beings; these students become adults who are as much a blessing for their work environment as they are in their personal lives.

Good education for the entire soul of the young person fosters both outer and inner growth, which benefits not only the individual, but also everyone he or she associates with. This requires a turnaround in the orientation of the teacher and the subject content as regards the significance of the education. Young people are not to be forced into a mold, but educated so that they are able to unfold to the greatest extent. We need to teach young people the same way sensible parents feed their children. We give children good food because that will enable them to grow well and develop themselves optimally. The goal is not the proteins and the vitamins or the body weight; the goal is a child who is ready to take on the opportunities of his or her life. Education can be similar in that the goal is not the reproduction of knowledge and methods, but the inner nurturing of the young people. Education enables them to become sufficiently human and to have sufficient knowledge so that, when they have grown into adults, they are able to form inner relationships with the content of their work, society and each other.

The ever-increasing body of regulations, protocols and certificates indicates that well-trained adults can by no means always be trusted in their work. Such trust can be granted to a person who grew up in a healthy way. And such a person does not need a straitjacket of rules; he or she has the ability to take their own measure. This is the direction for worthy educational development of the human being.

Entelechy

In order to think and speak about teenagers and their career choices we have to step back to a concept of a more general nature, a concept that lies at the foundation of all choice: *entelechy*. Since a great deal depends on an adult's thorough awareness of this concept, I want to deal with it in some depth.

What does this difficult word *entelechy* mean? It is becoming what you as a spirit and organism are meant to become. It is living as a full expression of your essence. It is the revelation of who you are and what you have come to do on this earth in this time. It is the element in the human being that strives for meaningful realisation. You could call it the golden thread of a human life.

If you succeed in feeling and understanding your entelechy, and in giving it form, the thread of your individual life will unfold. You can then lead a meaningful life, because as a human being you are in harmony with your spiritual origin and intentions. This is different for every human being. When we look back, we can frequently discern the red thread in our life. It is what we have lived through, what lies behind us and has clearly become our biography. It would be ideal if the golden thread of our entelechy, which we brought with us at birth, would coincide with the red thread of our biography. If that is not the case, there will be a kind of discord between that which wants to become in our life and the reality that has actually happened.

Entelechy is a wonderful concept, but what does it mean in practice? As we are growing up we forget all about it. We no longer know who we are in our inner essence and what we have come to do. Yet our peculiarities show through. Attentive educators notice what we say or ask, how we look, the talents we have. These are often subtle traits that are part of this one human child. Real educators wonder what each new human child has come to do and where he or she is heading; this is why they observe each child so intently.

Educating also means influencing. The entire soul is suffused with the influences of others. Much of this is absorbed and helps us develop. But when the teen years begin, children want to find their way back to their inner origin, their own essence, to the starting line. In a way they try to remember who they were, what they came to do and what their capacities are. But they can't remember...

There is only one solution, and that is to follow the impulses that bubble up out of the soul now and then. If young people are lucky there are adults who help them with this because they understand these waves of individuality and respond to them. If they are lucky they then find the right school, the right field of study, the right job, the right friends and partner, the right place to live, the right opportunities to practice sports and hobbies. People with this degree of luck are exceptions who would be able to bring their entelechy to realisation almost automatically. But in practice, that is not the usual way. Most people find little pieces of the puzzle of life as they go along and have to discard other pieces because they don't fit.

There are significant moments in life. You could call them entelechy junctions. It is as if you are on a roundabout and have to choose one of many roads. Going around and around is not a solution – you have to make a choice. Toward the end of the teen years – usually around the end of high school – there is such a junction. So far, most of the choices you made were based on your intellectual achievements and preferences for subjects in which you were interested and performed well. But now you are facing inevitable questions that are grounded in the purposes of your life:

◊ What do I want to be?
◊ What do I want to study?
◊ What am I going to do in this world?

Then it is important that teenagers, together with adults around them, listen carefully to their own souls. Unconsciously, deep in this young person, lives the inner seeker who can help with these choices. Everything that was forgotten is still there, preserved in these deep layers of the soul. There lives the knowledge of the life question, there lives the engine of the entelechy. It is rare for people to regret their own choices, even if they have to make adjustments later. It is much more common for people to regret a choice they were talked into by 'sensible' adults, even if it helped them do well in life.

Parents and teachers who, through attentiveness and objective acceptance of a teenager's individuality, have developed a sense of the young person's entelechy, are able to help – not by making a choice for the teen, but by helping this young person look for what is his or her own.

The Potter – 1

Once upon a time there was a young man who, after long contemplation, decided what he wanted to do in his life. He said goodbye to his father, left his home and departed on a distant journey. After a long voyage over the ocean he landed near the mouth of a river.

He had resolved to become a potter, and it seemed to him that in this river he would find the clay he would need. He walked along the stream for a long time until he finally found a spot with wonderful river clay. He could see signs that people often came to this place to cut clay. Those people had to be potters, and they would be able to teach him the trade he so urgently longed to learn. The young man bent down, collected some of the wet clay, set it to dry on the bank, and waited for people to come by. But because of the clay, the ground was very slippery, and suddenly the young man lost his footing and fell, hitting his head on a hard rock. He lost consciousness.

He might not have survived if a man and a woman had not appeared soon after. They found the young man and saw that he needed their help. They did not seem surprised to find him there. With great care they brought him to their village and laid him on a bed. Full of love, they took care of him in his complete helplessness so that gradually his mind cleared, he learned to eat again and to stand up and walk. The man and woman cared for him like new parents. But the young man's memory was gone – he could not remember anything that had happened before.

The people in the village were woodworkers, including the new parents of the boy. His new father taught him to cut trees and saw them into logs. The young man learned to make wooden furniture and objects, and from his new mother he learned the complex patterns she skilfully carved into the wood when the chairs and other objects were ready.

One day the young man had a strange dream. He could not remember the content of the dream, but that day he was restless and looked at his familiar surroundings with different eyes. He did not know what was the matter, but he had a feeling that he did not belong there, as if he were not himself. These were strange thoughts and feelings, and he did not know what to do with them. The dreams continued, and now and then his days were also disturbed by vague impressions and feelings that emerged from his memory. He became increasingly restless and it became obvious to him that woodworking was not for him.

He started to visit other people in the hope that he would recognise something in them, but he always came back disappointed. As time went on he became angry at the people around him, who were acting as if nothing was the matter. They may have picked him up out of the river, but he did not belong to them.

He often wandered around; he wanted to leave, but did not know where to go. He was thus forced to stay, but did not know what to do with himself and felt more and more frustrated. At his wit's end, he finally took an axe and cut himself a way through the forest that surrounded the village, leaving a trail of destruction behind. It took a long time and was hard work, but he knew how to cut a tree without having it fall on him and kill him.

He finally came to the end of the forest and found another village. He walked into it and looked around at what people were doing. They were potters! Something in his inner being leaped for joy. He asked the potters if they would be willing to teach him their trade, and they took him in. His head cleared: here he had found his home; this was what he had been looking for.

He became a good potter. In the clay, he drew the patterns he had learned from his woodworking mother, to the astonishment of everyone. He gained all that the people of the village were able to teach him, and wanted to start his own pottery business. First he built himself a house by cutting trees and sawing the wood into pieces for the walls and roof. The villagers loaned him a cart and an ox and showed him a trail along the riverbank. This took him to a place with beautiful clay. Whistling and singing he was collecting the clay when he heard his name being called. Surprised, he looked up and saw his woodworking parents. He realised then that he was collecting clay in the river that flowed by his former village. Full of joy he greeted his parents and told them where he had been and what he had done. They listened to him close to the spot where they had once found him.

12. Boredom

Boredom is something that occurs frequently these days. On the one hand we never have time, on the other hand we do our best to fill time. Many people are bored.

Teenagers often suffer from various forms of boredom. The behaviour that comes about – or is lacking – because of this soul condition is a never-ending source of conflict between parents and their children, between teachers and students, and between adult society and teenagers.

What is boredom? How does is arise and what can we do with it?

What is boredom?

Boredom is the condition in which we have an inner need for liveliness, for life, yet we experience lifelessness in our soul. The soul has three realms, or functions: thinking, feeling and the will. Every realm has its own degree of liveliness. The life of the soul can be stimulated by inner impulses or by impulses from the outside world.

Inner impulses come from our spiritual core, our 'I'. Through this core, impulses of a spiritual nature enter into the soul. For example, ideals, artistic impulses and urges toward self-realisation are awakened in the soul by our 'I'. Because our true essence is connected with our spiritual core, it can receive these impulses and communicate them to our soul body.

Impulses from outside come through the encounter with other human beings, with animals, plants, knowledge and culture: with the entire world as it presents itself to our senses.

People who are bored may look lazy because they are not doing anything. However, they may also look very active – what we see then is a kind of forced busyness without any engagement out of the soul: lifeless busyness, always doing things, but nothing really coming of it. This form of boredom is like being stuck in a traffic jam – you are on your way but you can't move.

What Causes Boredom?

Boredom can arise when impulses are not penetrating into the soul. When the soul is closed off, impulses cannot enter. The soul can be spiritually closed, so that it cannot hear the spiritual core of our being, or it can be closed off against the outside world. It may have grown a thick elephant skin or erected blockages of one sort or another so as to prevent impulses from the surroundings penetrating into it. Boredom will result, for the soul is then insufficiently enlivened by influences from inside or outside.

Another cause of boredom can be that impulses reach the soul, bringing the soul to sparkling, seething life, but that it proves impossible to express this intense liveliness. For example, when you take children along on a social visit and all they are allowed to do is sit still and respond when they are spoken to, their soul may be alive but they can't do anything with it. Boredom is the result.

Apparent boredom can also be caused by sheer lack of energy. Energy is an indication of life, a condition of life. For the soul to be lively, it must live in a human being with sufficient life force. When we are tired, exhausted or ill, we lose much life in the soul. Blunt and insensitive reactions often indicate a lack of energy. A small child at the end of the day, a teacher at the end of the academic year, an overworked employee, parents who work two jobs and want to maintain their social lives – everywhere around us we see excessive fatigue and lack of energy. To a greater or lesser extent the soul then becomes silent – it does not have enough life force.

WHEN ARE WE NOT BORED?

When we are not doing anything outwardly but we are at peace with that, and experience it as positive, we are not bored. These are times of listening for the soul. When our inner life is active we are not bored either. This is like an answering time for the soul. When we are inwardly active but not yet ready to come into action in the world, again, we are not bored. That is a time of making plans, of preparing for future deeds.

A healthy soul experiences a rhythm of highs and lows, fluctuating movements between inner and outer activity, between listening to impulses and acting on them.

When people are in their natural element they will not be bored. Just as there is no unemployment in a primitive culture, but this comes about only when a society has become 'civilised' and complex like our own, so boredom cannot exist when humans are in an environment that is truly theirs. Children in playgrounds are not bored (until they become tired). A nature person is not bored when outdoors in the natural world; a thinker is not bored in a library; football enthusiasts are not bored with a ball at their feet. A bored teenager – is that perhaps someone who is not in his or her element?

Boredom and the Three Soul Functions

BOREDOM IN THINKING

Living in the soul function of thinking means having questions and working with questions. When we wonder about something and thinking comes to life, many questions will arise in our minds. Thinking in the soul grows through questioning – questions we ask ourselves, and questions asked by others. Cut and dried answers will quickly bore us; they are dull. Answers found in a lively thinking process, with or without others, stimulate the soul.

The simple transfer of knowledge, learning by rote, is a recipe for creating boredom in the soul realm of thinking. A transfer of knowledge that leads to *answers* for questions that have arisen in the soul will never be boring. You could almost say that all people should direct their learning to those subjects on which they have developed questions in their individual souls. Lessons adapted to children's age and stage and interest will be vastly more effective than information they have never thought about.

Highly talented children tend to be bored. Handing them more knowledge is not the solution. In my opinion, the boredom they unfortunately often experience is much more successfully dealt with if we confront them with questions. The many, many questions alive in the world around us can bring their souls to life; they may feel challenged and want to go to work on them.

Teenagers find themselves in a world of knowledge transfer. Are they looking for this knowledge? If they are, they may be satisfied. But if there is a gap between their inner questions and the mandatory knowledge, they will be bored in school –they are not in their natural element, and they are not interested. Students can be sprawled in their seats, yawning and lazy during one lesson, and in the next one be full of life reacting to the riddles the teacher is throwing at them. This striking difference may be caused by the atmosphere the teacher creates, but also by the teaching method. There are maths teachers who first let the children try to figure out what to do with a problem before they explain it. This is one way to overcome boredom in thinking.

> The profound meaning of thinking lies in understanding the riddle of the world.

BOREDOM IN FEELING

Let us first remind ourselves that the feeling phase of the teen years is the middle period, between the thinking phase and the phase of doing.

Life in the realm of feeling is connected with the ability to make an inner image of something, to imagine things. We create an inner image that corresponds to the outer world when we sense what lives in someone or something, through empathy or compassion. An impression that comes into the soul is then brought to life. A spiritual impulse that comes to life in the soul also enables us to create such an image. When someone tells us a story that stirs us in our feeling life, we can imagine what that story means for the other, how it came about, and so on.

When we speak about the unimaginable things that happen in the world, we refer to events in which feelings were not alive. When there is horrible slaughter of people somewhere, we can be sure that the feeling life of those who committed the acts is full of dead spots. Someone who is able to imagine the suffering of a mother does not kill her child.

Empathy in the soul connects people with that from which they are physically separate. Whether it is events in the past, things going on right now, or plans for the future, life in the feeling realm of the soul brings the outside inside. When businesspeople have to map development into the future, they have to engage their thinking and their force of action. But a really lively imagination of things in the future will only come into being if the soul's feeling realm connects with the plans and enlivens them.

Teenagers have a way of closing themselves to others and to what others consider important. Their soul is then not alive in that regard, and they can do things without imagining what their action may mean for others. If this were not true, bullying, destruction and aggressive behaviour would not occur as often as they do.

Good educators and parents will always try to let teenagers feel the full meaning and outcome of their behaviour. By having to repair what they have damaged, teenagers will often develop a response to what at first left them cold. It is always a question of bringing their feeling soul to life on the matter over which they have misbehaved. If we only appeal to their common sense (thinking), they will just be bored.

Many things young people work and play with in our time have a hardening effect. Boys in particular often want to appear emotionally invulnerable. The fact that this brings a little bit of death into the soul is something they are not aware of. We can harden ourselves by watching scary movies until our stomach stops churning because our imagination has stopped working. The same thing happens in a computer game full of aggression, speed and frightening moments. Since we gradually get used to these effects we need ever more and stronger excitement to produce the pleasant surge of adrenaline in the body. Getting used to such things means that we are hardening ourselves. The same thing happens when we look at pornography. We can also harden ourselves by regularly behaving crudely. The first few times we may be ashamed, but pretty soon we get used to it. We no longer imagine ourselves in the suffering of the other, which we have caused; we don't imagine anything any more. People with a rich inner life may be astonished by the insensitivity of a lifeless soul.

Lifelessness in the feeling realm causes boredom in teenagers. They may be invulnerable, but they do not feel much about anything any more: it is like an inner death. This is the kind of boredom that leads to [a search for stimuli] actions of last resort in the attempt to feel something – in the attempt to feel sensation.

SENSATIONS

Sensations are stimulants for dead parts of the soul. Everyday gossip has that function, as do theme parks and horror movies. We ingest sensation stimulants such as scent, colour and taste additives in our food. Then there are the sexual stimulants in movies, reported scandal and experiments. Parties, alcohol and drugs bring about incredible sensations.

When the lifeless parts of the soul are stimulated in this way – which is really a sham – it is like cracking the whip over a sick horse. A small flame is blown into a bright torch, yet the result is nothing but ash. Sensation stimulants extinguish soul life instead of bestowing life on the soul, as they had promised. Ever more is needed to enable us to feel anything. The result is a dead and empty soul.

When we want to bring feeling into the soul, therefore, we have to look for that with which we can feel empathy, and for a little corner in the soul where there is still a connection with something on the outside. Even if there is only one friend, one animal that stirs something in the soul, feelings like empathy will still have a chance. A person can then imagine something of what another experiences.

> While thinking has the task of solving the riddle of the world, feeling has the task of solving the riddle of our fellow humans.

BOREDOM IN THE WILL

Boredom in the will is the kind of boredom we are most familiar with. When you are bored in the will you can't think of anything to do. Total inactivity. A teenager just hanging about the house during the summer, or a young person without study or a job presents a problem for any parent.

Bodily movement is the means by which the will comes to life in the soul. Our inner life in the soul realm of the will is founded on our awareness of earthly relationships, especially those of our own body. At puberty, our bodies grow out of balance. Some children become fat, others grow gawky with long arms and legs that seem to be forever in their way. It is normal that we lose the youthful harmony of our bodies at this age. At the end of the teen years the body reaches a new state of balance. The young man or woman has then found a new relationship to his or her physical being.

Movement of the physical body engenders experiences that are beneficial for the life of the will. In Greek antiquity young people had to spend as much time on sports and games of skill as on intellectual development.

Restlessness and fecklessness may be indications of a teenager who is bored in the realm of the will. The urge to do things is asleep; only a great restlessness is left. Apathy, indifference to work and body are often expressions of the same kind of lifelessness in the will.

In contrast, a great deal of liveliness in the will usually shows up as desire, as striving straight for a goal, as ambition that still needs guidance.

In traditions of intensive meditation from East Asia and South Asia, the soul is quieted by sitting still. We can also relax by taking a walk in nature, but a yogi, who aims at stilling the soul and vivifying only the spirit, does not take a walk in nature. He or she will sit still for hours and hours, days and days. That is lethal for the part of the soul where the will lives.

At the computer we sit still. In school we sit still. Watching television we sit still. In the car we sit still. Teenagers are then bored to death. They look for activity, movement. Dancing helps perhaps. Or a nice fight with soccer fans! Action! It would be better for them if they could express their urge to move in sport and work.

In the chapter about the body and its relation to the soul I mentioned the importance of the sports teacher. It is important that teenagers do not give up sports because of their homework load. Whether they play football, ice hockey or go surfing, the point is that they experience their bodies in movement. In this regard, city dwellers are at a disadvantage compared with the children of a farmer, who have to help on the land in the summer. But a newspaper route, an active summer job or a hiking trip can also do wonders for the activation of the will. Doing things or being on the go through the activity and strength of the body is a constant source of life for our inner world.

> The will has the task of solving the riddle of the human being on the earth, in the world. This is the task for teenagers in their final teen years: this is when the riddle of our place in the world presents itself.

The Purpose of Boredom

Parents should not be overly afraid of boredom. Every new period in life is preceded by a stage of expectation, a period of brooding in which something new is hatched. Children who are ready for something new will first be bored. Out of this boredom arises the need for new impulses, and only once that need has arrived can you help them. In teenagers, boredom can have a very useful function. It awakens the inner longing for life.

Many parents get so annoyed when their child is bored

that they will use any means to prevent it. We can see striking examples of this during the first year of the child's life. A baby lives in the womb for nine months. During the last few months it is already complete, all the senses have been developed. No one is worried that the child might be bored in that little space. But as soon as it is born, we provide it with toys and pictures around the cradle. You can even buy 'activity centres' for babies, and three year olds are offered games. The child might otherwise be bored!

In reality, toys are needed only very gradually and in small quantities. A few – good quality – toys stimulate children's own imaginative capacity. As they grow over the succeeding years, this capacity of imagination will be the basis for the development of intelligence and social skills. By offering things too early, we run the risk of supplying answers before there were questions. We may prevent the boredom characteristic of teenagehood, but we impede development. Compare it with learning to feel thirst. If we prevent children from ever feeling thirst, how can they develop a living feeling for drinking, a living awareness of thirst and water?

Children who are spoiled in this regard frequently grow into young tyrants who demand that their surroundings entertain them. They always want to go out, always demand attention, always want to be amused. When children are small there is absolutely no need to play with them every time they ask for it. And once they have become teenagers it is not necessary for the parents to fill every minute of their time.

A simple method of overcoming boredom is to be constantly busy with your social network, your sources of information or games. But that means meaningful boredom is prevented. All the digital gadgets we use more and more actually overwhelm meaningful boredom. An instructive experiment with a class of young people is to agree that everyone will switch off every electronic device: cell phone, computer, television, tablet – everything. It is important to make this experiment at school and at home, not during a school break. It produces surprising experiences of time, social relationships, boredom and sleep. The young people then become worried about missing out on things. They begin to realise how dependent they have become on all these boredom chasers.

Lifelessness in the Soul

Too little life in the soul realm of thinking leads to imitation. It also creates knowledge fanatics – people who collect the thoughts of others as their own store. And it can turn people into victims of indoctrination by undesirable friends, sects or other influences.

Too little life in the soul realm of feeling may lead to loneliness, isolation or autistic symptoms. That causes depression – loneliness that can feel so deadly in an extreme case it may even be a motive for suicide. When such lifelessness turns outward, we see people who, through soulless acts, aggression, power, and through cold, hardened behaviour, break the hearts of their parents, their contemporaries or their partner. This lack of feeling is a kind of social bankruptcy. In an extreme case such a person may murder someone in cold blood, literally and figuratively.

Too little life in the soul realm of the will produces desertion of different kinds: dropping out, anorexia, truancy, getting into a rut, not making choices and letting others push you on, never living up to promises, always being late everywhere, and using the energy of others for your own achievements. Sometimes such lifelessness hides behind its opposite. Then we see a passion for work, which masks the fear to confront one's own lifelessness. This outer activity is not a true living in the will, but merely the appearance of it.

In all cases, a shortage of life in the soul brings insensitivity for one's own goal in life. In fear, the soul senses the question of the meaning of this life, without being able to reach the answer in the depths of the soul. It is an impediment and blockage of the entelechy.

When the souls of teenagers are sufficiently alive in all three realms, the teenagers will find their direction in life and bring it to realisation, full of originality and loyalty to their own entelechy and rightly connected and tuned into the world and the people around them.

13. Money

A Different View of Money

Money consists of coins, notes and balances in bank accounts. It represents a certain value; you can do and buy all kinds of things with it. Superficially, this is what it looks like to your child.

In my experience, it is important that we, as adults, develop a deeper understanding of money and finance. Then we can better teach young people how to handle this aspect of their lives.

If we seek the origin of financial value, and we look back far enough, we see at the source an effort, a force, representing the labour of a human being and/or a labour of the earth. Every dollar, euro, yuan or rupee represents the work of a farmer, a factory worker, an inventor or scientist. And at the same time, money represents the forces of our earth. Every substance, whether it is vegetable, animal or mineral, is extracted from the earth. This is obvious in the case of natural gas or oil. How much time has passed, how many forces have worked together, year in, year out since the far, far distant past, for oil to develop? These forces, this gift of earth's development, of earth's labour you could say, form part of the flow of money, the means at the disposal of human beings. The fact that we owe wool and silk to nature is something most people are aware of, but that petroleum is the origin of plastic and other synthetic materials is not as well known: this too represents riches of the earth.

Why is it so important to stop and realise that behind every coin stands labour donated by earth and humanity? Because it means that handling money is not something abstract; it can never be without commitment, without engagement. In money the flow of labour has solidified, has come to a halt. When we receive money, we also receive the task of ensuring that this stream of donated force is fruitfully used, so that the results of solidified labour can be augmented and given back to the earth and humanity. This requires commitment, and an engagement in what we do with money. The point is not to continually increase the amount of money, but to liberate the forces that are reflected in it by using them for a meaningful purpose. It is like what happens when we cut down a tree. The tree dies, but we use the wood to construct a house, or to make furniture, or for a work of art. In this way the tree becomes fruitful again. The same is true for money.

When this does not happen because the money is not properly used, something will weigh on the person who failed to recognise it. That person undertakes the obligation to replace the wasted labour and find another way to make it fruitful. If this task is ignored, money will work like a vacuum sucking up potential labour. Then we lose our own energy, we become lazy and develop all kinds of incapacities in relation to labour. It is like a sponge in water: if we don't see to it that the sponge is first saturated with water, then it will absorb the water until it is full.

Money is a totality of captured gifts. Money is transformed into a relentless force in the life of the one who gives no gifts but only takes.

Let's look at the fairytale 'Rumpelstiltskin'. The miller's daughter has to spin straw into gold for the king, but is unable to do this herself. The gold is given to her by Rumpelstiltskin. In return she sacrifices her own capacities in the form of her necklace and her ring. In the end she even has to give up the fruit of her union with the king, the royal child. Fortunately, the young queen possesses a sufficient amount of energy, for her servant travels all over the country and finally finds Rumpelstiltskin. Through the forces of the servant she is able to overcome the danger. This is an image of the power of our labour, which we can commit to a cause.

When we supply our teenagers with too much money for

too long a time, we put an improper burden on them and their capacities. When we teach them at an early stage, however, that money demands the effort of labour in some form, and we charge them with such tasks *according to their capacities*, we will lay the foundation for healthy growth to adulthood.

If young people have fruitfully used money and have added their own labour to the money they have obtained, they will not experience this as an attack on their labour power but, on the contrary, as an increase in their own work potential.

There is much talk of working too hard, of needing relaxation and leisure time. What a lot of rest we need compared with so few hours of work! Perhaps we don't become so tired due to too much work, but to an excess of unfruitful consumption of money and goods. This robs us of labour energy to such an extent that we can never get enough rest. Rest does not fill this emptiness. What we could do is examine our possessions and the way we spend our money – examine their value as gifts and fruitfulness. More wasteful holidays only add to the problem.

Teenagers and Money

When a child is young and lives exclusively from the forces of others, the whole subject of financial value and labour is not yet applicable. The parents take care of the child and accept the resulting consequences. When a child grows up and reaches teenagehood, this relationship changes. As children become older and more independent of their parents, and frees themselves inwardly from the influences of youth, transforming these into their own individuality, the extent of this independence and inner freedom indicates the degree to which they can become personally responsible for their financial and material conduct in life.

Many young people can't wait to earn their own money. They often have the experience that money they've earned themselves feels good. It makes them stronger and creates self-confidence. Parents are expected to react to this: it marks a change in parenthood from taking-care-of to guidance and coaching, and, finally, letting go.

POCKET MONEY

Most parents don't give much thought why they give their children pocket money. It is usually accepted as a general practice. The amounts vary quite a bit and generally children want more than they are given. In the early teen years this can cause serious clashes.

Pocket money can be a means of learning how to handle money. You can spend it on sweets or treats, you can use it to buy presents for people, or you can save it. You learn about the money system and the financial value of things. The fact that a fishing rod is more expensive than a bag of sweets soon becomes obvious.

Waiting, saving, wasting, these are things that can be experienced with a little pocket money, provided children do not get it too early and, most of all, not too much. I think what the parents do with their own 'pocket money' – the discretionary part of their income – is also very important. A child learns from the relationship parents have to their money.

Further, it is a very good thing to avoid talking about money with children. They won't fail to pick up what you want them to know. All early thinking and talking about money makes them age prematurely, lessens their spontaneity and robs them of their natural reactions to it.

As children grow and begin to sense their own individuality, they will also want to have more financial leeway. In the first instance, they will then approach their parents. In itself, this is a healthy thing, but in a broader sense teenagers are looking for ways to strengthen their individuality, not for dependence. If we give them a lot of pocket money without them having to do anything for it, we make them dependent. And yet, they do want more money. The ideal solution is that they try to get more money by working for it. From their fourteenth or fifteenth year, teens are perfectly able to have a summer job, do some data entry work, deliver newspapers, babysit for the neighbours, or perhaps put the neglected filing at Dad's or Mum's office in order. Parents can certainly help them find such work.

Working for money results in a real inner appreciation of its value and in much more careful and deliberate ways of spending it. Should you as parents want to give something anyway, then give something tangible, for instance, a season ticket to the local skating rink, or a nice trip away. But don't overdo it. Things received too early lose their attraction and enriching value. Growing up in deep poverty is bitter suffering, but wealth is a poor educator. Will power and responsibility will flourish when wealthy parents live soberly with themselves and their children.

HOUSEWORK

The household with all its endless tasks is in principle the adults' responsibility. But please teach your child at an early age that dirty underwear belongs in the washing basket. Everyone is able to contribute to the management of the household.

In a good family, teenagers are used to taking a small part in the household work. Don't just take your own plate to the kitchen: there is also a social gesture – put all the plates into the dishwasher. If they are not used to this by the teen years, the parents are too late. The kids throw out much of what the parents have taught them anyway, and it is not easy to make them take on new habits.

No matter how they grumble and how often they sneak out on you when it is their turn to do something, be consistent. Keep insisting that your sloppy teen does the dishes and cleans up. Obviously you can't hold growing young kids responsible for the whole household. But if they always leave you with hours of household work and let others fix everything, it becomes a question of spoiling them in the realm of work, which is just as bad as spoiling them with money and presents.

Many labour problems that take the form of a lack of commitment arise in the teen years, and are not the result of bad character traits as many people think. A hard-working farmer once said to me: 'Before they turn sixteen, the kids must have learned to work, otherwise forget it!'

Young people who get the chance and time *to be teenagers during the teen years, to study at their own level during the teen years, and to work during the teen years* will in later life find the right work for the right compensation. If during the teen years they look for a connection with their own 'I', and this 'I' begins to manifest itself via the masculine side of the soul, they will soon feel a need to express themselves in work. There they will find the strength and energy to bring to realisation that which wants to be accomplished in this life, in this human society.

We receive financial compensation for work, but there is also non-material compensation in the form of enriched labour power. We also receive work for compensation, for all money gives us a task in a non-material sense. Perhaps lethargic, languid, lazy people avoid making mistakes in life, but they become hard of hearing for the impulses and activity of the 'I', which runs aground due to a lack of 'servants'.

Let us go back for a moment to 'Rumpelstiltskin'. Besides the miller's daughter, we should also notice the king. He wants the gold. He forces the girl to spin gold out of his greed. But because of this he too loses his child; unknowingly, the king loses his child because of his greed. He thought he was sitting pretty, but without realising it he pays a high price.

I always consider 'Rumpelstiltskin' as an image of uncontrolled passion, of the greed of the king. Only when the queen becomes conscious of this force, and is able to name it through her servant, Rumpelstiltskin loses his power. It looks as if the girl solves everything by herself in this fairytale, but it always strikes me that when the king marries her he never again asks her to spin straw into gold. It seems as if he has overcome his desire and no longer wants to be rich without doing anything for it.

HANDLING OUR OWN AND OTHER PEOPLE'S THINGS

Under this heading I want to give a little attention to the frequent complaint that young people are careless with valuable things. Their bicycles, books and clothes, but also the seats in the bus and the flowers in the parks demonstrate the sad consequences of this.

Young people feel a kind of inner anger against all this wealth for which they have done nothing. This is because the use of these things demands a toll in the form of inner strength – in a way it works like a sponge soaking up inner strength, and young people experience this unconsciously as being robbed of strength. They vent their anger on the luxury and wealth around them without realising that this causes even more damage to themselves.

When we see children begin to exhibit a tendency to damage or neglect things we could consider giving the care for those things into their hands. Give children clothing money and there is a good chance they will stop losing their garments. Just let teenagers earn their own book money and they will stop destroying the books. If they are careless with their bicycles, let them get much better ones, but let them earn the money themselves. When a teenager works and through working acquires a bicycle, the inner anger will disappear. The money earned has taken form in the bicycle. And an inner capacity has received physical existence. If teenagers use money they earned to build a cage for their rabbit, for instance, they see the valuable results of their own efforts every day. In a quiet little corner of the soul the self-confidence will grow that their forces will one day be sufficient to take care of themselves and others when they grow up.

THE HOARDERS

There are also young people who have a tendency to hoard; they don't consume anything and keep all the forces of labour trapped in the money. Such teenagers often suffer from a kind of fear of life. They are afraid that life, the free flow of forces, will leave them behind with emptiness and want. They don't recognise, or hardly recognise, the enriching influence of standing strongly in the stream of life. The fruitful use of the stream of life and its forces works like irrigation in a dry soil: it brings new fertility and riches. Hoarders anxiously keep these streams within their narrow banks and do not dig irrigation channels.

Parents can try to work with these teens to find positive and fruitful uses for their money. When they really enjoy something beautiful, or learn to surprise someone with a gift, their confidence in life will grow. They will stop obsessively hoarding money and start trusting their life and their potential forces. This will enrich their lives and make them more fruitful. Frequently they will spend money on materials or instruments for projects. A good pen, wood for some construction, or a DVD their father had long been looking for, may bring them to free themselves and the forces inherent in money from fruitless imprisonment.

WASTEFULNESS

Spending everything even before you have received it is also possible: 'Mum, can I get next month's allowance now?'

Many young teenagers lose or waste money and its forces. Parents can help by giving small quantities of money with short intervals – for instance, weekly rather than monthly. Help them out of their financial problems, but let them do something for it. Don't allow them to get into debt. If it takes a year or longer to pay off debts it becomes a suffocating experience for a child. It is better to help them bring some order to the chaos of their desires and wishes. The wisdom of the saying 'Never go shopping on an empty stomach' can find a very practical application here. Go to the mall nicely dressed and with a full stomach, decide first which single DVD to buy, and then go and find it.

In this regard, online shopping is like opening the floodgates of desire. You always find too many things you want. It is pretty obvious that young people will lose themselves in this 24-hour shopping centre. First they have to learn to get themselves under control in real stores and when they are going out. Only then will they be able to control themselves online. Parental coaching and education in online shopping and paying is a necessity of course. Just going shopping often leads to purchases that exceed the available funds. If a teenager is not yet up to restraint, the parents will have to manage this process. Don't let them jump in the water before they can swim!

The Blossom Tree

Travellers who have visited faraway countries often come home with the most surprising stories. There was a time when travellers who had been in the Far East returned with stories about a blossom tree. The tree grew there in the warm sun and under the mysterious starry sky. It was enormous in size; it had thick branches and a colossal trunk. The people who lived there said that this tree was the home of the mother soul of their country.

This surprised the travellers, but they were even more fascinated by the blossoms of the tree. Large, fragrant, pink and white flowers hung from all the branches. They spread a delicious scent and, if you were lucky, a drop from a flower would fall on your head as you were walking under the tree. Your hair would then smell of it for months, and the tree would appear in your sleep and give you the most wonderful dreams.

Ever more travellers went in search of the tree. It was always blooming, even when it was carrying fruit. The fruits were small and green and looked like little apples. The travellers gave the fruits no thought, but the locals carefully harvested and preserved them, dried them and kept them for their children. When they were sick or there was not enough to eat, the parents gave their children the small, green fruit of the mother tree. The children then soon healed and their hunger disappeared. It was as if one single little fruit carried in it the strength of the entire tree.

Everything would have been all right if the travellers had loved the tree as much as the people who lived there. But they came from the West and had never learned to love trees that way. They only came to look at it and to catch the wondrous drops from the blossoms. Then they could brag at home about what they had done. They were always in a hurry and often did not want to wait under the mother tree until one of those wondrous drops fell from its magnificent blossoms. They had to go on, always travelling farther – their aeroplanes had strict schedules. They were in a hurry. They roughly picked the blossoms and looked among the petals for a drop of the liquid. The flowers were then thrown away and the travellers lost interest.

Some clever travellers came with little perfume bottles that they filled with the liquid. One drop had no meaning for them; they wanted a supply. Some of them sold these little bottles at home and became rich.

And so the tree was constantly picked clean. More and more travellers came; they fought each other for the most beautiful flowers. They climbed into the tree in order to tear off entire twigs and branches and then came down and picked them clean. The tree groaned and moaned, but that was only heard by the local people. The travellers thought it was the south wind blowing through the branches. Because wealth makes poor, the rich travellers returned time and again to collect even more of the liquid in their longing for the feeling of being rich, which was their sense of happiness.

The tree groaned louder and louder. Now that its blossoms were plundered it could no longer grow fruit. The little green fruit became a rarity so that the people of the country could collect them only now and then. Their children fell ill, and increasingly they remained ill and died of all kinds of diseases and weaknesses. When they were hungry and there was no food, the parents were helpless. Frequently, the children then stopped growing and remained small.

Thus the children, the parents and also the great old mother tree were suffering. In grief the tree let its branches droop to the ground, but that made it even easier for the travellers to plunder its flowers. They wanted the sweet-smelling drops from the blossoms, the gentle, delightful dreams – this was the only thing that counted.

In the end, the great, ancient mother tree fell ill, no new buds grew, the leaves changed from green to brown and fell off. It was as if the winds knew what had happened; they blew furiously over the land with storms never known before.

The travellers and rich people forgot the tree. They had come like a cloud of locusts to eat what was edible, and now that everything was gone they disappeared to other countries to plunder those in turn.

But the local people did not forget their tree. They gave it more water, fed it herbs and surrounded it with loving care. But nothing seemed to help.

There was an ancient custom in that country. Every girl who was no longer a child would come to the mother tree. She would then cut off a long lock of her hair and bury it among the roots of the tree. Root beings understood this silent question, for in this way every girl asked for health for the children she would have. The root beings then worked extra hard for the mother tree so that it would grow much fruit to feed and heal the children. But the root beings also could not do much any more. The mother tree was ill, and no matter how hard they worked, it remained bare and empty.

One day a girl named Warande came to the tree. Following the old custom she buried a lock of her hair by the tree, but she immediately forgot it. For as she was digging, she sensed how ill the tree was, and she wept bitter tears. She did not return home, but slept under the bare old branches. The next day she made a rope ladder out of grass and threw it over the lowest branch, so that she could climb up into the tree, higher and higher until she reached the top. There she heard the groaning and moaning of the tree.

Warande took a careful look around. Where did that voice come from? She looked and looked among the branches and twigs, until she found a hollow in a thick branch. Carefully she looked in. She saw a little ladder! Her nimble feet quickly found the rungs; fortunately she was small so she fitted through the opening. As she climbed down deeper and deeper she noticed that the space became larger; she was now climbing down through the trunk. The trunk was hollow!

Finally she saw a little campfire below. It was surrounded by stones so that it could not burn the inside of the tree. There was a lot of space, for the trunk was many feet thick, but the fire was very small. By the fire Warande saw a wrinkled little old woman. 'Hello my child,' said the old woman, 'I am so cold, can you do something about my fire?'

Warande poked in the fire until the flames were dancing happily and the old woman rubbed her hands together with satisfaction. 'Finally, I will get a little warm again,' she mumbled. She had hardly finished saying this when a little black manikin jumped into the space. 'Hot, hot,' he shrieked and he threw his black cloak over the flames, which then almost disappeared. The old woman groaned and moaned again with a loud voice, and the girl vaguely understood that this was the sound the tree had been making.

The black manikin disappeared as quickly as he had come, without paying any attention to the girl. The only thing that remained was a disgusting smell, which made the girl hold her nose. The old woman told her that the manikin had jumped into the tree during a moonless night. Most of the time her fire burned strongly and then the flames burned any intruders with bad intentions. But in recent years her fire had become so small and poor that it only had very tiny flames. These had not been able to burn the manikin. He had dug a dwelling place for himself in the ground, and now he put out every flame that grew large.

The girl was astonished. She asked the woman how they could get rid of the manikin. A deep sigh was her reply. 'O child, no one can restore what was made by the gods and damaged by people. This tree is so old. Now that the black manikin is in charge here, I will be cold for eternity!'

But the girl was young and understood nothing of eternity. She stoked the fire again higher and higher. The little black manikin jumped in again and threw his mantle over the flames. But Warande was waiting for him. Quickly she snatched the mantle and climbed as fast as she could up the ladder with it. The manikin ran after her crying out: 'Give it back! It's mine!' Breathless, the girl reached the opening high up in the branch and threw the mantle out. It was a pitch dark night. Suddenly she felt strange bats flying around her tearing the mantle into little pieces, which they scattered in all directions.

The manikin had now also come to the top, but too late! His mantle had disappeared. A bolt of lightning rent the air and struck him right in his evil heart. Warande saw a brief blue flash, and no more. But then ... she heard it! The tree was singing! Deep down, from the bottom of the tree the voice of the old woman was sounding, and she sang full of joy by her warm fire.

Warande climbed out of the tree and built a little cabin under it. After some time she saw that the tree was making buds again and that new blossoms appeared from these. New leaves grew, and the tree looked green and beautiful again. The mysterious perfumed drops had disappeared and did not come back, but fortunately the tree did grow new fruit, which the girl collected in great baskets and gave to sick and hungry children.

A year later she found two newly born children among the tree roots. One of these had red hair and the other black. Warande took them in and cared for them as if they were her own. They grew up healthy and strong, both the girl whose hair was red and the boy whose hair was black.

When these children had grown into adults they collected many fruits of the tree for themselves. The dried them and took the seeds out of them. The following year they put the seeds into the ground, and thus, years later, many new mother trees sprouted from them. Everyone who came received one of these, and when they had all been given away the two young people kissed Warande goodbye and departed. No one ever saw them again, but Warande sometimes heard their voices when she was lying in bed, voices that seemed to come from deep in the tree.

PART 3

YOU, THE PARENTS

The Gardener

Faithful, he is always there,
Full of knowing care,
Protects the stem so soft and tender,
Knows the force of wind and weather.

He works without determining
The fruit the tree will carry
Or when it will be full-grown.

But he is aware of the labour pains
Of a tree so full of life:
He wants to give it strong support.

He claims neither fruit nor tree,
He nurtures no secret dream.

In the end, when time is full,
The gardener knows no complaint.
He looks back and smiles quietly:
The tree became what it would be.

14. The Fear of Losing Your Teenager

Many parents have a great, underlying fear: that they will lose their relationship with their child in the teen years. We see in some families that there is a lasting breach.

Sometimes this is an outward breach: the teenager leaves home and cuts off contact, or the parents cannot manage the trouble the teenager is causing and throw their child out of the house. In both cases much damage is caused to the souls of parents and child, not to mention the risks children run if they have to fend for themselves between their fourteenth and eighteenth year. Normally, no parent desires such an end to the educational process. And, all things considered, no child desires such an end to the years of childhood. Besides, after such a breach there is a great risk that teenagehood will be cut short and prematurely transformed into early, and perhaps desperate, adulthood. In these circumstances it is also possible that a teenager will regress into behaving like a child again, becoming totally dependent on others, who have to take the place of father and mother. These others may be friends, some group or a religious sect. The teenager then becomes an imitator, like a small child, and stops exercising her or his own critical judgment.

Sometimes rather than an outer breach there is an inner one. This may be just as serious. It certainly generates the same kinds of risks as an outer breach. Here, too, we can observe both premature adulthood and childish dependence on surrogate parents. The breach is less conspicuous: the child lives in the home as in a hotel, preferably at no cost, but the human relationship with the parents is broken. Except for an occasional quarrel or superficial talk, there is nothing left between them, and not just for a little while – such as often happens in a family. All that is left is this indifferent or artificially polite form of contact.

I want to emphasise here that it is normal for this form of superficial contact to occur during the teen years, but if it is handled well it will be temporary. A real inner breach has occurred if there has been no warmth, no sharing, no closeness for years. Just as in the case of an outer breach, we can speak of an inner breach only if the child does not return. Many teenagers will try to leave home once or twice but via the street corner, a friend or neighbour they are soon back again.

There are a few straightforward ways to lose your child during the teen years. They occur over and over, and parents only realise what has happened when it is too late. I welcome the opportunity to discuss these tragic and unnecessary errors here.

Do We Own Our Children?

'Whatever you receive in this life, consider it a temporary loan. That will forestall much unnecessary pain.' This wise saying has general validity, but especially in relation to the children who have been entrusted to us it is, in my view, the most fruitful position.

Looking down out of the spiritual world, the child searches for the right parents. Out of an unlimited faith and trust in those parents the child is born as a totally dependent little entity. Since children are not able to bring their own 'I' into the world right away, they are dependent on the 'I' of the parents. Children are indeed really ours, because they give themselves to us, but *for a limited and necessary time!*

It would not be right if you could not feel deep in your soul that your toddler is your very own flesh and blood. That feeling gives the child security and tranquillity. However, this feeling should be time-bound. Until teenagehood children give themselves to their parents. But in the teen years, the gift of your child comes to an end. (Whether or not the parents enjoy their child is immaterial. For does not a child that requires extra care put even more trust in their parents? To surrender yourself to your parents when everything is fine and healthy is one thing; but if you come into the world disabled in body or soul, you trust your parents even more.)

Until about the tenth year, your child is simply your child. For most parents this is a natural feeling. But from ten on, children begin to remember that they have not given themselves to their parents for all eternity. Now and then they begin to sense that deep in their souls the 'I', the spiritual core that was still asleep there, is waking up. And this 'I' is the rightful 'owner' of the child. When teenagehood begins in earnest, we have to take on this change, because the inner master has risen: 'Until now I belonged to you; now I belong to myself!' Since this master is not yet experienced by the child as a real entity, as it is inside adults, we witness only the working of an inner, hidden force – just as in a lawn we do not see the moles but only their molehills. The 'I' of the teenager is as yet unborn, un-free, but its effects already throw up a lot of molehills in the form of restlessness, defensiveness, explorations, and so on.

Parents who continue to feel that their child is their possession suffer from egoism or fear in the soul. It demands a lot of soul strength to become conscious of inner egoism, especially because it hides comfortably behind all kinds of parental love. It is even more difficult to overcome this egoism and ensure it does not determine how you act.

The same is true of the anxiety we may feel for the child, and more general, deep anxiety about life. To deal with such anxiety we may need help from our partner, friends or a therapist. Working on it can create the right conditions in our own soul for maintaining connection with our teenage children.

Why Do I React the Way I Do?

You can go through life like an unconscious cauliflower, and most of the time things will come out right. But with a teenager in the house, you are compelled to reflect on your own soul and to become conscious of who you really are as a parent. Teenagers confront us with the way we react, but in truth the confrontation goes much, much deeper than this. Children mirror the behaviour they see around them from the moment they are born. Teenagers confront us with who we are. In the struggle to discover their own individuality, to find a connection with their 'I', they also continually struggle to discover the 'I' of adults.

Teenagers will faultlessly bring to light how their parents relate to their own 'I'. Are their parents' lives really no more than a semblance, or do they follow their own red thread? Has the soul of the parent gone through real teenagehood? Is it free of unconsciously copied content? Does the soul body fit the content? How much respect do the two parents have for each other's 'I'?

I don't believe there is an adult in the world who can pass this test. Somewhere the 'I' in each of us is not connected, and we live in routine and indolence. There are always things we have never thought about, never tried in a different way, but kept doing in a way that always seemed obvious. And then there is the shock of realising that, although after much wrestling through and beyond the teen years you have been able to transform your soul content into genuine content of your own, you can't get out of your soul body despite the fact that it does not quite fit the soul content any more. Your teenager will let you know head on that while you think about something in a certain manner in the present, you betray in little ways that you still carry the old around with you in your habits. That hurts.

When parents are out of balance because of emotional problems, if they quarrel with each other or give in to impulses out of desire, a teenager will be quick to name and criticise these unprocessed facets of the soul. And they are often painfully right.

To summarise, the risk of a parent losing their teenage child outwardly or inwardly depends on things like the following:

◊   Recognising that your children are not your possessions but individuals in their own right;
◊   The extent to which the soul of the parent went through the teen journey;

◊ The degree to which the parent strives for a realisation of a meaningful life goal out of their 'I';
◊ The extent to which the parent is willing to reflect on themselves and their self-knowledge;
◊ The parent's willingness to give up their attachment to their own ego, their pride of personality.

The last point has to do with our complacency, our pride and security, our status and arrogance. We all have these things in our inner being, no matter how modest and insecure we appear on the outside. Perhaps such insecurity or modesty is really our pride or our security.

Any encroachment into this realm of the ego evokes pain. Pain frightens us – we run away or react with aggression. When dear daughter or son steps on our ego again, we may pull back in silence, or in tears. Or we may fight back with sharp words or a violent row.

WHAT CAN YOU DO?

Lack of trust in your child, in the future for your child – it is often so understandable, but also senseless. When children are teenagers, are in their sojourn in the lock in the river, they crave trust – parents who, in spite of all troubles, know that things will come out all right. Whether the teenager smokes and drinks, misbehaves sexually or hangs out, don't be misled. Maintain inwardly the iron conviction that this child of yours will make it to the other side of the swamp she or he is in, and will capably realise her or his own plans for the future.

But be careful! These are not *your* dreams for the future of the child. What counts here is the future that is right for the 'I' of the child, her or his own master.

The inner wisdom the teenager is struggling for will lead her or him to a future home. That is the genuine trust teenagers crave, even though they will rarely show it. Naturally you will lose your trust time and again; you are in anguish and terror when you see what your child is up to. That is all right, provided you take charge of yourself again each time, and you put yourself resolutely behind your child again and face the unknown future full of confidence.

It will be clear that parents with lots of fixed notions about what the future is supposed to look like – studies, accomplishments, money, prestige, or just the opposite like simply being free and enjoying things – are vulnerable in this regard. They will look askance at everything their child does that clashes with their beautiful picture. What healthy teenagers do may not be so pretty, but later they will find their own life pattern, which could include anything – perhaps even what their parents had in mind for them! But if the child's dream is different from the parents' dream, the parents will perhaps never trust the child – they may consider the child a failure and yet may continue to hope that she or he will still... Some parents persist in this until their children are sixty!

For children, 'success' only means searching for the way toward the meaningful realisation of their own life goal, out of their own 'I'.

Parental Love

Teenagers may fall in love repeatedly, but genuine, deep love is still hardly there. They may become desperately attached to someone, but usually it is a case of being highly dependent on that person (as discussed in the section on sexuality). The great love they should experience in this period is what they should still encounter as a gift, the gift of their parents. What is love? I will leave that to the poets. But what does it look like in teenagehood? What is it that one gives them?

The love of the parents is what the teenager encounters in: *patience – acceptance – forgiveness – tolerance – interest – attention – authenticity – trust – constructive criticism*; but also in *confrontation – struggle – directness – anger!*

There is something else I also want to mention. It is the willingness to keep to yourself as much as possible the pain you feel during and because of your child's teenagehood. Don't burden your children with your difficulties in parenting them. Renouncing the desire to mirror your pain is a sacrifice that strongly indicates a loving parent. Don't burden them with feelings of guilt, which they won't know how to resolve. When we inwardly process the pain of rearing our children and allow it to grow into insights, we let our children go on their way unburdened.

Parents who practice this continually build bridges across the chasms that erupt between them and their children. Those are the bridges that make it possible for the teen years to end without us having lost our children.

The Potter – 2

Once upon a time there was a man and a woman. They were woodworkers, just like the other people in their village. They lived together in their house and longed for a child. Eventually they sensed that it would not be long before they would be a household of three. They made sure everything was prepared.

When they arrived at the river one day they saw a beautiful child who did not seem to belong to anyone and who urgently needed their help. The woman went into the water and tried to keep her footing in a whirlpool while she lifted the boy out of the water. Her husband helped her from the bank. They took the boy home and tried to make him drink. They saw to it that their house was nice and warm, and together they washed the child and took care of him. It took a long time before he could stand up, walk, speak and eat all the food they offered him. But they delighted in every small sign of progress and loved the boy as if he belonged to them for life.

When he was able to do everything people generally learn to do, the father began to impart knowledge of the forest to the boy. He taught the boy about the various types of trees, and which ones were the most useful for woodworking. He taught him the names of plants and animals, but also familiarity with tools such as saws and axes, and how you could use them to cut a tree without being crushed when it fell. The mother taught the boy how to carve and embellish the wood. She knew how to catch the most wondrous lines and patterns of butterflies and birds in the wood.

The parents delighted in their boy; he had talent and worked hard. He seemed driven, as if he wanted to be able to do everything.

Secretly, they were already imagining how he would build his own house, strong and graceful.

But their dreams were cruelly upset. After many years they noticed that the boy was changing, and they were concerned. He often did not look at them, refused to eat with them and merely wandered about. He would come home tired and dirty. Wood and tools were neglected. He was also quickly provoked to anger and yelled at his mother when she asked him what was wrong.

In the beginning he preferred to go into the forest with his father to fell trees. But the father was also unable to discover what was wrong with him. He let the boy come with him, provided that the work was being done in accordance with his orders. This was the cause of many quarrels between them.

Sometimes the parents saw the boy sitting by the river where they had found him. His head would be down, and they wondered what he was so sad about and what they had done wrong. Where had he come from all those years ago, and what had happened to bring him to them? Where had he been going? The boy withdrew more and more. He slept when they were awake and wandered about when they slept.

One morning he was gone. He had taken his tools and something to eat. That was all. They followed his tracks and saw that he had cut himself a new path through the forest, crudely and in great haste, but a beautifully straight path, competently made. They grieved for their son, wondering why they had lost him. They also cleared the damage to the forest, which took much time and energy, but the work did them good. The boy's track turned into a new path that was easy to travel.

The parents knew that the path led to a village of potters, but they did not follow the boy that far. They went back to their own labour. Days, months and years passed. But one day they heard a well-known whistle. Their hearts leaped for joy when they found their son by the river, now grown into an independent potter. They were glad and proud of him, and full of joy to see him again. Worry and grief evaporated in the stream of time.

15. The Picture Language of Childbirth

Parents are prepared in a most important way for the years of bringing up their children when the birth of each child becomes a deep inner experience for them. Just as the child perceives and inwardly adopts its life goals before birth, so during the delivery parents and child perceive the period of youth, not in some clairvoyant vision, but as a real experience. Everything that will be asked of them during the years of upbringing is lived through in the form of a brief but intense extract during the hours of the delivery. The entire delivery, with all the people and experiences involved, is one great panorama of what will follow afterwards for the parents and their child.

Somehow or other we do not realise this. In my many years of practice I have never neglected to ask questions about the birth of a child. It contains much information and is, in a way, like a passport and a condensed schooling of parents and child. No detail of the delivery, no event, no feeling is devoid of significance. We should learn to recognise this pictorial preparation, to appreciate and use it for the insights and support it can give during child rearing.

Once when I gave a course for parents and we discussed the rich pictures of childbirth, every parent had a 'delivery story' to tell. There were also people who told the story of their own childbirth on the basis of what they had heard from their parents. People were speechless when they discovered the wealth of information that was hiding in these stories. Because many of their children were already much older, they could observe the pictorial message relived in everything that had happened in later years; time and again the experiences during the delivery gave an exact image of those later events.

When a baby presents the wrong way and the delivery is difficult and extra painful because of it, deep in body and soul mother and child are prepared for each other in this experience. As this child is growing up it will also 'present the wrong way' in its relationship with the parents. It will cost the parents much pain and effort to follow the child.

Many mothers who spoke of suddenly arising feelings recognised them again in later years. One mother was given drugs intravenously to accelerate the delivery because it had to take place before the weekend. Later, the feeling of not getting enough time to take the upbringing of the child in hand in the way she wanted but of being hurried by others recurred time and again.

When you make this conscious and bring the pictures of childbirth clearly to light, you can learn to use these experiences as insight and stimulus. Then you realise that you have to make sure you have enough time for the upbringing of your child. Or you devote extra time, patience and energy to building a relationship of authority toward the child that was lying in the wrong way. For being human means that you have the freedom to make conscious choices to take your destiny in your own hands. By gaining insight into these pictures you know what to expect and prepare for. And sometimes you may see traits in your child that you had overlooked.

The Delivery

Naturally I can only speak about the picture language of childbirth in general terms, since every delivery is unique, just as every human being is unique. Every person starts out on their path on this earth in their own characteristic way. A similar event or picture may have a different significance in the life of one person than in another's. Dogmatic thinking along the lines of 'this picture means this or that' ignores the uniqueness of each human being. Repeatedly re-living, re-experiencing the process of childbirth, allowing the picture language to permeate the soul – this is what brings insight into the meaning of *this* picture for *this* child and *these* parents.

In a delivery we can distinguish three phases. Each points to a phase in the period of upbringing.

THE FIRST PHASE

In the first phase the mother feels that the delivery is beginning. The contractions are still light and irregular in intensity and duration. Is it coming or isn't it? Many things have to be prepared at this point. Is everyone reachable, is everything ready, is this the time? Are we going to the hospital or is it a home delivery? The partner comes home, the children are taken to friends or relatives, and the midwife or doctor is called.

This phase of the delivery is more or less a form-giving phase, a preparation for the second phase. When this phase is very short and proceeds immediately into the second one – one of those really quick deliveries – then that is the story of that one child.

The first phase of the delivery points to the first period of child growth – the first six to seven years are portrayed here. In addition, this first phase of the delivery indicates much of what will later have to be wrestled with in the realm of thinking.

THE SECOND PHASE

The second phase begins with regular, obvious contractions that have to bring about the opening of the cervix. In most cases these are painful contractions that have to be tolerated. Relaxation exercises, breathing techniques and other practices will help manage these contractions.

Viewed from the outside, this is the most uneventful period. The mother experiences the contractions together with the unborn child. Having too few of these contractions often results in an easy delivery, but emotionally this is not always so simple, because the mother is then not really ready for the third phase. When these contractions demand their time, energy and stamina, a moment will come when both mother and child 'have arrived'. The cervix is fully open and the third phase can begin.

> The rhythmical contractions, this balance between effort and relaxation, are a picture of the second phase in the life of the child, the period between age six or seven to puberty. This second part of the delivery also indicates much of what will be experienced in the realm of feeling by parents and child.

THE THIRD PHASE

The third phase begins when the cervix is completely open. It is time to start pushing, and the contractions have a different nature. Slowly the child travels from inside to outside through the birth canal. Birth is approaching.

Now there is a lot of outer action. Mother and child are working together extremely closely, and those around them – father, midwife, nurse or doctor – are immediately involved. They help, stimulate, encourage and support the mother. The contractions continue until the head of the child has passed through the mouth of the vagina. One more little push and the child is born. There it is – a complete, separate little being. No, not yet. Not until the first breath, and until the blood is no longer beating in the umbilical cord. When this is bound and cut, the birth of the child is complete. Now there is a new and separately living human child on earth.

> The third phase of the delivery pictures the third period of the growing child: the teen years. In this physical process of separation, of expulsion, the images arise that are of importance in the teen years. In addition, this last phase represents what will have to be experienced by parents and child in the realm of the will.

Note that in a normal delivery first the head (thinking), then the chest (feeling) and finally the lower body and the legs (will) are born, the same sequence in which teenagers free themselves.

The Place of the Father

The mother gives birth. The father does also – or perhaps not – or perhaps somewhat. Becoming a mother is something unavoidable for a woman; becoming a father is something to which you have to give form yourself.

Formerly, men were not permitted to be present at childbirth. They waited anxiously in a little room for the first cries of the baby. Today most fathers are present at the delivery and take an active part in it. We see the same thing in the upbringing of the child. While it used to be mainly women's work, today the fathers are much less in the background and are much more active in the whole process of education and upbringing. Here, too, the outer changes around the delivery show a picture of the changes that have taken place in child rearing.

In some situations fathers are the parent most involved in witnessing the birth. When a mother has a caesarean section, she can be cut off from conscious perception of the birth of her child. I regularly meet fathers who were present at such a birth. They are the ones who then consciously observe the child in the process of the birth, and they can later tell the mother, who is now at some distance removed from it, what they have seen, heard and felt.

In caesareans it remains important to observe what is happening in each phase of the delivery. The mother experiences the first phase. She may not experience the second phase, or perhaps she does in part, or perhaps in its entirety. It depends on the moment of the decision to proceed to the caesarean. By definition, she does not experience the third phase. Always ask the doctor and the nurses for the details about your child's emerging. Some information is better than none.

Some Stories of Birth then Teenagehood

FIRST EXAMPLE

In the last phase of her delivery, while pushing, a woman feels the contractions diminish. She is exhausted and her body is giving up. She receives help in the form of medication and through the words of the people who are present at the delivery. She gets a second wind and collects herself – the child is born. This moment of hopelessness, this feeling of exhaustion, leaves a deep impression on the mother.

She relives this moment when her child is a teenager. He is so difficult and causes so many problems that she is desperate and is ready to give up. She becomes indifferent and just lets the child go his way. But then she suddenly sees the similarity with the delivery, and this gives her courage. She brought the birth to a good end, didn't she? She looks for help and finds someone who is able to give her the support she needs to go on.

SECOND EXAMPLE

Toward the end of the final contractions, when the head of the baby is about to be born it turns out to be so big that the doctor has to make an incision. This frightens the mother; perhaps it hurts. But this intervention makes it possible for the child to be born. The mother is left with a wound that has to be stitched and then has to heal. Most of the time these wounds heal very quickly.

After the birth the mother looks at the child. She is confused, a little scared. But then she sees how quietly her healthy baby is lying in her arms and how she is looking at her with open eyes. She has the feeling that those eyes are telling her that everything is fine. It helps her find her inner equilibrium.

When this child is at the end of the teen years she runs away from home. She goes to friends, finds her own place to live and thus breaks loose. Was there too little space to become independent?

The mother remains behind; her soul is injured and wounded. Did it have to be this way?

When she remembers the delivery and the feelings she had at the time, the mother finds the right answer. She visits her child, who is now living in an apartment. She looks carefully around and sees in her child that it is all right, that there are no disturbances – that this was the way this child had to break out. She finds her equilibrium and is able to be at peace with the situation. The wound in her soul then heals quickly.

Because she knows that the delivery is such a great preparation for child rearing, she realises that she can find her inner balance again by meeting with her child and seeing the reality of her independence. Perhaps she would have realised it anyway, but the risk that she would not, or might do so when it was too late, would be much greater if she had not made a conscious connection with the great teachings of the delivery.

THIRD EXAMPLE

A father is present at the delivery of his daughter. Deep in his soul he sympathetically feels the pain of his wife and the struggle of his child. Then he sees the little head coming out. He is overcome by an intense feeling of joy and encourages his wife by telling her that he can already see their child. Someone then asks him to do or get something, which he does. Right then the woman makes the final push and when he looks again the child is born. Just missed it!

During the teen years of his daughter the father actively participates with his wife in the life of the family. He experiences deep in his soul the process of the child loosening herself from her home. Then he is offered a new job that takes him on many international business trips. As soon as he is away on his first trip the daughter leaves the home and finds a place somewhere else.

Should he have stayed? Or was it better that he left? When he remembers the delivery, things become clear to him. He remembers that the child made use of the opening she had because of his absence. Now he can accept the fact that later she also needed more freedom and space to become independent, when he was forced into the background because of his travels.

There is no end to the examples. The mother who literally experienced everything during the delivery. The child who had to be delivered with forceps. The deep impression made when the child is born just as the sun is rising. The presence at the delivery of people you love, or the opposite – their absence. The understanding, or lack thereof, of others. The pain and how you were able to deal with it, or weren't.

I hope that many people will be able to find access to this rich source of experiential knowledge of their child, themselves and the circumstances of child rearing.

The teen years are a time of loosening. The child is in a kind of birth canal. It is a tight space: between childhood and adulthood. There is no way back and the future is uncertain.

In the last phase of the delivery the mother pushes the child into the outside. Loosening, letting go the reins bit by bit, giving children their own responsibility – that is the 'push' during teenagehood. Not all at once, and not by holding on. During the delivery this stage is the most risky, both for the child and for the mother. Sometimes it is a matter of survival.

> The third phase of the delivery is also a narrow path to freedom, the outer freedom of the body. Teenagehood is the narrow path to the freedom of the soul.

16. Fathering Teenagers

Why Fathering Matters in the Teen Years

What is fathering during the teen years? Why does a teenager have such a profound need for a father? And what does that mean for a single mother?

When teens isolate themselves from 'home influences' and make their way through teenagehood to an adulthood based on influences they have made their own, they first orient themselves by their surroundings. It is not as if everything from outside is immediately replaced by the inside.

Earlier in this book I used the image of a lock in a river. A sojourn in the lock is a necessity – you can't simply jump from one level to another. If you try that, ship and skipper will most likely get dunked.

Usually the child will close the door to what is too close by, but open it wide for other influences. Like someone who wants to break their addiction to smoking: often first they replace the cigarette with something else, like sweets or food.

That is the way with teenagers. They free themselves by first rejecting the old, but accepting other un-free influences. As parents we are surprised when our children completely ignore us telling them to do or not to do something, but then meticulously follow the unwritten rules of their friends or club. They don't care a bit about the mess in their room – something that annoys us parents – but having the wrong kind of cell phone is a major disaster, because then they lose face at school. And of course, when something else is 'in' next year, they will cheerfully want that.

What does this have to do with fathers? For a child, the father is usually the person who is more oriented to the outside world than the mother. Many mothers work part-time, perhaps the father also. When the roles are totally changed around, teenagers will often also turn their father–mother orientation around. But fathers are usually more focused on the physical outside world. A child who is beginning to reject home influences can make the transition via the father. The father is like a bridge between home and outside world. Teenagers can afford to take their father seriously for a longer time than their mother. If they have a good father, they let go of mother's hand when they reach the teen years and let themselves be guided by the father a little longer. *Not by taking his hand!* But a father who sort of walks by your side for another year – that is okay.

Such fathers do have to satisfy a few conditions; they should:

◊   not be glued together with the mother and do everything together with her;
◊   make time to do things with the child;
◊   not talk all the time about what the child should or shouldn't do;
◊   refuse to be the bogeyman who measures out punishment and pulls the reins the mother cannot hold any longer;
◊   have been true teenagers themselves so they can look at their child's antics with humour and see them in perspective;
◊   not be absorbed by problems between the parents, at work or problems related to ageing.

A healthy father who supports a teenager in the transition from child to adult is in a way already a big friend. But if the father always pulls together with the mother, the teenager will write them both off. Not that the father has to take positions against his co-parent or should permit things that she has forbidden – that just causes confusion and quarrels. No, just set clear boundaries. But in your inner attitude toward a teenager it is fine when, as the father, you already treat the child as if she or he were a little older than she or he is. Repeat: a little. Begin to create a little distance in the parent–child relationship, while that is still a problem for the mother. For instance, a story about mistakes you made yourself as a young man can give perspective to the child's imperfections. Did the father also sometimes have bad grades in school? Did he also come home late? Did he also pull the wool over his parents' eyes? Most of them did!

The father that a teenager needs is therefore someone who puts himself beside his child, and transforms himself from parent-caretaker to parent-companion, earlier and more completely than most mothers are able to do. Such a father lets the thankless task of parent-caretaker continue with the mother. The child thus receives a little island halfway in the river between the bank of youth and the bank of adulthood.

The father then gets more opportunities to help as the child orients more and more to the outside world. The teenager will ask him more often and for a longer time for his opinion. And that is sometimes exactly the support that is needed. Your arm is then just long enough. Suppose your teenager meets a new group of people with fanatical religious or ideological ideas, she or he is likely to share that with you so then you have the opportunity to avert a looming one-sidedness by asking your child questions or by bringing her or him into contact with very different ideas. No commands, no prohibitions. Of course you can't just criticise – then your views are simply thrown out and the fanaticism is embraced. Through the right encounters give them the opportunity to get acquainted with real life and to discern truth. This will stimulate the development of the child's own 'I', which in due course has to take on the task of the father.

Naturally, it is extremely important that there is harmony between father and mother. Much has been gained if the mother can accept that her partner has a little more space for a special relationship with the child, so that these two can develop something together. But if the mother feels discarded and becomes jealous when the child tends toward her husband, who never devoted the same amount of time and attention to the family, she will make it harder for her husband to be a good father. This is a very difficult point for many mothers. If her husband shows understanding and attention for this pain, it will make things easier for her.

Physically doing things together can work wonders. The father does not need to be a great philosopher, but he should be there for the important matches of his teenager's football team. And let him faithfully pick up his teens when they are out late at night. Then they won't fail to tell him about the party.

Take your teenager to the opera or go to a famous city for a weekend: London, New York, San Francisco... Or perhaps a fun place closer to home. Fathers who take days off to go hiking with their teenage children, or take on some other exciting physical achievement, are worth their weight in gold.

Doing things together has great value. But make sure they are things you enjoy, because when you do things with your teenager you don't like, you cut off your nose to spite your face. They know it right away, and don't appreciate it at all. Teenagers are in search of truth, in spite of their own incapacities. Whenever they encounter 'nice' lies in adults, they will not mince words rejecting them.

The mother bridge and the father bridge

You could say that children cross two bridges in their development to adulthood: the mother bridge and the father bridge. Long before birth children step onto the mother bridge. Via this bridge they enter into the world. After birth children need the mother's mothering; they incarnate through this soul condition. Whoever takes care of a young child is addressed in the feminine part of the soul; from there the child is mothered. *This is also true for fathers!* Around children's ninth year the mother bridge turns downward. Mother's possibilities decrease, and they stop at the beginning of teenagehood.

The father bridge begins after the birth of the child. As the mother bridge begins to tend down when the child is about nine years old, the father bridge keeps growing through to the beginning of teenagehood. Then it levels off and starts turning down, but it can continue to accompany the child into adulthood.

Parents with growing children are gradually addressed more and more in their masculine soul energy; they are called to 'father' more. *This is also true for mothers!*

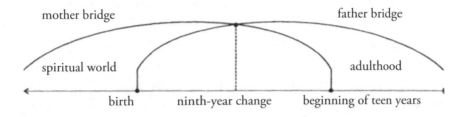

OTHER REASONS WHY FATHERING IS IMPORTANT

Every soul has both masculine and feminine energy. The soul has two poles: it can express itself through its feminine or masculine pole. This is true for both men and women. Most men are accustomed to live more out of the masculine forces of their soul than the feminine forces. When the higher 'I' seeks entry into the soul of a human being in order to work there and to stimulate that person toward her or his life lessons, it will look for such entry through the masculine pole of the soul.

When you allow this statement to work deeply into your inner being, it will lead to many consequences. It helps us understand why teenagers are so keen on standing their ground. This goes for both boys and girls; girls also want to assert themselves. The way in which this takes place is frequently a distortion of the original impulse, but you can still distinguish in it the searching and working 'I' that wakes up the masculine pole of the teenage soul.

A younger child is still so oriented to artistry, creativity, to receptivity and openness that the emphasis is on the development of the feminine pole of the soul – not physically, but of the feminine soul energy that lives in both girls and boys. In this phase they still look for beauty, images, for sweet and pure life.

The teenager begins to look for other things: truth, strength of presence, rightness, certainty. The masculine pole of the soul is awakening, and must awaken. This is the door through which the 'I' enters. Only when this soul quality has come to life and is working can the 'I' make a connection with the feminine pole of the soul. Just as in the creation story Adam came first, and then Eve, so in every young person, when the higher 'I' starts coming in, it irradiates and liberates the masculine pole first and then the feminine pole.

For this reason the teenager looks for an image of masculinity – a masculinity permeated by the 'I' force. Not egoism, for egoism is exactly counter to an 'I' force; it is a desire of the soul over which the higher 'I', the spiritual core, has not yet been able to exert its mastery. Masculine soul strength will express itself in strong, dependable love, true and sincere striving, and also in genuine fatherhood; in faithful support that never abandons but, through all the dust storms raised by growing children, always discerns the essential in them.

This is a golden opportunity for fathers. With all my soul I would like to advocate for the development of good fatherhood: the adult human being who opens the masculine, ambitious, earthly side of his soul so it can serve his own inner master. That will enable the great miracle of the second awakening to take place: one 'I' awakens the other 'I' in the young soul.

Good fatherhood with this inner foundation is an ideal worth striving for, but for which we have a long way to go. That does not matter. Along this inner path it is possible to become a genuine father, for your own children, and also for people who are still like children, for pupils or others for whom you have a responsibility.

Single Mothers

Here is also the answer for the single parent: *genuine fatherhood is a soul quality that every human being, man or woman, is able to develop.*

It will be clear that the mother who wants to develop this in herself because she does not have a partner who can do it faces an enormous inner struggle. She was the soul *mother*; now she is asked to become the soul *father.*

People who want to try this must not forget that going for

perfection does not help a teenager. Teenagers look for adults who sincerely seek, and work at developing themselves through trial and error. When your teen senses that you are striving for inner fatherhood, she or he will have the opportunity to develop through you. You do not need to have completed the whole course, as long as you always stay ahead of your child.

A parent who wants to take up this challenge faces three great life questions in the soul:

◊   have I sufficiently developed my masculine qualities?
◊   am I not being overwhelmed and blinded by an excess of masculine qualities?
◊   is my soul open to the spiritual call of my higher 'I'?

When the higher 'I' develops and guides a human being, it is possible to observe a social process unfolding at the same time. The higher 'I' develops the individual human being and, at the same time, serves the development of the individuality in others close by. Those who develop themselves without evoking development impulses in others, are servants of egoism. They betray the fact that the true 'I' is actually not present.

When children of divorced parents reach the teen years they may wish to switch from living mostly with the mother to the father. It is certainly true that the visiting parent has new opportunities when his child reaches teenagehood, but it is a rare case when a child successfully leaves the primary parent (mostly the mother), and moves in with the weekend parent (mostly the father). At this age, children do not grow new roots, and the risk of becoming a wanderer is great. It is better if in teenagehood the living situation does not change. The process of loosening then runs its course more naturally, and there is less chance of wandering, living here and then there.

Again, if fathers can be a bridge between mother and adulthood, the way described above is the better one, the way of attention, certain support and doing things together – no longer just physically, because the time of 'dear daddy' is past. Let teenagers fight the battle for their individuality at home!

Divorce and Composite Families

Many young people grow up in composite families or in families with one parent. A composite family consists of one of the child's own parents together with a new partner of their father or their mother, perhaps with half-brothers and sisters and children of the new partner from her or his prior relationship. Frequently we also see a shared upbringing in the sense that young people live alternately in the new families of the mother and the father. In the United States, 27 per cent of children live with one parent. In the United Kingdom, about one in four families with dependent children are single parent families.

There are, of course, great differences in these various family situations. Most of the parents have between one and four children; an increasing number of teenagers have between one and four parents. In essence, this means more possibilities. Growing young people may benefit from an extra educator in whom they have a better example than in their own parents. It may also happen that the contact with mother or father becomes more intensive after a divorce, because the adults now give the child their undivided attention.

Often fathers and mothers quarrel and fight for years before a divorce. When this stops, there may be more room for intensive individual relationships with their growing children. But there is a snake in the grass, for if they keep quarrelling, stirring up strife and criticising the past of the joint family – or, conversely, romanticising it – then big problems develop. Children of divorced parents are not divorced, only their parents are. When the parents gossip about each other, interrogate the children, keep on fighting about money and the children, the divorce will expand to include the children as well. In many cases the children then speak about the divorce as 'we'. When you hear a child say, 'We are divorced,' you can be sure that something has gone seriously wrong. Because they are so closely involved in the divorce, many children feel inwardly torn. They participate in the negativity of the mother concerning the father or vice versa. In both cases they end up, often unknowingly, in a false situation. Without realising it they participate in a game that for them is a false one.

The connection with one of the parents may be so close that they betray that with the other parent. That happens because they inwardly experience the negative content of the thoughts and feelings of the one parent as their own. They eagerly relate how unpleasant and boring the other parent was, without as yet being able to realise that they are permeated with the feelings and thoughts of the parent with whom they identify. Sometimes such a relationship becomes obsessive, and the parent and the growing child are unable to let go of each other. In other cases we will see a healthy teenagehood that leads to inner freedom from the overly influential parent. The teenager may then step over to the parent with whom the relationship was broken off, thus rupturing the connection with the primary parent all at once with much pain. When this does not happen, the relationship with the more estranged parent may remain broken for a very long time. In most cases these are father–child relationships.

To prevent such problems the golden rule is to avoid loyalty conflicts in divorces. Loyalty to mother and father is normal. The fact that ex-partners make this a source of conflict is a form of spiritual child abuse. We must combat this kind of abuse much more strongly than is currently done. Fortunately many parents have joint custody and the unhealthy situation in which judges ask twelve year olds whether they will choose Mum or Dad has become more unusual.

Because of their father or mother's new relationships, many young people have one or more extra parents. Teenagers do not accept any second mum or dad. An extra adult, who you can consult like a friend and who supports you by word and deed, who knows you well and wants to understand you – that is a gift. Such a person can be an excellent bridge to adulthood. Having to get used to the growing independence of a teenager and excessive anxieties are things a new educator will suffer much less than the child's own parents. An open, free relationship can then grow, filled with warm affection, a relationship that should be appreciated with gladness by the real parents. If that does not work, and jealousy and reproaches become the norm in the new relationship, a second divorce is usually just around the corner.

There are many complex situations that may develop in a composite family. 'Patchwork families' they are called. Half-brothers or sisters are born, or the new partner brings children of his or her own. Sometimes these are discoveries of a lifetime, bringing friendship, companionship and close connections. Finally the girl has a big sister, or the boy a playmate. Perhaps all the young folk go out or on holiday together. For the teenagers who babysit the small children who have come to live with them it is also a social enrichment.

But we should learn something from the fairytale of the Frog Prince. Just like in the fairytale, the young person will at first often want to keep the door closed, will refuse to sit at the same table with the new parent. In brief, the teenager will refuse to live together with him or her. Before young people can gain socially from the situation, they have to throw the frog against the wall, you could say. Only then can the prince appear. Loving but strict parents should take the king in the fairytale as their example. In the end, the frog has to go with the recalcitrant princess to her bedroom; of course we should not take this literally, but as a picture. Taking it with you to your bedroom means taking it into the night, forging a new connection that can grow roots in the deepest depths of the soul. This takes time and may be difficult.

It usually takes a long time before the parent's own enthusiasm for the new relationship can be shared by the teenager. Naturally, the parent will have to control her or his impatience. Quiet confidence and clear choices full of understanding and warmth will usually overcome initial estrangement and resistance in the end. Parents and young people who support and strengthen each other full of understanding in this process of accommodation keep their connections intact. Otherwise, there may not only be another divorce, but the young person may yet run away from home.

Out of my own experience, and from that of many parents who have confided in me, I know that the people around the family – relatives, friends, colleagues and teachers – have great influence on these processes. They can be the cause of success or failure. Every person around such composite families should therefore observe a few rules of behaviour:

◊ not gossip
◊ accept the divorce and inwardly process your grief
◊ do not judge
◊ welcome and accept new relationships
◊ do not form 'camps' pro or con
◊ overcome loyalty problems (grandparents: do not stop your visits on birthdays!)
◊ do not reinforce or aggravate difficult memories
◊ do not romanticise the past
◊ do not write off the ex-partner and the absent children – they might come back!

The reality of divorce and changed family composition is part of our time. Many parents have feelings of guilt relating to divorce. This is caused in part by stories about the number of children who get into trouble after the divorce of their parents. Besides the fact that such guilt feelings are unfruitful, these figures should also be carefully weighed. It is most plausible that parents and families with problems will fall apart. That which is carrying a heavy burden, may well collapse. When we investigate the children in such divorces, we will naturally see a lot of problems, but it is distorting to ascribe these by definition to the divorce.

We see around us how people from different religions, countries and origins are brought together. It looks as if the strength of family ties wants to grow into a deep experience of ties among humanity. Perhaps the difficulties of composite families are the harbingers of a new era in which people are learning to bridge the gap between what is theirs and what is foreign.

Masculine and Feminine Soul Power

LACK OF MASCULINE SOUL POWER

Fathers *and* mothers are able to work at strengthening their masculine soul powers. Suppose you are a very shy mother who hardly dares attend a parent-teacher evening at school, or who lets herself be pushed around by stronger personalities. When your child is growing up it is very important to learn to strengthen such weak spots in the soul: to gather new forces to request a conversation about your child, to put your pushy neighbour kindly but firmly in her place, and so on.

Your children will pick this up. If you have an active child, chances are that she or he will challenge you to show those more masculine forces: 'I challenge you! I will continue until you become mad at me and draw a boundary.' Yes, your child is then offering you your underdeveloped areas on a silver platter.

If you have a more passive child she or he will mirror your example and influence back to you in even greater shyness or victimisation. Do not weep. Every one-sidedness can be overcome, and also leaves its own riches behind. For a shy mother never terrorises her children but always quietly listens to them; that is something the children take with them.

Always keep moving; never stand still. What has been was good, it provided its own riches, but when your child grows older it becomes time for the second part of parenthood. Now the emphasis is no longer on the development of all the instruments in your child. Now, at the beginning of the teen years, the emphasis is on your child's potential for a meaningful life through their inner musician.

Excess of masculine soul power

If as a father you still have to prove yourself at the expense of your children... If you always want to be the cleverest, the strongest and the best... Or if as a mother you want to be the prettiest, slimmest, most intelligent and conspicuous... If father and mother always want to hold forth at school meetings or at the dinner table... If they dominate every party... If the child's room has to look the way the parent wants... If father makes all the rules and everyone nervously follows them... If mother writes angry letters to everyone and determines every relationship her children can have... Yes, then your parents have an excess of masculine soul forces. And it is perfectly clear that at moments such as those described here they put these forces in service not of their higher 'I', but of their daily little 'I' – their egoism.

Just controlling these forces, however, leads in a straight line to their unresolved accumulation and eventual explosive discharge. Should we therefore not control ourselves? We certainly should, but at the same time we should find a way to release these forces. *It is through the feminine parts of the soul that they can flow out and be freely given away in service to someone else.*

In order to be able to make masculine soul potential available to the feminine pole of the soul, we have to make use of the higher power that comes from the spirit. The spirit has the ability to drive the two horses of the soul. That is why the higher 'I' needs to be called on in this situation, so that the soul forces then have their master and allow themselves to be used for a meaningful purpose in service of the human being and the world.

Imagine that as a father you decide to stop bragging about all your accomplishments. Keep your mouth shut. If you work at it hard enough, you might succeed. Then one day, preferably when you are a bit overtired, your son starts bragging about how quickly he has understood his math problems. Suddenly you can't stand it any more and you erupt in a torrent of blame and reproof: why did he then get an F for math on his report card last semester? And then comes the litany of all father's wonderful grades, and the son is swept off the table. The end is a loud fight, the son is insulted and withdraws into his room, and dad is angry and disappointed in his well-meant resolutions.

How can the father prevent this? His higher 'I' can help him. It can lead him to feel that he does not need to look for security in what he is capable of, but in who he is. That will deflate the situation in that the father can then look for ways to use his strength rather than emphasise it. Could he perhaps help his son with his math homework? He could learn to listen to his son's vulnerability, which hides behind his bragging.

The father could try to use his strength for something another member of the family would like to have. Would his son like to get a nice new bookshelf? Or a particular birthday present? When you look for such small gifts you always need both strength and love. Strength is not the problem in this father; love is an invitation to the true 'I'. With these two together we are able to give gifts and to help. The loving 'I' then consumes the excess of strength by applying it in a positive manner. Thus the father does not need to explode – he is no longer living on a powder keg.

Excess of feminine soul power

It is not hard to recognise when an adult has too much masculine energy and regulates and dominates everything and everyone. But it is not so obvious when the feminine soul energy predominates. Such a parent is often rather docile; everything seems possible. But when you look a little closer, things may be changing, but nothing much seems to happen – a lot of talk and flexibility, but nothing actually gets hands and feet. Such people may have many ideas but they leave it at that. They may have no end of compassion, admiration and love for their child, but never set limits when something goes too far.

The number of teenagers who are literally longing for their mother to resolutely put them to work, to give them a kick in the behind, might surprise us. Imploring them with buckets full of tears is perfectly useless. Fathers too can keep treating their children playfully and never develop into real fathers. The higher 'I' that works in the soul evokes respect in the child. If a child has no respect for you or for what you stand for, it gives you something to ponder.

Of course, respect is about the last thing teenagers will show their parents, and yet... when it really counts... And a younger child should have a basis of respect.

When as a parent you have shown too much of your feminine side to your child, you will quite likely experience authority problems. There are other causes of authority problems, but this is one of them. And if that is the basis on which you enter into the child's teenagehood, this lovely child will step so hard on your soul to force you to stop making sacrifices and playing with her or him. The teenager will call for the masculine force of boundaries to wake up in you, and will do so in a far from attractive manner.

Again, the issue here is to do with egoism. When the feminine predominates and is not guided by the higher 'I', everything seems as if it is nice and sensitive and beautiful, but what we are actually witnessing is an avoidance of resisting the child out of egoistic motives. The focus is then not on the development of the being of the child, but on the comfort and feeling life of the adult. Such parents may well blackmail their children: 'If you do that you will break my heart,' or, 'If you talk that way to your father he will be upset.' This kind of blackmail obviously makes a child unfree. And freedom is the linchpin of a healthy development toward adulthood in which the 'I' can unroll the red thread in its life.

In the end we will notice that speaking about fathers and good fatherhood results in speaking about good *parenthood* – that balance in soul development is a prerequisite for both men and women. While children will usually look to the father for good fatherhood, they can find it just as well with the brave mother if she takes this life question seriously. She can place everything we have said about the father also in herself. She can nimbly switch from one role to the other and thus by herself form an island between childhood and adulthood.

Many single mothers can try this. Many fathers who see their children only every other weekend can try it. Teachers who are fond of young people are able to try it. But whoever has no interest in young people, who views them only as factors causing disturbances, is not yet up to this.

PART 4

MOVING ON

17. Loss of Energy in Parents

In the womb, in birth and in the childhood years, children build their development through the forces they find in their immediate surroundings. At first, the child needs the physical and life forces of the mother. Later, the forces of the father and of all the people who interact with the child are added to these. The child also absorbs many life forces from nature.

Besides physical and life forces the child also needs soul force. Soul forces are taken in primarily in the family situation and later at school and from others. What we call 'atmosphere' and everything that takes place with constancy and regularity nourishes the child. Not just one story, but every evening a little story before falling asleep. The Christmas tree not just once, but as a constantly returning rhythm of the beautiful green tree in the house every year. The heart forces of the parents, and most of all the mother, are a great gift for the souls of their children,

I mentioned especially the mother's forces, but fortunately there are also more and more fathers who know how to 'mother'. I am including those fathers just as much as the mothers. Similarly, there are also the grandmothers and others who take care of children while the parents are at work. They 'mother' too, and are sometimes better than the father or mother they are substituting for...

When children reach their teen years they begin to separate their soul from all the surrounding soul forces. They want to build up their own soul content and soul body. You can't take this literally enough. Even though you can only observe this process if you are clairvoyant, believe me, it is happening. As with a keen knife, the connecting threads between the parents (and I am including all the others involved in the upbringing) and the child are cut. The energy that flowed from the parents to the child no longer returns; contact with the source is lost.

Sensitive people sometimes experience in all its reality how during their children's teen years they are cut off from the soul forces they have bestowed on them. It is as if from the runners of a strawberry plant new little plants have grown, and when these are large enough the connection is cut and the new plants are transferred to a different place.

Something like this has already happened once. Right after birth – the process during which everything is experienced in miniature – the umbilical cord is tied and cut. The child is no longer nourished by the blood of the mother, but its own little body takes on that task. The umbilical cord falls quiet, the young life separates from the life of the mother.

If it is done well, the adults will wait until the baby no longer uses the flow of nourishment through the umbilical cord, and then close it off. In the same way, the parents wait in the teen years until the child no longer absorbs the flow of soul force, and then they give the child his or her freedom. Of course, everyone knows that keeping a physical umbilical cord alive is nonsense; but that is no less true for the psychic umbilical cord!

When these soul connections are cut, not only does the child separate from the parents, the parents also loosen themselves from the child. That is the way it should be. But the parents have now also loosened themselves from the energy they gave. That is also the way it should be, but I want to put some emphasis on this because most people do not realise that they may feel terribly tired in their soul as a result of this separation; they may even feel a loss of life forces.

We always think that we lose so much strength because teenagers make life so difficult for us. That may indeed also be a reason, but even the most congenial teenager feeds on your soul, because in the first instance the separation process brings with it a kind of amputation of soul forces. In the face of this, it is of enormous importance that our reaction should not be an effort to hold on to the child. That is self-defeating and just means that we will lose him or her even more rapidly; or we bestow new soul forces on the child, which then cannot properly grow to maturity because they disturb the development of independence in the child's soul.

Thus, we are clear about what we should not do, but what should we do? Protecting and nurturing the soul forces the parents have left is essential. When they don't succeed in doing this, they will become depressed, overwrought, ill, weak and hard to get along with. Much of what is usually ascribed to menopause is really connected with the transition the children are going through and its consequences for the parents, not to the transition of the mother due to her age.

Protecting and Nurturing the Soul Forces

Protecting soul forces? Yes, not those that were given away, they are gone for good, but what is left needs to be carefully husbanded. Fun outings with a good friend, with your partner, or time with a good book; going somewhere to be pampered for a few days; learning something new you've wanted to learn for years – it doesn't matter what, but all such small, nice things are now more important in life. Attention, warm interest, the chance to talk and cry your heart out and, most importantly, understanding for your loss, are then precious. In addition to this the challenge is to look for an orientation or deepening of a more spiritual nature. When one force is diminishing, another force may generate much new energy.

Imagine a time when children are in the middle of the teen years and the end of this period is in view. Is the parent who has gone through all this able to find a new, meaningful content for him or herself? Our time demands of us an individual search for the essence of things, for a connection with the forces from which our humanity comes forth. This is really exactly the reverse of what is happening between parents and teenager. The adult seeks, often unconsciously, to connect inner threads that are hanging loose, so that forces of a spiritual nature can give themselves to the soul.

Maybe this is a distant picture for many adults, but such a search often begins with very practical things such as looking for a new job, for a better place to live so that you have a chance to realise what is essential in you. It does not matter whether or not you have already found an answer to the spiritual question in your life; what is important is that you look for the threads that connect you with what is essential in yourself and in everything else. It will create courage and enthusiasm. When the old life goal is gone, don't stall, but go in search of new goals!

If your forces fall short, you can find nourishment in forces from a higher energy source. The soul can nourish itself from the spirit, the life forces can find nourishment in the soul, and finally, the physical body can be nourished by the life forces. When your forces fall short and you continue to consume them, you are likely to end up accelerating the consumption of lower energy sources. The life forces consume many physical capacities during illness, for instance. The soul consumes life forces in times of suffering and trials. The spirit consumes soul forces when there is a spiritual crisis, a problem involving the life goal.

When the soul can be nourished from spiritual forces it will be a big support for parents with a teenager. It is especially important for them to pay attention to their life forces when the soul is under great stress. The soul consumes a lot of life force when it falls short and still continues to do its work. Mothers in this situation become completely exhausted. Healthy food, fresh air and a time in nature are just as important for adults in this phase as warmth and coziness. A new sport or some other activity in the outside air can also be an answer.

In this context, I want to put the spotlight once more on high school teachers and other adults who continually interact with young people because of their profession. For them what I have described here holds true even more than for parents. True, the children are not their own, but when they commit themselves with heart and soul to young people, they may experience the same problems in the course of the years as parents toward the end of their children's teen years. When you see such kids come into high school and you start teaching them your subject, you will find that when they finish school they take a chunk of your soul forces with them. The warmth with which you teach brings the content of the knowledge into the souls of the children, and that is a wonderful thing. Let us realise that en-souled teachers are precious resources, so that they do not run on empty but have the opportunity to nourish themselves from time to time.

18. The End of Teenagehood

The end of teenagehood is an important time. If things have gone well, the parents have stepped back and the young people, now young adults, are standing in the front line facing the future. Teenagehood is behind them.

This is the beginning of the period (from about age twenty-one to twenty-eight) in which young people will learn to live life out of the ever clearer voice of their own 'I', an inner voice that can sound more and more distinctly in the now fully grown, self-remodelled soul. When a person has learned to listen to this voice, has learned to know it and distinguish it from other impulses, only then is she or he a real adult – usually toward the thirtieth year.

In the final phase of teenagehood – roughly between the seventeenth and twenty-first year – many young people will already be making choices for a life of their own. They go to college or find a job and live by themselves or with roommates. In one way or another they already show a great deal of outer independence. Every child has an individual pace of development, and this may be very different from one person to another. For this reason there is no rule of thumb for the age when a young person is capable of her or his own independent life. It is always a question of observing how your child has developed.

Children who live on their own still have a need for support in the background. This does not need to come from the parents; sometimes they chose other adults on whom they can fall back. That is not so important, and the parents should not find this painful. When children in their individuality choose someone else for their background support they show their own autonomous personality.

Don't burden them with disappointment or jealousy. That is your own homework, and you will do better finishing it yourself.

How Can You Know that a Teenager is in the Final Phase?

You will notice that a teenager has reached the final phase when there are fewer confrontations. You know again where you are with your child. You could say that the deck of cards has been shuffled, and now the game can proceed more quietly. In addition, and this is most exciting and essential, the young person begins to make her or his own decisions with more originality than before, and with consequences she or he recognises and accepts. In brief, you can see the first workings of the 'I' in the choices she or he makes and carries out.

For instance: 'I am going to share an apartment with Henry,' or 'I want to change from my school to this other school,' or 'I am going to look for a job.' They are assessing professions, relationships and many other things, and real judgments are made. Such resolutions quickly turn into action – suddenly they know what they want.

Father and Mother: make sure you back them up now! For now you will see that they have not only kicked against their parents, but that they are able to set their own course without their parents' help. It may be a hard thing to swallow. Now your child is truly not yours any longer; the time has come to let them go their own way.

Even if you can predict that a relationship will not last, or that they still have a lot to learn about living on their own, do not fall back into a parent–child reaction. Were we so perfect ourselves when we left our parental home? And did we not acquire most of what we know about life after that moment? It may be useful to remember our own lessons. Protecting our children from their own life lessons is impossible and undesirable. It is their life and their path of learning.

It works much better if you give them a lot of confidence. They know where to find you when you stay in the background, and they will need your advice later. But if you do not let your children go they will break loose, and then the risk is great that they will prefer to find out everything for themselves rather than ask their parents for advice or share anything with them. Let us remember the doors of the lock in the river: if they are not opened, the little ship will ram them open with much unnecessary damage on both sides.

Besides, aren't many of these parental worries based on your own worries that you can't handle things, and your anxieties about what is going to happen with this piece of your life work? For every child is indeed a life work of the parents. If things go well, you give this work away to your child, and a gift means that the receiver may do with it what they want. Right?

But secretly, under these parental worries hides the desire that the big investment made should produce a return that becomes visible in the successful adulthood of the child – one with which the parents can feel satisfied. A kind of delayed report card! Many children feel such expectations, and it makes them un-free. It is better to give them the space they need. Whatever they do, your self-evaluation should be based on the investment you put into parenting, not on what they are doing with it.

There is also something new in this young woman or man. They are so conscious of everything. They are so conscious of who you are as mother or father, woman or man. It makes you feel as if you are naked. In perfect equanimity they can give you a description of your inner world or habits. At the end of the teen years, teenagers have acquired a lot of understanding of the adults around them. They know how to handle them, although not always perfectly. In brief, they have pretty well learned what their parents are able to teach them.

Problems in the Final Phase

Some young people are forever teenagers. Do you know them too? Those young folk in their thirties who just do a bit of this and a bit of that and never really commit to anything? Those young people who flit from one relationship to another, and just when it begins to look serious, take to their heels again?

It is so tiresome to deal with adults who never become real adults and are forever teenagers. All the characteristics of teenagehood are still there, but now rigidified. The way they kicked against things when they were sixteen, they still do later. The way they shirked tasks and responsibility then, they still do after twenty years. Slippery and convinced that they are right, they go on living like teens. You will often see them break off study, jobs or relationships, and then years later want to start again with a much younger girlfriend or boyfriend, start a fun little café, or start work on a doctoral degree. After further years, when they are facing consequences, they start something else again. Their biographies show much that is unfinished and neglected.

How come? These are often children who were a little 'light'. I mean children who did not possess a strong personality. They feel perfectly at home in the years of their youth. Everyone sometimes enjoys golden oldies, or getting together with former schoolmates; these people stay there. Perhaps the parents have spoiled them, or have been too strict. Perhaps they have lost the capacity to work. Perhaps they lack self-confidence.

Whatever is at the root of it all, they increasingly desert everything that relates to the task of their age, to what is being asked of them on the basis of their age. Frequently they will seek a partner who in a certain way acts as their guardian and makes decisions for them, but whom they will not hesitate to deceive when it suits them. They avoid every commitment.

WHAT CAN YOU DO?

As parents you can try to be a mirror for them: let them experience the results of what they are doing. When that surprises them, an opening may emerge that allows them to grow toward adulthood. It does not matter whether you confront them with the consequences of their dealings with relationships, with money, drugs or whatever

– the only truth that can reach them is their own truth. Don't try to convince them with your own pain or suffering; they don't feel it. But show them who they are when they live in the way they live. That creates an opportunity.

See to it also that you don't always protect them. There are parents who are almost in love with that beautiful, big daughter or son. Loving looks that rest so tenderly on son- or daughter-dear merely serve to keep them childlike, and smooth over all their failings. There are parents who after twenty years still keep paying the debts of their dear child; or they go and take care of their child's children because the adult child does not face up to the task of parenthood.

That just serves to preserve the old. It is better to let them take care themselves of the damage they cause. Only then can they come to a new and strong resolve. After all, life itself is a strict but just educator, which continues where the task of the parents ends.

19. Four Final Stories

The four final stories are meant to show a picture of the inner path of a child toward adulthood. The three realms of thinking, feeling and the will are portrayed in the first three stories, while the last story gives a picture of the path of the human 'I'.

The way of the life of thinking is that of 'The Little Fisherman', who loses his childlike nature in stormy waters and develops his intellectual powers over a number of years. This enables him to make a lot of money but, in the end, he sails the high seas all by himself in a boat full of fish. Only after having developed social consciousness can he find the way to his spiritual origin again.

The way of the feeling life is the way of 'Little Miriam', who becomes blind and loses her childlike happiness. Inwardly she can find it again when she has located the narrow path to freedom. Her happy feeling life is then revived by the discovery of spiritual beauty, the true 'I', in the image of the queen.

The way of the life of the will is that of 'The Young Blacksmith'. This path leads straight through the reality of earth and darkness, involving commitments and encounters with all that life demands of a human being. Will power thus becomes a wise servant who is able to make a connection with the queen of the middle. As a result of this process, will power can heal the 'middle', the warm heart forces; it can then unite with them with the king of the heights' blessing.

'Backer and His Boy' gives a picture of the way of the 'I' in the human being. Although spiritually protected in the beginning, the young 'I' is nevertheless taken along by the adversary powers working in the world. These can obscure the 'I', but sooner or later the human being will set out to retrieve the land of his birth so as to unite himself with his higher 'I' and enter into dialogue with it. This is a long road, but the relationship between the earthly 'I' and the spiritual 'I' is restored. The shepherd with the golden thread in this story lives in every human heart.

The Little Fisherman

Once upon a time there was a little boy with a little boat and a little fishing rod. Every day this little boy rowed his little boat onto the lake and caught a few little fish. He baked the fish in a skillet on his fire and ate them. There was always just enough to fill his stomach, most of the time not too much and not too little.

The boy sometimes dreamed that he would become a big strong man with a large boat and a real fishing net, and that every day he would catch hundreds of fish and would be able to eat as much as he wanted. But these dreams never came true, and every day he had the same small catch; his dreams never made a difference.

One warm afternoon the little fisherman was dozing in his little boat. In the heat with the quiet rocking of the boat he slowly closed his eyes and fell asleep, so that he did not notice that the weather was changing. Huge clouds were gathering and in the distance lightning flashed – a thunderstorm was coming.

All the boats on the lake made for a safe harbour, and soon there was only one little boat left on the choppy water. The little fisherman did not wake up and did not know that his fishing rod had been thrown overboard and that his boat was heaving and rolling on the waves. The little anchor gave way, so the boat was a prey for water and wind, drifting hither and thither as if it were a toy of the elements.

On its western side the lake had an open connection with the sea. When the water rose too high, it would flow through that opening and then through a canal into the sea. The winds were having fun in their game, for they pushed the boat with the boy in it at a furious clip through the canal, farther and farther until it was in the open sea. The little boat would surely have capsized there, and the little fisherman would have drowned, but for the fact that his time had not yet come.

At the last moment he woke up. He did not know where he was and had no idea what had happened. Frightened, he looked about and suddenly realised that he was in mortal danger. He heard the roaring noise of the winds and waves, and without giving it another thought he jumped into the deep water. The little boat that had served him all his life drifted away, capsized and disappeared.

Desperately he tried to swim, but his arms and legs were still so short. When he tried to yell for help he almost suffocated because of the salt water that rushed into his mouth. He tried to float quietly on his back, but the wild waves always rolled him over and over. Finally, he could not think of what to do any more, and he resigned himself to waiting to see what would happen. Silence fell in his head, and he felt homesick for the safe shores of his lake and his meal of fish. But the little boat and fishing rod were gone, and he knew they would never come back.

Suddenly he felt himself lifted up by a wave that was bigger and stronger than all the others, and he was thrown onto the beach of a distant, unknown island. There he was, more dead than alive. He did not feel how a pair of strong arms lifted him up and carried him to a large house where he was tucked into a soft bed and slept for two days and two nights.

Slowly, life returned to him and he could open his eyes. He saw that he was lying in a bed, and beside the bed a large dark man was standing. The man smiled kindly to him and spoke to him in a strange language. The boy did not understand a word of it, but it sounded reassuring. He got up and, though still shaky on his legs, followed the man. The man gave him food and drink and also some new clothes. Then they went outside.

The man had many animals that he cared for with great attention and warmth. The boy helped him. When they had finished, the man went to his fields and cultivated his land; again the boy followed and helped him with everything he did.

Every day they cared for the animals, but after that every day also brought some new work. The second day the man worked with his little helper in his carpenter's shop, and the third day in his smithy. The fourth day they wove rugs on his loom. The fifth day they worked on the house to clean it and repair whatever was broken. That day they also did the laundry and scrubbed the floors. On the sixth day the man went fishing with a large fishing rod on the sea. On the seventh day they baked bread for the whole following week. The little fisherman helped him with everything and pretty soon learned the language the man was speaking and how to do each job.

In this way days, months and years went by. The fisher boy was zealous and grew big and strong with all the work he did. Eventually he became just as competent as his master.

One day the master called the boy, and together they walked to the beach. The sea was calm with friendly little waves murmuring in the surf. There the young man saw a big vessel riding at anchor, a fishing boat with fishing nets hanging by its side. The man gave the ship to the young man as a reward for all his work. The young man now felt like a real fisherman. He had long forgotten the dreams of the little fisherman, but the ship made him feel happy and proud. It was a strong, beautiful ship, filled with provisions and tools. The sea beckoned him, and thus he said goodbye to his master and rode out to sea.

Every evening he hauled in his nets and hundreds of big, shiny fish cascaded onto the deck. Then the great fisherman baked them in his pan and ate as many of them as he wanted. Every evening he left countless fishes lying on the deck; he had much too many of them, and when he had stuffed his stomach with them there were still so many left that you could not see that he had taken any for his meal.

Thus he went on for some time but eventually it was not a pleasure any more. What was the use once you had filled your stomach? He surprised himself when he wondered what he should do when he could only use such a small part of his catch. It was a question he had never asked before.

Eventually he turned his ship around and went back to shore, where he dropped anchor in a small bay. On the beach there were many little huts standing in the sun. Small children played around them, and they ran to the waterline to see the beautiful big ship. Their mothers and fathers came also, some of whom possessed a little boat with a fishing rod. When they came closer the fisherman saw that they all looked very skinny and some of them even looked sick. They were looking at the fisherman full of expectation. What was he doing here?

He flashed a broad smile, hauled in his nets, overfull of fish, and that evening all the children and their parents had plenty to eat.

During the time that followed, the little bay became a busy place. People cut, sawed and fashioned wood to build great ships. They made fishing nets. Blacksmiths made stoves and tools, new tools with which to work the land!

And the fisherman? He smiled every day even though sometimes he had no time to eat because he had to be everywhere at once. He brought prosperity and joy and health into the little bay, and the people were grateful to him. When all the work was done and the fisherman left again, a few small boys went with him to work and learn on his ship.

Thus he sailed the high seas, and everywhere he came, he brought good work and good food.

The years flew by, and the fisherman grew old – old and content about what lay behind him. In those days he had dreams of a lake, of safe harbours, a little boat and a little fishing rod, and of a few little fish for dinner. When he woke up he would feel that he knew that lake, but he could not remember it distinctly. But one morning he woke up and saw the lake; it sparkled as never before and a silver boat approached him. A silent figure stepped out of the boat and stretched out his hands to him, full of warmth. The old fisherman recognised his master and joyfully went on board. Together they sailed away, far, far away.

The Day that Miriam Stopped Smiling

Once upon a time there was a little girl named Miriam. She had a father and a mother, brothers and sisters, and they lived in a small house at the edge of town. On one side of the house there were streets and houses; on the other side green fields and a stream with frogs, ducks and birds. Cows grazed in the fields, which in spring and summer were coloured gaily by countless flowers, especially the haying fields where there were no cows and the flowers were able to come to full bloom.

What Miriam loved most was picking flowers. For hours she would wander through the fields and along the stream to collect bouquets of flowers, perhaps all kinds of yellow ones, or blue and white ones. Sometimes she put together all the colours she could find; every time she went collecting she thought of something new. When she came home she always found a little vase, bottle or can the flowers would fit in. Then she gave them to her mother or to a neighbour, or she set them somewhere in the house, or even on a post by the garden path so that everyone who came by the house could see them.

Miriam knew all the flowers and also knew when and where they would be blooming. She did not know what their names were, but that didn't matter, for flowers do not talk. She knew exactly how they smelled. She could smell the flowers from a great distance and knew which scent came from which one, so that she could easily find them. Her mother sometimes teased her and said that she had a flower nose!

There was something else that distinguished Miriam from other children: she was always smiling. Morning or evening, her face always had a happy smile. She beamed happiness as if she herself was one of the flowers. No one had ever seen her angry, sullen or out of sorts. Miriam was a real flower child.

The years went by and Miriam grew up. One day when she was looking for lilies by the stream she slipped and fell in the water. That wouldn't have been so bad, for she was quite able to swim, if she had not hit her head on a piece of old rusty iron that someone had once thrown into the stream. Her head hurt terribly and was bleeding badly. She could not see anything and her face was full of rust, blood and water. She called loudly for help causing some startled chattering ducks to fly up with much noise.

Fortunately her father heard her calls and he ran to her where she had managed to get back on firm ground. He was very frightened when he saw her lying there; carefully he picked her up and carried her to the house. Her mother gently washed and dried her face. Where was the injury? At first they saw nothing because the bleeding had stopped.

But then they saw something they had never seen before: Miriam was not smiling. Her pale face was set and still. And when her father and mother took a close look, they saw that Miriam's eyes were not moving; they were just staring straight ahead. Then the parents heard Miriam's voice, very softly: 'I can't see anything!'

From that day, Miriam was blind; no doctor was able to help her despite the fact that her parents travelled all over the country with her looking for the cleverest doctor they could find. Miriam's eyes remained cold and still, she saw nothing and she never smiled any more.

Her parents bought her a large rattan rocking chair with a soft cushion so she could sit in the midst of the flowers in the garden. She liked that, for her nose recognised the flowers even if her eyes could no longer see them. She drew in the scents of the flowers in the garden, the flowers in the fields and by the stream, and then she knew exactly which flowers were blooming.

She discovered something very special. When she had filled her nose deeply with the scent of a flower, she could see that flower somewhere in her mind. Not the way she used to see it, but much more beautiful, with colours that were much deeper and more radiant than she had ever seen before. The scent of the flower would then become even stronger, and her heart became warm, very warm, and wide open, and then... then Miriam smiled again!

O, those were golden moments – if only she could hold on to them! But the colours faded, the scent dissipated, and Miriam's smile disappeared again.

One day Miriam decided to go travelling. Her parents and her whole family were against it. No, she should not do that – how would she be able to take care of herself with unseeing eyes? And where did she want to go anyway? Weren't things nice at home where everyone did their best to mitigate her suffering? No, she should most certainly stay at home.

But Miriam went. Very early in the morning, when the scent of marsh-marigolds and daisies was in the air, she left the house. From all that her parents wanted to give her, she took only a few things, leaving her backpack, coat and extra shoes behind. She did take with her the little white bunny rabbit that was completely used to her.

Did Miriam know where she was going? Did the bunny rabbit know where she was going? Regardless, the girl walked confidently along without any sign of doubt. She had a sturdy walking stick and when she was not sure if she could go on, she used it to feel her way. She walked until she was tired, ate what she received from compassionate people and went to sleep wherever she happened to be along the way.

At first, Miriam smelled well-known scents, but after a while she encountered more and more strange smells of flowers she did not know. She enjoyed them but she was sorry that she could not see these new flowers.

The bunny rabbit faithfully followed her and helped her across roads and bridges. They slept closely together and the warm little rabbit gave Miriam a sense of security.

The trip had lasted seven days and seven nights when Miriam approached a big white house, as large as a palace, surrounded by a park, with a pond in front. A large white swan was swimming in the pond. With some hesitation Miriam continued walking. She went through the park, walked by the pond, and finally the bunny rabbit brought her to the big white door of the house. She rang the bell and waited.

No one appeared, but the door opened by itself. Behind it was a large hallway with marble floors and white statues along the walls. There was a sign that read: 'Closed to strangers.' But Miriam could not read. She went in.

She walked through the hall, through a room, through another, bigger room and stopped, unsure of herself. She had a strong feeling that this was where she had to be. Suddenly there appeared a large figure dressed in white, who seemed like a queen. She looked at the girl with eyes full of understanding and love, and said: 'Tell me, Miriam, what have you seen?'

Miriam told her of all the flowers she had seen at home when she was still a child. She spoke for a long time, for she had seen many flowers. When she had finished, it was quiet, very quiet.

Then there was a sigh and the figure in white asked again: 'Tell me, Miriam, what have you seen?'

Miriam thought for a moment and told the lady of her parents, brothers and sisters, and of the garden, the many birds, frogs and butterflies, everything she could think of.

It was becoming dark when she had finished, and after her words it again became very quiet, even more so than before and for a longer time.

Now the royal lady moaned as if she was suffering from pain, and very softly she asked once more: 'Tell me, Miriam, what have you seen?'

Miriam thought and thought. What did this lady mean? Feverishly she wracked her brain; she had a feeling that she had to hurry. But no matter how she puzzled and worried, she could not think of anything more. She had told of everything she had seen before she had lost the light in her eyes, and after that she had seen nothing!

Or perhaps she had? Miriam now began to tell of the flowers in her mind, the wondrous depth of their colour, more beautiful than she had ever seen in a flower before. As she was speaking full of enthusiasm about the flowers in her mind, she smelled their scents again and her heart opened itself wide and warm; she saw all the flowers at once and the scents of thousands of flowers surrounded her. She smiled so happily – even more happily and radiantly than ever before.

And her smile – her smile caused a miracle to happen, for suddenly her eyes were able to see again. In front of her she saw a sweet face, a royal figure, a lady who opened her arms wide to her. Miriam let herself be cherished and held close. It was as if she had come home. Later she could not tell how long they had been standing there, but eventually they let each other go. They went outside and took the bunny rabbit with them.

Together they travelled on, and wherever they went the flowers bloomed and people smiled. A lovely scent went with them and in the places they visited some of this scent lingered behind, and the people would sing. The sick felt strengthened, grieving people found consolation, and the disgruntled ones found peace. Fearful people found rest, and angry people forgot themselves for a while.

Thus they brought the strength of flowers wherever they went. Far, far away, the parents heard of the miracle, and they smiled, joyful and deeply happy.

The Five Hundred Anxious Nights of the Earth

In a far away country lived a remarkable people. These people lived very high up in the mountains, not in houses but in caves and chasms in the rocks. They were able to leap and jump like mountain goats, see as far as eagles and make themselves invisible by hiding like groundhogs. Everything they were able to do was part of the mountain environment in which they lived, in the thin air and close to the starry sky above them.

They never came down into lower-lying areas, to the forests and fields where people built houses. They were afraid of those people and of forest animals and beings. They felt oppressed in the heavy air where they would be forced to walk erect and straight, always at the same speed instead of leaping and climbing. Without the mountains around them they became fearful and sick, and therefore they preferred to stay in their homeland.

Occasionally, however, there was someone who wanted to see more of the world. Their king had to give permission for that, but it was a rare person who asked him. It was known that, in order to get to know the world beneath them, they had to go through an unusual trial, a dangerous assignment that most people preferred to avoid.

One day there was a young blacksmith who decided that he wanted to see more of the world. He was an expert blacksmith who had been thoroughly trained in his trade. There was no iron tool that he could not make with his skilled hands. But he wanted more – he wanted to know where this earth iron came from. He wanted to go down the mountain! Thus he took his duffle bag, food and drink and his most important tools, and strapped it all on his back. He had broad shoulders, his feet stood particularly strongly on the earth, and his arms were muscular and strong because of all the ironwork he had done. He would have no trouble, he thought.

The smith went to the king and asked for permission to depart. The king took a good look at the smith and saw who he was. He warned the young man of the many dangers he would face and impressed on him that *he should never turn back*. The king knew that there was no way back for those who seek the downward path.

The king gave the smith permission to go, and gave him his blessing. The smith thanked the wise king and promised to follow his advice. He felt happy and cheerful and went on his way full of courage.

First he had to climb many mountain ridges to find the downward path. When he eventually saw it in front of him, he heard a sweet, well-known voice. It was the voice of his mother: 'My dear son, stay in our country; I will care for you, I will cook your favorite meals and prepare your warm bed. Do not go, for you are certainly heading for great danger.'

His mother's proposition sounded pretty enticing to the smith, and he began to turn around. But right then he remembered his promise to the king. 'I can't, dear mother of mine!' he cried, and he went on.

He stepped onto the path that would lead him downward and saw below valleys full of forests and meadows. He exulted and ran down the incline. In the process he stepped on countless rocks that came loose and rolled with great noise down the mountainside. Where they landed the smith didn't know, nor did he care. His mountain people were not used to worrying about such things. The loosened rocks hit other rocks and after a while an avalanche of rocks rolled down into the lower lying areas. They damaged the fields and houses of the people who lived in the valleys.

Astonished, the smith saw what was happening; it was the first time he had realised that what happened higher up had an effect

down below. Just a few rocks higher up but so many down below –
would he still be welcome there?

Now he continued down more quietly, reflecting on what he
had seen. In the first meadow he reached, he saw a mountain cabin
where a lonely shepherd sat on a bench, seemingly waiting for
someone or something. The smith asked him what he was waiting
for and the shepherd replied: 'I am waiting for someone who will
bring me fresh fire.'

The smith took two flints from his bag and struck fire for the
shepherd. Soon the latter was warming himself and cooking some
food. The shepherd shared the warmth and the food with the smith
and in his gratefulness also gave him a little jar of sheep fat. 'Save
this fat for cold nights; if you smear your body with it you will
not freeze,' said the shepherd. The young man thanked him, said
goodbye and continued on his path down the mountain.

For the first time he felt soft ground under his feet rather than
rocks. He smelled the earth, and a warm feeling in his belly told
him that that was good. Farther down he was approaching a dense
spruce forest. The trees rose dark and sinister against the sky. At the
edge of the forest, a hunter was sitting on a log. It looked as if he was
waiting, so the smith asked him what he was waiting for. The hunter
replied: 'I am waiting for new arrows, because mine are too blunt.'

Immediately the smith made a fireplace of boulders and formed
new sharp, shiny tips on the arrows. The hunter thanked him and
gave him a bearskin in exchange. 'If you wrap yourself in this skin
you will be able to make it through anything,' said the hunter, and
he disappeared in the forest.

Surprised at the things he was seeing and experiencing in the
world, the smith took the bearskin and walked into the dark
forest. In the middle of the forest he saw a round hill, crisscrossed
by countless tunnels and passages. The smith peered into these
passages and called: 'Hello, is anyone at home?'

A scorpion with sharp claws crept out and asked him what he
was looking for. The smith answered that he wanted to get to know
the earth. The scorpion replied: 'He who wants to get to know the
earth has to go through the trial of the five hundred long nights. If

you survive that you will know the secrets of the earth; if not, you will forget who you are and where you came from.'

The smith agreed to go through the trial for he was a brave man. He followed the scorpion into the inmost part of the hill where there was a large cavern in which the scorpion left him behind.

The young man sensed how the earth around him began to speak and implore: 'Free us from our imprisonment!' the earth spirits around him beseeched him. The smith had compassion for them and promised to help them. The earth then opened itself and a long passage leading steeply down became visible. Cold air rose up from it and it felt as if strange hands took hold of him.

The smith thought: 'This is the beginning of five hundred cold and dismal nights!' He remembered the sheep fat and smeared it all over his body; he also wrapped himself in the bearskin he had received from the hunter. Thus protected, he let himself sink down; above him the earth closed itself noiselessly. The passage seemed endlessly long, for the smith forgot time on his way. Finally, the passage ended in a large cave, a hollow space filled with bats. Old, cold stone walls surrounded the smith, grimly grinning, and icy cold fell upon him.

But the smith was safely wrapped in his bearskin. He saw that the walls were covered with signs from age-old, ancient times, and he tried to decipher them. The bats flew around his head and tried with their cries to divert his attention from the secret signs. But the heart of the smith was beating warmly and evenly while he read what the earth had preserved.

When he had read everything and had stored it in his iron memory, he suddenly heard many voices, groaning and whining voices that frightened him. Cold and deathly darkness assailed him, and through it all he heard again the worried voice of his mother. She called him back. He came back to himself, sat up straight and said with a loud voice: 'Sorry, dear mother, but my path never ends and I will not turn back.' And in the dark he loudly spoke all the words he had read on the walls of the cave.

Once more the walls of the earth opened and he went on, without light or air, deeper and deeper into the earth. After much time he heard a dull growling, and dark earth gnomes rushed at him. They carried lanterns and in great excitement they cried: 'An explorer!' Completely composed, the smith asked them what he could do for them, and they gave him blacksmith work to do. They made him make so many things that he collapsed under the workload. But at that point they had everything they wanted: hammers, chisels, chains and rods – everything they needed.

They let him rest and thanked him by placing a shiny stone on his forehead between his eyes. The stone radiated a clear light so that the smith saw everything that otherwise could not be seen but yet wanted to be known. He wanted to thank the gnomes, but they had already disappeared.

The smith considered that he had been travelling for a long time – would the five hundred nights have passed by now? He had not counted them, and his path had not reached its end, so he just went on since there was no way back anyhow.

Eventually he reached the inmost part of the earth. A great fire was burning there, for the heart of the earth burns with love for the one who can find it. The smith threw off his bearskin and flung it into the fire. It burned until nothing but ashes were left.

Suddenly the smith saw an old man whom he had not noticed before. The man tended the burning and suffering heart of the earth. His eyes shone like the stars high above the mountains where the smith had grown up. The old man gave the smith a golden girdle and asked him to bring it to the Queen of the Middle Realm. The smith had never heard of this queen, but he had compassion for the heart of the earth and agreed to do it. Thereupon the old man bestowed much new wisdom on him, and when he knew that the smith had taken it all into his heart, he showed him the way he had to go.

The smith took his leave and went on again. But now he arrived in the region of the black serpents. They lived on the subterranean path in countless numbers and swarmed around him. The smith had no time to reflect, but he immediately reached in his duffle bag and pulled out his hammer with which he struck every serpent on its head. One by one they collapsed on the ground with their skulls crushed, and, undaunted, the smith walked on. The light from the crystal on his forehead enabled him to see where he was. He was no longer in one single tunnel; he found himself in a maze of passages and knew that if he went in there, he would never come out again.

Not only did he know this deep in his inner being, he also knew another way. He dug a new tunnel, straight through the maze, straight ahead, on and on. He had to bear terrible things, but he did not look back and fought his way forward, until the five-hundredth night had passed.

But the smith did not know that. Imperceptibly his time had come: the earth above him broke open and he struggled upward. He emerged in a wonderful green meadow full of flowers. Breathing in deeply, he filled his lungs with the fresh air. He noticed that the shiny stone had hidden itself inside his forehead and the golden girdle under the skin of his waist. By now, the smith was no longer so easily surprised and therefore this seemed very natural to him. He continued on his way and did not forget his assignment. He asked everyone he met about the Queen of the Middle Realm. He wandered about for a long time, but one day he saw her castle. However, the windows were closed because the queen was lying in bed, seriously ill.

People told him that it was said a golden earth girdle would heal her. The smith hastened into the castle and asked to see the queen. She let him in right away and asked him the reason for his visit. Without a word, the smith pointed to his waist where the golden girdle had hidden. A golden radiance lit up the room, and the queen felt the warm power it spread. She was healed at once and stood up from her bed. She thanked the smith, took him by the hand and asked him to govern the middle realm together with her. The smith felt his heart beating faster and did not need to think long about her offer.

Thus it happened that the queen told the smith all about her realm and about governing, and he was a fast learner. The great wisdom he had acquired during his journey through the earth served him well, especially since much of it was a revelation for the queen. The smith promised allegiance to the middle realm and the queen.

Thereupon they departed together for the mountain country along a different way and visited the old king. The king rejoiced about the young couple, gave them his blessing and let them depart full of confidence to the middle realm. There the smith and the queen married and served the land as king and queen. They were wise and just, and found a solution to every problem.

In this way a smith grew into a wise king, who knew about great heights and bottomless depths, and who was a human being with a heart that never lost its warmth.

Backer and His Boy

Many people say that they are looking for the land of silence. But most of them are afraid of silence, and just when they are in sight of the border of the land of silence, they turn around and never go back. Others continue and take a holiday in the land of deep silence. They come and rest, and when they are satisfied they quickly travel back to their own country. Only very few people actually live and work in the land of silence.

In this country everything is silent, not only the people but also the wind and the sea, the animals and the trees – everything is silent. The people who live there do not speak. Stillness deeply permeates their souls and has made its home there; stillness has become part of their being. They are able to be silent because they understand stillness. For them everything speaks in the land of this deep, deep silence. They hear in stillness everything that wants to be spoken, and silently they live in harmony with that.

This land is the birthplace of the children of the word. Surprisingly enough, they can only be born there and be nurtured by the people who live there. When there are no people who find them and take care of them, they disappear as mysteriously as they came. Then they are born in other countries, no longer as children of the word, but deaf and dumb, and they go through life with their heads down.

In the middle of the land of deepest silence is a clear mountain lake. In the middle of the lake is a little island with a hut, and in that hut lives Backer, the great watchman. This is the story of Backer: the great Backer and his boy.

After long, long, silent years a child was born in Backer's hut, a child of the word. The child showed no resemblance at all to the great Backer. He was a delicately built little boy, while Backer was big, strong and hairy. The child never noticed any differences. He smiled at Backer, and the lonely, still soul of the big man opened itself wide to the child, and all the love that lived in him streamed toward the little boy.

Backer took good care of the child, better than any mother and father could have done together. The child was a happy boy and grew up healthy and strong. He had a little boat to go out on the lake and to dive into the water with the fish. All the fish knew the child of the word and had promised Backer to take good care of him.

Although Backer never spoke, when the boy grew a little older he began to speak all by himself. Pure, crystal clear musical sounds resounded in the land of silence, and they created no disturbance. It was as if they made everything even more silent. Everything understood the remarkable language of the boy and listened to him.

One day, when the boy was ten years old, he fell asleep by the edge of the water. As he was sleeping a dark ship came across the lake with two ominous figures on board. The sails of the ship were a drab grey. Backer heard the ship approaching although it made no sound. He felt a strange fear in the pit of his stomach. With rapid strides he walked to the water's edge, took the boy into his arms and carried him into his hut. When he looked out through the window, the strange ship was gone. But every day when the boy was by himself it came back. And always Backer then hurried to the boy and kept him safe.

One day Backer was working behind the hut. He was splitting logs for their fire. There was one more heavy log that Backer wanted to split, although it was already getting dark. Backer did not want to stop. With his powerful arms he swung the axe up and down, up and down, until the log had been changed into a heap of perfect looking firewood. Now Backer sat down and felt content.

That feeling did not last, for only now did he hear the boy calling to him in the crystal clear tones of his pure voice from far across the water, until the sound was abruptly stopped by a rough pair of hands. In the distance, on the other side of the lake, Backer was just able to see the dark ship disappearing, carrying away what was most precious to him. He did not waste an instant but jumped into his rowboat and rowed as fast as he could to the other side. By the time he arrived there, however, the mysterious ship had disappeared together with the child of the word.

Backer succumbed to deep despair, and huge waves of bitter regret and rage burst forth from his soul, which felt as if it had been ripped to pieces. He yelled in desperation, and the land of deepest silence was filled with his shrieks. There was no answer... Everything remained still, and for the first time the silence oppressed Backer; for the first time he fled away from this terrible stillness. He ran and ran past the borders of the land of deepest silence, because his ears could no longer bear the sound of the silence.

He came to other countries where silence had disappeared and people spoke with each other. He asked everywhere for the child of the word, but no one had heard of the child or seen him. Backer did not give up. Restlessly and with a gnawing pain in his soul, he drove himself on and on, farther and farther, to look for the dark ship on lakes, rivers and the high seas. But it was nowhere to be found, as if it had never existed.

And still, Backer did not stop searching. Why should he? What else was he going to do? Go back to his hut? That was impossible, for the land of the deepest silence now pained him; the memory of the beautiful times he had had there, that were now so cruelly ended, tore his heart apart. Forward, always forward – ask, search, hope and lose. How many years had this nightmare lasted? Backer could not remember.

And yet, the end did come. One day Backer met a man who lived as a shepherd in a hut on a high mountain. The shepherd had become old and wise in the mountains, and long before Backer asked his question, he had already read it in his eyes. He invited Backer to join him for a simple meal, gave him a bed and clean clothes and told him that he could help. Backer could not believe his ears. Really? The shepherd smiled and told him the story of the boy.

The dark ship had kidnapped the boy and taken him out of the land of deepest silence. It had sailed far away to the land of darkness and obscurity. He was taken there so he could bring clarity to that place with his crystal clear voice. But they forgot that the boy could not live without love, for they did not know what that was. The boy lost his happiness and his voice broke for grief.

When the boy spoke he no longer sounded pure tones but only dull, sad words without sound or colour. The obscure inhabitants of the dark country were enraged and threatened the boy with horrible punishment. Nothing helped; the boy could utter nothing but dark, obscure words of a kind with which those people were quite familiar. Jeering they chased him away and threw rocks after him. The boy fled away, farther and farther away. He went through many lands and regions, and slept in caves or under trees.

And then, clear sounds welled up in him again, but he was not able to give them form any more. They only sounded deep in his soul without finding a way to the outside. The child of the word longed for silence; he missed Backer. Grief gnawed at him in silence, year in, year out. Now a young man, he came to know people, shared joys and sorrows with the animals and learned to distinguish one plant from another. He knew which ones could feed or protect him, and was grateful to the plants and animals.

He did all the work he was asked to do. Sometimes he had to solve great riddles; sometimes he had to toil with heavy stones for many days. Every job was fine with him. In the end he had become an adult and decided to return to the land of deepest silence. Would Backer have waited for him? Everyone and everything alive helped the young man and thus, after a journey of a full year, it came about that he reached his birthplace again. He travelled into its center and enjoyed the deep silence that took possession of him. Finally he arrived at the lake, built a wooden boat and rowed to the island in the middle. Here a cruel disappointment awaited him. The island and the hut were abandoned and the hut was tumbled down. Had Backer died? Grief overwhelmed him, and he felt more lonely than ever.

This was the story of the shepherd. How did he know so much? Who was he? Before Backer could ask him these questions, the shepherd gave him a ball of the purest golden thread and tied the end around Backer's waist. 'Follow this thread and you will find him,' said the shepherd, and he whistled for his dog and sheep and disappeared at a fast pace into the mountains.

Backer jumped up and shouted his thanks after him. Then he followed the ball of gold thread, which happily skipped along in front of him. Up and down mountains they went, along rivers and through woods – there was no end to the thread.

And thus Backer found the land of deepest silence again. The silence no longer pained him. He hastened on, longing to find his lost child. He came to the lake, built himself a rowboat and rowed to the island. His hut had been fixed up and the door stood wide open. A tall young man was standing in the doorway, waiting for Backer. In silence they embraced each other.

As they were standing there, time and history fell away, and Backer knew that everything had been worth it. He listened to the boy who had become an adult. The inner sounds made their way out again, and the air vibrated with the pure tones. Everything sang with them, winds and water, plants and animals. Even Backer found deep, powerful tones in his chest that pushed their way out.

Together they sang, and the land of deepest silence changed into the land of the word, the word through which people know and understand each other, and through which everything changes.

Bibliography

Brink, M. van den, *More Precious than Light*, Hawthorn Press 1994

Dunselman, R., *In Place of the Self*, Hawthorn Press 2007

Grimm Brothers, *Illustrated Treasury of Grimm's Fairy Tales*,
   Floris Books 2013

Hans Christian Andersen, *Favourite Tales from Hans Christian Andersen*,
   Floris Books 2013

Goldberg, R. *Addictive Behaviour in Children and Young Adults*,
   Floris Books 2012

Lusseyran, J., *Against the Pollution of the I*, Parabola Books 1999

Meijs, J., *De diepste kloof*, Zeist 2004
   Liefde en seksualiteit, Zeist 1999
   De puberteit voorbij, Zutphen 2005

Sleigh, J., *Thirteen to Nineteen*, Floris Books 1998

Staley, B., *Between Form and Freedom*, Hawthorn Press 2009

Steiner, R., *How to Know Higher Worlds*, GA 10, Steiner Books 1994
   *The Bridge between Universal Spirituality and the Physical Constitution
   of Man*, GA 202, Anthroposophic Press 1958
   Education for Adolescents, GA 302, Anthroposophic Press 1996
   Balance in Teaching, GA 302A, Steiner Books 2007

Zeylmans van Emmichoven, W., *The Anthroposophical
   Understanding of the Soul*, Anthroposophic Press 1982

Index

Addictive Behaviour in Children and Young Adults

The Struggle for Freedom

Raoul Goldberg

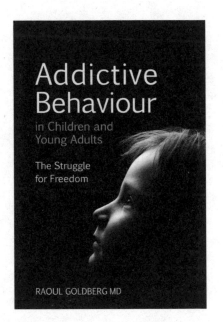

Addiction is one of the most critical problems of our modern world, affecting children as much as adults. We face not only a widespread dependency on illicit substances, but also addictions to food, beverages, cigarettes and alcohol, as well as electronic gadgetry, online social networks, and entertainment media within a culture of violence, along with excessive and unhealthy sexual practices.

This book explores the overall health consequences of addictive behaviour in children and young people, as well as its underlying causes.

florisbooks.co.uk